Witness to Integrity

Witness to Integrity

The Crisis of the
Immaculate Heart Community of California

Anita M. Caspary, I.H.M.

THE LITURGICAL PRESS

Collegeville, Minnesota

www.litpress.org

Cover design by David Manahan, O.S.B. Cover illustration: detail of serigraph *Fiat*, by Corita Kent, 1953, from *Arca Artium Collection* at St. John's University, Collegeville, Minnesota, with the acknowledgement of the Corita Art Center, Immaculate Heart Community. Photos provided by Susan Maloney, S.N.J.M., and the Immaculate Heart Community Archives, Los Angeles, California.

1   2   3   4   5   6   7   8   9

Library of Congress Cataloging-in-Publication Data

Caspary, Anita Marie, 1915–
    Witness to integrity : the crisis of the Immaculate Heart community of California / Anita M. Caspary.
      p. cm.
    Includes bibliographical references and index.
    ISBN 0-8146-2770-6 (alk. paper)
      1. Sisters of the Immaculate Heart of Mary.   I. Title.

BX4522 .C37 2003
271'.97—dc21

2002029841

DEDICATION

To my mother and father, who gave me life

To the Immaculate Heart Community, who enriched my life

To my friends, living and deceased,
who sustained my life for these many years

Contents

Foreword

Catholic tradition holds that religious life is a gift to the Church. Historical accounts record that communities of religious women have emerged to serve, educate, and aid those in dire need. In the past twenty-five years a revived interest in Catholic women's religious orders has assumed an important place in the work of historians, social scientists, feminists, and theologians. Amidst these stories of heroic deeds, studies give evidence of a recurring theme of conflict between Church authorities and women religious when women begin to assert control over their own lives and ministries. Conflict with the Catholic Church hierarchy has emerged as a commonly recorded theme in the chronicles of Catholic women's communities. Many of these stories are situated in the paradoxical context of clerical familiarity and clerical hostility. *Witness to Integrity* is more than another story of a clerical bureaucracy treating women as children. The story is singular, uncommon, and unique because it is a collective story in which truth speaks to power, honesty overcomes the lies of silence, and women claim their own lives.

In these pages Anita Marie Caspary, I.H.M., carefully sets the context and leads the reader through the complex past that brought the Immaculate Heart Sisters into direct conflict with the male hierarchical system of the Church. I use the term "male hierarchical system" deliberately. Contrary to the popularized notion that the Immaculate Heart story is simply an account of a conflict between liberal, rebellious nuns and a rigid, conservative cardinal, Caspary, in exhaustive detail, chronicles the evolving antipathy of male Church authorities toward the Immaculate Heart Sisters prior to and during the call to renewal as dictated by the Second Vatican Council. Her evidence, recorded in letters, memos, interviews, personal notes, and community meeting minutes, would make any historian green with envy. More important, it places in the historical public record original sources that enrich, expand, and correct the inaccuracies and myths that have grown around the verifiable facts of this story.

One of the myths in Catholic American folklore popularized by the public media is the role of Caspary herself. Many journalists not familiar with the inner workings of community life casually assumed that Caspary alone, as mother general and later as president of the new community, was a fiery, fearless leader of a community of rebellious nuns. Quite the contrary is true. Caspary anchors her story in her stable family life. Born into a loving but firm German-Catholic family, she learned to live a devout Catholic life in the American context. As described, her life is that of the quintessential Catholic woman, from a Catholic family, Catholic educated, destined to be an obedient nun—who else would accept the religious name of Sister Mary Humiliata?

Caspary would seem to have been the most unlikely candidate to head an order that would eventually challenge the Vatican and its treatment of women. Trained in the rigid and semi-monastic spirit of Catholic religious life in which obedience was paramount, coupled with personal characteristics of shyness and deliberation, Caspary obediently consented to a ministry in higher education. She was to live in the Catholic literary world of Gerard Manley Hopkins, François Mauriac, and Flannery O'Connor. One of the first IHM nuns educated at Stanford (her doctorate is in English literature and medieval studies; she still recites poetry in Middle English), her idealism, perfectionism, and sharp ability to analyze, compromise, and negotiate prepared her well for the office of mother general, with a mandate to renew but not to challenge.

In a style that is nuanced, Caspary reveals slowly her reflections and motivations during the period of controversy. What sustained her and the other members of the community to demand their right to educate their women, adapt their lifestyles, and experiment with different forms of prayer despite the intrusive questions of the male hierarchical authorities? Her answer is quite simple. It lies in the deeply ingrained virtue of obedience and the IHM understanding of the philosophical and theological shift in religious life proposed by the Second Vatican Council.

The reader will find rooted in Caspary's book the religious belief that one obeys the call of God and follows the Spirit as transmitted through legitimate authority, in this case the general chapter of the Immaculate Heart Sisters. The collective understanding of the teachings of the Second Vatican Council was, for the elected delegates, the highest ruling authority.

The Immaculate Heart story portrays a woman and a group of women in tandem, a leader and a community both with the enviable experience of a dialogic, idealistic yet heart-rending relationship. In our age of post-modernity, when the fragmentation of the individual and the rhetoric on the need for community abound, this story is instructive for those yearning for a sense of collective identity and purpose. Yes, it is possible to live in community, struggle with the ideas and ideals of a shared life, and live them into the future, but one pays a high price for this type of integrity.

For orders of Catholic women, there is a more direct lesson and challenge. In the past few years the Vatican, through its various agencies, has publicly reprimanded individual women religious for their support of the ordination of women, reproductive rights, and homosexuality. In each of these contemporary situations, the individual woman religious was singled out, silenced, and/or threatened with expulsion from her religious community. Many hold the opinion that the resistance by the Sisters of the Immaculate Heart of Mary, Los Angeles, to the male Church authorities in the sixties is still a vividly unpleasant memory for Vatican bureaucrats and local Church officials. The hierarchy, ever reticent to receive negative publicity, does not want another confrontation between churchmen and an entire congregation of sisters. Thus the scrutiny given to the individual woman religious by contemporary Church officials.

For contemporary Catholic religious orders of women, this book challenges the efficacy of the principle of recognition. In the sixties the Sacred Congregation for Religious was the Church agency with the authority to recognize, to legitimatize, and to "protect" a Catholic religious order. Catholic pundits predicted that the Immaculate Heart Sisters would not survive as a community if they withdrew from the traditional canonical status of a religious order. Caspary's book provides the theological and philosophical argument of why contemporary religious orders of women need to consider non-canonical status as part of their future options.

Witness to Integrity demonstrates the clear but painful understanding these women had of their original commitment to excel in everything for the love of God and service to others. They wanted the best education for themselves in order to better educate their students; they wanted new prayer forms and horaria in order to experience God more directly; they experimented with new forms of garb in order to better relate to their peers and the contemporary world. This book deals with a common problem in the sense that conflict between Catholic religious orders of women and the hierarchy will be a continuous struggle until Church authorities and Church law accept women religious as full, adult persons in their own right.

Witness to Integrity is an uncommon, singular, and unique history because in it we can read the story of women who met in this struggle the God of their heart and conscience. In keeping with the tradition of Catholic orders of women, they have given a great gift to the People of God (the Church)—and they did it together.

SUSAN MARIE MALONEY, S.N.J.M., PH.D.

October 6, 2001
Feast of Blessed Marie Rose Durocher

Preface

This book relates the history of why four hundred Immaculate Heart Sisters of Los Angeles (IHMs), a community I served as mother general, in 1970 elected to surrender our vows and status in the Roman Catholic Church to become a lay ecumenical community. To some observers, the efforts of the Immaculate Heart Sisters to stand firmly with the choices we made to renew the community was a stubborn rebellion against authority, an insistence on doing our own thing. To others, the crisis centered around an exchange of religious values for secular ones. For yet others, the changes we sought were fearful symbols of the tumultuous society of the sixties. Some observed our struggle as a psychological dynamic—a protest against an unreasonable male prelate of advanced years by a group of intelligent women who were (relatively) young and headstrong.

What many did not comprehend was our collective understanding of the element of risk coupled with a passionate love and vision of the Catholic Church and its future. We could not have risked jobs, relationships and thousands of years of collective commitment to the Catholic Church without an ideal and inspiration that was both sacred and practical. We envisioned ourselves as women of a renewed Catholic Church, ready to participate in creating a world in which none are poor or alienated, in which hatred of other countries, races, and gender exists no more.

In 1967, as a community we were not explicitly conscious of feminism as a theological base or cause for action. In many ways we foreshadowed the contemporary (and vibrant) feminist movement within the Catholic Church. Our ideas matured with the call for renewal from the Second Vatican Council. We were able to articulate the ideals of responsible personhood and full community that would be the message of

feminist theologians in the seventies and eighties. A passage from the
IHM decrees from our 1967 Chapter of Renewal expresses our vision:

> Women, perhaps especially dedicated women, insist on the lati-
> tude to serve, to work, to decide according to their own lights. Our
> community's history from its beginning, including its early mis-
> sionary activities in California and its eventual separation from a
> Spanish foundation which was inevitably removed from and indif-
> ferent to peculiarly American conditions, speaks of our readiness
> to abandon dying norms in order to pursue living reality. It ex-
> presses, also, our willingness to seek human validity rather than
> some spurious supernaturalism.
>
> Women around the world, young and old, are playing decisive
> roles in public life, changing their world, developing new life
> styles. What is significant about this new power for women is not
> that it will always be for the good, nor that it will always edify, but
> that there can be no reversing of it now. Women who want to serve
> and who are capable of service have already given evidence that
> they can no longer uncritically accept the judgment of others as to
> where and how that service ought to be extended. American reli-
> gious women want to be in the mainstream of this new, potentially
> fruitful, and inevitable bid for self-determination.[1]

The media, interestingly enough, sensed this theme and personalized
it in dramatic fashion as "The Cardinal and the Nuns." So the stage was
set for the encounter in terms of traditional gender-related roles. The
denouement, as it was seen then, would be defeat or triumph for one of
the two forces, the male hierarchy or the community of religious
women. In many ways the IHM story has continued to develop over
more than a quarter century. It is past time, certainly, for the beginnings
of the present community to be traced and documented before less
accurate accounts gain wider circulation.

But the story told here is that of the various ways in which the Immaculate Heart Sisters of Los Angeles gave witness to the signs of the
times, to personal and responsible fulfillment, and to loving and caring
community. The tensions we felt as we faced ecclesiastical forces ex-
acted a toll of morale, membership, and clarity of purpose. The particular historical moment of our renewal under highly conservative

[1] Prologue, Immaculate Heart Decrees of the Chapter of Renewal 1967.
A/IHMCOM (Archives of the Immaculate Heart Community, Los Angeles, California).

Church leadership forced decisions that left little time for alternative considerations. Under almost insupportable pressure, we found that choices for personal and group expectations could not always be made as in a less troubled context. But the ultimate choice, that of a status we did not originally intend, was one made in utmost integrity and sincerity, in sorrow but in love and fidelity to the Spirit. We could choose no other road.

Our dramatic struggle, with its strategies and decisions leading to the formation of the renamed Immaculate Heart Community of Los Angeles, appears increasingly in works written from a religious perspective, whether historical,[2] sociological,[3] literary,[4] psychological,[5] or specifically Catholic religious life.[6] Dissertations,[7] several TV documentaries,[8] and at least two plays[9] have been written on the conflict of the Immaculate Heart Sisters with the cardinal archbishop of Los Angeles. However, the story I present is unique in that it combines my personal reflections and a historical perspective on one of the most controversial moments in U.S. Catholic history.

[2] Jo Ann McNamara, *Sisters in Arms* (Cambridge: Harvard University Press, 1996) 640.

[3] Mary Fainsod Katzenstein, *Faithful and Fearless: Moving Feminist Protest Inside the Church and Military* (Princeton: Princeton University Press, 1998) 224; John Seidler and Katherine Meyer, *Conflict and Change in the Catholic Church* (New Brunswick, N.J.: Rutgers University Press, 1989) 80–81; Helen Rose Fuchs Ebaugh, *Women in the Vanishing Cloister* (New Brunswick, N.J.: Rutgers University Press, 1993) 139–141.

[4] James Patrick Shannon, *Reluctant Dissenter* (New York: Crossroad Publishing Co., 1998) 130; Marcelle Bernstein, *The Nuns* (New York: J. B. Lippincott, 1976) 149–154.

[5] "To Be Beautiful, Human, and Christian—IHM's and the Routinization of Charisma," in Mark S. Massa, S.J., *Catholics and American Culture* (New York: Crossroad Publishing Co., 1999) 172–194.

[6] Lora Ann Quiñonez, C.D.P., and Mary Daniel Turner, S.N.D. de N., *The Transformation of American Catholic Sisters* (Philadelphia: Temple University Press, 1992) 42.

[7] Marshal H. Mercer, "'You People Don't Pray Right': A Study of Organizational Power and Superordinate Goal Conflict" (Ph.D. diss., Claremont Graduate School, 1994).

[8] "Nuns in Conflict" in the *Man Alive* series was produced by the British Broadcasting Corporation in 1968. CBS produced the TV documentary "Lamp Unto My Feet" in 1970.

[9] *Immaculate Heart*, written by Hugo Leckey, ran for over a month in Los Angeles in October 1985. Also a play by Jack Frankel, *The Mother General* (1990), in a revised edition called *A Lion at the Door*, made it to the semifinals in the play-writing competition of Siena College in 1994.

It is difficult to relate all the events leading to the departure of the Sisters of the Immaculate Heart from canonical status and the subsequent formation of a new community. Such an exposition necessarily involves the narration of our differences with Cardinal James Francis McIntyre, archbishop of Los Angeles, and at times necessarily involves criticism of his actions and the role he played in our history. Although this book highlights the IHM-McIntyre interface, it in no way purports to give a complete picture of the life of the community or to pass judgment on the life and work of Cardinal McIntyre. His vision for the Catholic Church of Los Angeles, his varied charities, and his concern for the welfare of the aged and the ill are all well documented in other biographical works. The specific focus of this book is the experience of the Immaculate Heart women and our struggle to renew our religious life, not a commentary on those who did not understand our vision.

The significance of the book is fourfold. First, from a perspective of religious history, Immaculate Heart Community is one of the first U.S. Roman Catholic orders of women to change its canonical status with the Vatican and survive as an independent ecumenical community of women and men. Second, although several books and dissertations have been written about this event, this is the first book written by one who struggled personally through the conflict with the Vatican. I am keenly aware that many accounts and personal reflections on the Immaculate Heart story could have been written. The whole community was involved in our struggle in varying degrees; thus there are many perspectives on this period of our history. As president of Immaculate Heart College (1958–63) and mother general of the Immaculate Heart Community (1963–70), it is my intention to give a first-person account of the conflict, intrigue, and betrayal of women challenging the hierarchy of the Roman Catholic Church and choosing a new religious life based on our experience as women. This book also corrects the inaccuracies that have grown up around the verifiable facts of the story.[10] Third, in addition to personal reflections, I am able to use original source documents from the Immaculate Heart Community archives that have not been available to scholars or the public. Fourth, at the beginning of the new millennium many women and men seek models of community grounded in a spirituality relevant to the American (USA) experience. My story attempts to provide an understanding of how a group of

---

[10] Msgr. Francis J. Weber, *His Eminence of Los Angeles: James Francis Cardinal McIntyre* (Mission Hills, Calif.: St. Francis Historical Society, 1997) 2:416–441.

American women living as traditional nuns redefined their own spirituality, which led to the transformation of their lives, relationships, and institutions.

Witness to Integrity is both a history and a future. It documents an unparalleled event in American religious history for women and provides evidence of a new form of ecumenical community relevant in an age of globalization. As a central player in this historic controversy, I recount the story and analyze its significance. I have waited many years to tell this tale.

One of the most formidable tasks of this project was the space limitations required in publishing a book. After much reflection, consultation, and advice, I chose to include the 1967 Chapter of Renewal Decrees in an abbreviated form. These writings, so dear to my heart, I offer to the reader in Appendix D.

Many of my source documents were written before inclusive language became a common practice of writers and scholars. Out of respect for the authors of letters, memos, decrees, notes, etc., I did not change the language to be inclusive. I assume the reader understands my decision to honor the original wording of these documents.

Acknowledgments

It would be absurd to attempt a community history like *Witness to Integrity* without strong communal support. And so I acknowledge first the Immaculate Heart Community for the encouragement, patience, and trust with which they gifted me. In particular, my gratitude is addressed to Mary Kirchen, I.H.M., and to Julie Friese, I.H.M., of the original leadership team of our community, who with risk and generosity made possible my long task with all its interruptions.

Every story has a prelude. Memories of Mother Eucharia Harney's visionary leadership and determination, a woman whose spirit continues to influence my life and the life of the IHM community, propelled me at many intervals to write this story. For her unique personality and gift in my life, I will always be grateful.

To Marian Sharples, I.H.M., who wrote the early history of the California Immaculate Heart Sisters in a scholarly and delightful style in her invaluable text *All Things Remain in God*, I am thankful.

The change of the reportorial style of my first version became a more readable story with the research skills and intense dedication of Fidelia Dickinson. Thank you, Fidelia.

The same gracious Providence came into play when the leaders of the IHM community, through support and a strong recommendation, suggested Susan Marie Maloney, S.N.J.M., as my research associate. Dr. Maloney's passion for writing and her commitment to the study of Catholic religious orders of women assisted me greatly in every facet of the writing and editing process. Her unquenchable interest in the meaning of the IHM story for the future of religious life for women and all women of the Church was evident throughout our joint venture. To her a loving salute of deep appreciation.

To Catherine Ferguson, S.N.J.M., my gratitude for the innumerable times she rescued me with her editing, computer skills, and general insights into the writing process.

To Rose Eileen Jordan, I.H.M., a lifelong friend in community, my appreciation, which words cannot express, for all the tasks she performed so generously, thus enabling me to have the time to write.

To Elizabeth Anne Dunn, I.H.M., for her support and whose insistence on the historical importance of the story guided the book to publication, my appreciation.

To Gretchen Teeple, I.H.M., for her expert photographic skills, my gratitude.

To Doris Murphy, I.H.M., and her assistant Jeanne Albert, I.H.M., who worked tirelessly in the IHM offices organizing the archives, thus making them easily accessible, I give my thanks. And to their predecessors Anna Cecilia Hatfield, I.H.M., and Anita Weyer, I.H.M., who for years guarded with care and precision the documents and legacy of the IHM history, I owe a deep debt of gratitude. Unless otherwise indicated, all photos in this book are courtesy of the Archives of the Immaculate Heart Community.

To my dear friends and companions at the IHM Kenmore community in Los Angeles, whom I have known and lived among for over a quarter of a century, I am deeply grateful for your many acts of kindness and comments of endearing encouragement.

To Helen Kelley for her friendship, lively discussions, and reading material while this work was in progress, my appreciation.

To the Sisters of the Holy Names of Jesus and Mary of the California province, for their restful Stuart-Marshall House, where many chapters were written and revised, my gratitude for sharing this wonderful accommodation.

To my sisters Gretchen, Ursula, and Marion and my brother Gerard and their spouses for never losing faith in my long and sometimes tedious project, my prayers of thanks.

To James P. Shannon, former Roman Catholic bishop in St. Paul, Minnesota; Father Charles Curran; and Mr. Jim Douglas Henry, formerly of the British Broadcasting Corporation, my gratitude for their unfailing insistence that the story be told from my perspective.

To Kathryn Crosby for her friendship and support during our struggles, a lasting thanks.

To Marshal H. Mercer for his generosity in sharing his research, I am grateful.

To Stella Matsuda and Julia Felker, two wonderful women and friends who have continued to give me life through dance, discussion, and prayer, my heartfelt thanks.

To the "Friends of the Immaculate Heart Community" for their interest, care, and treats to me during this writing period, my thanks.

To my former students for their loyalty and love these many years, my gratitude for remembering.

To Richard W. Clark, M.D., David S. Cannom, M.D., and Richard D. Hornichter, M.D., three specialists who have made my life these past few years more comfortable and secure, my thanks for their medical care and personal concern.

To Camilla Broderick and Henry Ben-Zvi for their expert legal advice, my gratitude.

Finally, to the entire expanding Immaculate Heart Community, whose hopefulness about reading their biography never diminished between several editions, my thanks.

Chapter 1

The Accusation

"You will suffer for this," the cardinal thundered at us. His threat to the five of us who were the elected administration of the Sisters of the Immaculate Heart of Mary of Los Angeles betrayed years of rage. With little notice James Francis McIntyre, the cardinal archbishop of Los Angeles,[1] had stormed into my office at the motherhouse in the hills of Hollywood. He was angry. There were no greetings, and the days of cordial amenities were over. The purpose of this hastily assembled meeting was painfully evident.

That final sentence of his tirade, uttered some thirty-seven years ago, still resounds in my ears, not simply as a warning of danger but as a promise of punishment. It was May of 1965 when His Eminence[2] James Francis McIntyre spoke those fateful words. On short notice he had demanded to see me and my sister councilors at a meeting to be held in my office as mother general of the Immaculate Heart of Mary Sisters.[3]

Surprise, fear and even anger at the threat hung in the air over our five veiled heads. Acting without benefit of Church law governing such

---

[1] The title "cardinal" is bestowed by the pope and indicates status within the Roman Catholic Church. The position grants a place in the College of Cardinals, which is the body that elects the pope. An archbishop heads an archdiocese and has legal and juridical authority over a specific territory. Usually, but not necessarily, a cardinal is also the legal and canonical (arch) bishop of a(n) (arch) diocese. Not every archbishop is a cardinal, nor is every cardinal an archbishop.

[2] "His Eminence" is the traditional title of a cardinal.

[3] Members of the General Council of the Sisters of the Immaculate Heart of Mary (IHM) were Sister Elizabeth Ann Flynn, Mother Regina McPartlin, Sisters Charles Schaffer, Eugenia Ward, and Gregory Lester. Minutes of the meeting with Cardinal McIntyre and Monsignor Edward Wade on May 13, 1965. Archives of the Immaculate Heart Community, Los Angeles, California (hereafter cited as A/IHMCOM).

matters, the cardinal had notified us that this meeting was an "Extraordinary Canonical Visitation."[4] The unusual wording of his official demand for a meeting could mean only one thing: that we were to hear more drastic accusations. Listening to our misdeeds as pronounced by His Eminence, along with condemnation of the Immaculate Heart Sisters, and especially of our leadership had become a common occurrence during my years as mother general.

Since the close of the Second Vatican Council in 1965, our adoption of its spirit of renewal and openness to new theological ideas were a source of constant tension between the cardinal and our religious community. His Eminence was not comfortable with the direction in which the Second Vatican Council was moving. But on this particular May day, his dislike for the general updating of the Church known as *aggiornamento* focused on the Sisters of the Immaculate Heart. He had early been aware of our enthusiasm for the spirit of Vatican II, and thus we were particularly vulnerable.

As the minutes ticked away, the cardinal chronicled the "this" and "that" of what we would suffer. We were subjected to a vigorous condemnation of our alleged errors and told of numerous anonymous accusations against the sisters which he had received. The list was long:

> Why are you allowing the young sisters to read Cardinal Suenens' book *The Nun in the World*?
>
> Do you not understand that guest speakers at your college must be approved through my office?
>
> Is it not clear to you that I am the judge of religious life in the diocese?

[4] Canon 397 §2 of the Code of Canon Law states, "The bishop can visit members of religious institutes of pontifical right and their houses only in those cases expressly mentioned by law." The commentary on this canon states, "The law distinguishes between religious institutes of pontifical right and other [diocesan] institutes of consecrated life. This implies in practice that institutes established by the Holy See [Vatican] or approved by it with a formal decree are less subject to episcopal supervision than other religious, especially regarding the internal life of the community." *The Code of Canon Law: A Text and Commentary*, ed. James A. Coriden, Thomas J. Green, and Donald E. Heintschel (New York: Paulist Press, 1985) 334. The California Sisters of the Immaculate Heart were established as a pontifical institute in 1924. Cardinal McIntyre's authority to visit us in this manner and under the rubric of extraordinary canonical visitation was questioned by our administration because of our canonical standing as a pontifical institute. This was one in a series of questionable visitations and acts of intrusions into the internal life of the community.

Why have so many of your community asked for dispensations from their vows?

Why do you permit the use of modern art to portray religious subjects?

Do you know that the Christmas cards designed by your art department and the sisters are an affront to me and a scandal to the archdiocese?[5]

Question followed after question in such haste that we barely had time or the presence to answer, although everyone tried at first. Stunned by the vehemence of the cardinal's tone as the interrogation continued, we heard each of his charges resounding in the room.

At first we tried one by one to counter the indictments against our using the directives of the Second Vatican Council as our defense. Never had we expected our first mild experiments in religious renewal to encounter such impassioned resistance. His Eminence, during that painful meeting, demanded over and over that we abandon our plans for a program of renewal in the community and return to a traditional form of religious life, including a hierarchical view of clerical authority. He contended that the sisters must follow the Church and its tradition rather than present-day theological thought. The cardinal, not modern thinkers, he said, represented the Church in Los Angeles, and there was no room for new ideas that had not been evaluated and accepted by him. Once we saw the futility of argument, we resorted to silence without defense. As could be predicted, the cardinal became more and more frustrated by our lack of response.

As I think now of how the sisters were beginning to discuss a new identity and a new concept of service to the Church, I understand better the angry outbursts of the cardinal and his advisors. The members of the hierarchy were threatened by the changing position of women in general, but most clearly, by that of women religious. As individual women and as a community, we experienced a patriarchical system that fostered a clerical culture, thus allowing this verbal abuse. JoAnn McNamara writes well of the roots of this system. A male celibate clergy had come to the conclusion that "women religious had to be confined behind walls and grilles."[6] But then, ironically, "clergymen

[5] Minutes of meeting on May 13, 1965. A/IHMCOM.
[6] Jo Ann Kay McNamara, *Sisters in Arms* (Cambridge: Harvard University Press, 1996) 5.

feared women entirely withdrawn into a world without men even more. This complementary threat of female autonomy always drove them back to the *cura mulierum,* the care (and control) of women."[7]

The history of nuns in the Church saw, with very few exceptions, little change on the part of the male hierarchy for the better part of two thousand years. As for the Sisters of the Immaculate Heart, our newer understanding of our worth as women, and particularly as women religious, had been slowly evolving. This development occurred through advanced education, wider religious and secular reading, and retreats. Our relationship with male authority in the Church would never be quite the same again. So the present crisis was inevitable: for men to allow self-determination to women religious meant the surrender of power.

Although Vatican II's Decree on the Up-to-Date Renewal of Religious Life, or *Perfectae Caritatis,*[8] was only months away from publication, this document was not yet issued when this dramatic confrontation with the cardinal took place. Yet certainly the cardinal sensed in our meetings and discussions that we were modeling changes in our lives based on the views expressed at the Second Vatican Council. Indeed, the IHM General Council of the sisters, elected in 1963, had designed a five-year plan in the spirit of the times for renewal of the community.[9]

Thus, in spite of his awareness of our early experimentation with aspects of the internal life of the community, the IHM Decrees on Authority and Government, which developed out of our Chapter of Renewal four years later, were indeed shocking, even heretical, to the cardinal. For those of us who had conscientiously lived our canonically approved Rule, it was a challenge to convert our former attitudes and principles of docility and obedience into freedom of conscience and an all-encompassing personal responsibility. That this crisis of renewal should be translated into a practical change of the structure of religious life was for some Catholics almost unthinkable.

Therefore, it is important to point out, lest the complexity of the sisters' dilemma be underestimated, that the Immaculate Heart story is not simply a matter of the pitting of ecclesiastical might against a small band of dedicated women. Nor should it be seen as merely a conflict of personalities, since in the Immaculate Heart Community almost the

[7] Ibid.

[8] *Perfectae Caritatis,* in *Vatican Council II: The Conciliar and Post Conciliar Documents,* ed. Austin Flannery, O.P. (Northport, N.Y.: Costello Publishing Co., 1981) 611–633.

[9] See Chapter 6 for an extensive discussion of the five-year plan developed in 1963.

entire body of sisters would consent to be involved in the move for progress and renewal. At the heart of the controversy, the real protagonist may well have been the unchanging (and unchangeable?) male hierarchical system, and the antagonist, the female agents of change, viewed as inevitably destructive of that system.

For many sincere persons, the Church has always had as one of its chief values its immutable nature. It was especially the religious orders that symbolized the absolute character of the Church. Any change, especially on the part of nuns, instilled in many pious Catholics a deep fear that any modification would eat away at the stability they had come to expect of the Church. These Catholics preferred to rely on authority rather than to take personal responsibility for examining their beliefs. Many good Church women and men believed that they should enforce this position by urging complete reliance on those in authority as teachers.

Those of us in leadership positions in the Sisters of the Immaculate Heart knew that our stance toward renewal would mean the strain of making an increasing number of choices. We knew that we were facing the possibility of standing alone, especially when no one knew what "renewal" really meant. We had no pattern to follow. Yet we knew that this was the way we had to go if we, as women religious, were to make any difference in the modern world. Thus the ideologies represented by the cardinal and by ourselves in my office that day in May were in irreconcilable confrontation, each side sincerely believing that a greater good was at stake.

This extraordinary visitation of the cardinal ended on an extremely unhappy note. Our silence was interpreted, as indeed it had to be, as a refusal to obey the cardinal's demands. This provoked an irrevocable challenge on his part. By our silence we were stating that we refused to acknowledge his right to interfere in the internal affairs of the community, his "right" being subordinated to our right as a pontifical institute,[10] and, further, that we believed in the "new" Church evolving from the Second Vatican Council. As the cardinal rose from his place at our council table, he warned, "Because you refuse to answer, I must tell you that you will suffer for this." And the meeting ended abruptly with a slam of the door signaling the exit of His Eminence from my office.

The silence continued as we glanced at one another after the door closed. We now knew that we faced an unavoidable challenge. But we

[10] See note 4 above.

could not retreat from our position, for we were determined to set in motion a program of renewal authorized, we knew, by the Second Vatican Council. Before we left the room, I requested the council members not to reveal the message of this shocking interview, for if we informed the community now, many sisters whose dedication to a new life was just beginning would leave the community and thus be lost to the service of the Church. Obviously some day the community would have to be told, and some day, too, the entire community engaged in renewal would meet open opposition and suffering not only from the cardinal but from many conservative Catholics. But it was our feeling that this was not the proper time. There was also the chance that the attitude of the cardinal or his advisors might soften or even change.

We did not know then what form the threatened suffering would take. Would our sisters be asked to leave the Los Angeles area? Would our college be closed by ecclesiastical dictum? Or our high school? Would the whole community be banished from Southern California dioceses? Would our institutions—our convents, hospitals, and the many parochial and high schools where we had served so many years, watching the children grow into Christian adulthood—be closed by the chancery office? Would our sisters be publicly castigated? Or even excommunicated from the Church? All these questions and others now troubled the General Council. Sick at heart, the five of us retreated to our own rooms to think and pray, keeping the words of the cardinal to ourselves for a later day.

In retrospect, my own life and ideals underwent a transformation. But then I was just beginning to see. At times in this renewal period the community seemed to present a picture of utter chaos. Doubt and fear often seemed to prevail. We had to grasp the fact that it was not the "little black rule book" of community life that united our members, nor even our regularity in following its precepts. Our renewal demanded time and infinite patience on the part of both administrators and those we served.

Yes, James Francis, at this distance of time, I can perhaps begin to under-stand. Sometimes when I am praying in the impressive edifice that might have been your episcopal cathedral, St. Basil's Church, I let my eyes rest on the tasseled red hat, the galero that was once yours hanging high in the sanctuary. It is almost on a level with the tortured figure of the crucified Christ that is suspended high above the altar. There is infinite pity in the eyes of that wooden, spread-eagled figure. When your eyes last rested on that figure, what, I wonder, did you see?

Chapter 2

Memories of a Catholic Girlhood

Anyone observing me as a child would hardly have visualized me in the role of a mother general of a Catholic religious order of women, much less the leader of a band of independent women doing battle with a cardinal. I was not by nature a fighter, a revolutionary. I was shy, one to avoid conflict when I could; in later life, I was able to disguise this timidity when duty demanded it.

I was the third of eight children born to Jacob and Marie Caspary. Maurice, the first-born son, died at birth. Two years later, at the age of two, Ruth, the first-born daughter, died after a one-week illness. Her death occurred only a few months before I was born in the November cold of South Dakota. My parents were highly protective of me, and this parental attitude remained part of my relationship with them throughout my life. Children were precious—more treasured than material wealth in the Caspary household. This was exemplified when we moved to Los Angeles in 1917. At that time I was not allowed to play with neighborhood children. My infant sister, Gretchen, was still too young to be a companion for me. Separation from other children was thought by my parents to be a protection from mysterious, perhaps fatal childhood diseases, which they had experienced in the death of their first two children.

I can remember a little blond boy looking in at me through our iron gate. Beneath the stern enclosure of the gray grill fence surrounding our front lawn he rolled a lovely bright orange toward me. Turn between not wanting to hurt his feelings and my mother's warning, "Don't take food from strangers," I slowly let go of the orange and spun it back to my anonymous friend. New to the city, I pondered over my mother's order to see neighbors as strangers. Only after a kind priest observed me playing alone in our front yard did his gentle reprimand move my mother to allow the gate to be opened for a few select play-mates.

My paternal grandparents, Friedrich Caspary and Josephine Simons, had moved from the Midwest to California some few years before we took the same route. They settled in a grand Victorian home in a residential area of central Los Angeles. We purchased a less pretentious house just a half block from them. Since they were very sociable people, to visit them meant a whole round of introductions to strangers. To escape from the ordeal of being shown off to the visitors, I would scurry to hide behind the large davenport in the parlor. Sometimes I was discovered, but sometimes I succeeded in not meeting the family friends.

I was almost equally shy with children my own age. My grandfather had a study known as a "smoking room." To a child my age it seemed to be a secret place for my grandfather and his cronies. The room was small, tucked away, hidden from plain view just off the entry hall. Clouds of blue pipe smoke always swirled about the men. Only occasionally did we children get a stolen glimpse inside.

So I grew up the product of a German-American Catholic enclave in our area of Los Angeles, the descendant of generations of devout and utterly loyal Roman Catholics. There is even a story, probably apocryphal, of my grandfather standing guard at the bolted door of a small Catholic church in South Dakota, forbidding the poor parish priest, who had reportedly joined the Church-condemned society of Freemasons, to celebrate Sunday Mass. Certainly the story is a paradigm of the spirit of devout and defensive Catholicism with which my growing years were surrounded. I can't remember any family members or friends ever questioning any official dogma of the Church or the multiplicity of devotional practices customary at our parish church, St. Joseph's, located in what later became downtown Los Angeles. There was no threat in this conformity; Catholicism meant family and unity. We lived in an almost exclusively Catholic atmosphere.

Accordingly, I was sent to the nearby Catholic school staffed by Franciscan sisters. The building itself was part of a large complex dominated by a steepled American Gothic church and flanked by a fenced-in residence for the Franciscan friars. On the other end of the property were a house and a garden, also fenced in, where the sisters lived. The "school" was actually only the second story of a kind of community center. The third floor was an auditorium that easily accommodated five hundred or more people. The stage was well structured for the innumerable plays, ranging from pious drama to comedy, portrayed by parish groups with perhaps more enthusiasm than talent. Of course, the school had its share of performances for the edification of parents and friends. On the ground floor were spacious meeting rooms and a kitchen and dining area, where breakfast was served each morning after Mass to the children who had received Holy Communion. Since home was only two blocks away, I was expected to return there after Mass for breakfast. Occasionally, as a rare treat, I was allowed to buy the hot chocolate and buttered toast that were sold at school for ten cents.

Classes began promptly after the required daily Mass and a pause for breakfast. The subjects were well taught, and there were few disciplinary problems. Besides the regular curriculum, there was ample opportunity for stage productions. At one point physical exercise in the yard to the accompaniment of a blaring record player was introduced. At the end of the day there was a grade-by-grade, four-abreast exit march to the accompaniment of a drum. It was my ambition from my first years at the school to play that drum. After eight years of practice on the instrument at my grandparents' house, I achieved my desire. Unfortunately I played so rapidly in my first enthusiastic attempt that the ranks almost ran from the school.

The sisters moved through our childhood world as somewhat mysterious beings, quick to disappear into the convent after school hours. Brown-clad, white-coifed, with black aprons for classroom wear, they never spoke of themselves or ate in our presence, and only rarely did we glimpse their hooded heads touching as two of them exchanged some comment we were not to hear.

I was eager to please these ethereal beings and deeply disappointed whenever my papers did not receive the coveted gold star. I was even more concerned to excel among a group of my classmates in discovering by secret glances whose head would remain bowed longest after receiving Communion.

Religion classes I remember only faintly, mostly as competitive question-and-answer series from the Baltimore Catechism: "Who made you?" "God made me." "Why did God make you?" "God made me to know Him, to love Him, and to serve Him in this world and to be happy with Him forever in the next." And so on. Success was measured less in grades than in collections of brightly colored "holy cards." More memorable were the services in the church, where the sweet, exotic odor of incense and candlewax never quite vanished. The eloquence of the friars in delivering dramatic homilies impressed me deeply, so much so that I still remember the themes of some of those sermons. So beyond the little-girl contests and rivalries, there was created slowly, unforgettably, a heroic Christ-figure I would never quite outgrow, although at intervals I tried to shut it out. And this figure was created by the priests whose eloquence shaped my religious imagination. Always through this time I cherished the moments of prayer that I could snatch from busy family doings. Mostly this would happen late at night when I could take time to enjoy quiet recollection communing with God.

At home I never discussed my feelings or thoughts about these "private" religious matters. There my mother too claimed that what "Sister said" was to be regarded as more significant than her own dictates. Yet she was probably secretly pleased that all her four girls, Gretchen, Beatrice, Marion, and myself, and two boys, Gerard and Gilbert, fit so well into the ideal patterns set up for us; even the boys were seldom involved in anything but mild mischief, such as teasing the girls.

My mother's elaborate preparation for each child's first Communion and Confirmation, the pride she took in our proper clothing for innumerable processions, her insistence on special prayers we said together with her for special feast days—all were affirmations of the atmosphere at school and church. During the month of May she would erect a small altar before which the whole family would pray the rosary each evening. There were also stories of the lives of the saints, rewards of "holy cards" for religious lessons well memorized—all these molded us in a rhythm unbroken by skepticism or deliberation about the Church or its representatives.

Mom had been a teacher in her late teens, answering with some reluctance the request of a pastor for teachers at his school in her home state of Iowa. She was lively and fun-loving and did not relish the thought of living in a small town away from her friends—and boarding in a convent at that! She had only another lay volunteer for a companion and told us often of their carefully laid plans to escape convent supervision by visiting the local post office, where young people gathered in their free evening hours. She had undertaken teaching only at the urging of her mother, whom she worshiped. One of a family of seven girls and two boys, she grew up happily in her Midwestern farm home.

Mother was small in stature, but she had an air of authority about her. She held herself erect until her last years (in her nineties), a sharply etched figure only a little over five feet in height. She dressed tastefully, and as a young woman she had sewed for herself and for "her girls." One of the most vivid memories of my childhood is seeing her dress to go out, leaning forward with a great cascade of brown silken hair being brushed out and then flung back and formed into a knot. Her eyes were a deep blue shaded with a bit of melancholy, but she held her head proudly, as if conscious of her classical features.

My father was not part of our family's devotional program. His religion was a private one, probably thought of then as more manly. His affirmation of our beliefs was evident on Sundays when he was head usher at the central door of St. Joseph's. For this occasion he wore his best suit and vest, freshly cleaned and pressed. As a finishing touch there was always a tiny rosebud in his lapel. Although he was fairly tall and somewhat stout as the years wore on, he moved with dignity down the aisle, handsome with a marvelous air of assurance. How I loved seeing him there!

My relationship with my father was a special one. When I began to take part in plays both at the parish and later in college, he would sit through many endless evening rehearsals waiting to escort me home, since we lived in an area that was becoming unsafe. After we drove up in front of the house, we would remain in the car talking, as good friends do. These were partly times of learning for me and, I suppose, enjoyment for him. He would listen to my questions and, I think, take paternal pleasure as I listened carefully to his responses. It pleased him when I understood his work, the cares and worries that were so much a part of his life. He loved explaining how businesses were run, how money was invested, how this process earned money, and his plans for the several relatively small but profitable enterprises he started on his own.

When I was a little older, I was sometimes called in to be a part of family discussions with my mother and father. Both seemed to value my opinion. At times like these I grew a little apprehensive over their attention to what I had to say. At the same time, I am sure, my self-confidence grew, for I began thinking of myself as an adult long before my years warranted it.

Among the members of our extended family, there was an awareness of the roles that women could play, roles not limited to housekeeping or to married life alone, and interestingly enough, roles that were shared by both men and women in the family. My mother's sisters, especially the younger ones, were teachers, as my mother had been. In my father's family, both men and women played musical instruments well and formed a creditable family orchestra. My aunt Angela spent many years of training in voice, and her sister Dorothy was a gifted pianist and organist, employing her talents at the great organ in St. Joseph's Church in Los Angeles. Both women were expected to perform profes-sionally on the concert stage, and only Angela's failing health pre-vented that from becoming a reality.

My father, for his part, had made a firm decision for all his children: both boys and girls were to receive a college education, in spite of the Depression years in which we grew up. In this he was at odds with his own parents, for whom college was appropriate for boys alone. He would say to us, "No matter what life may bring you, no one can take your education from you," and it was college he had in mind.

And so I grew up, not a saint certainly, but the descendant of gener-ations of fervent, loyal Roman Catholics. This was not a matter of coer-cion; all in the family stood on firm ground and had no desire to move from it. We were neither fanatical nor puritanical; feast days as well as birthdays were celebrated royally. On Sundays there were trips to the beach or the mountains, with frequent stops for sweets or fruit. Our table was seldom without friends and playmates as family policy grew more liberal. I had some companions of other religious beliefs, al-though I must confess I looked on them with some pity as not sharing my special favor with God as a Roman Catholic.

My high school years were spent at Catholic Girls' High School on Pico Boulevard in Los Angeles. It was unique at that time, since it was taught not by one but by a number of different religious communities of sisters. By the time I arrived, there were seven or eight communities represented on the staff, each of which would have a role in my educa-tion. The students daily compared nuns with great, fluted, white coronets, nuns in violet-blue habits with sheer black veils and stiff coifs, nuns with great black bonnets whose profiles were always hidden. So my world moved from teachers in identical Franciscan robes and similar mannerisms in walk and gesture at St. Joseph's into something altogether new.

It was in this varied environment that I began to be influenced by the nuns who taught Latin, mathematics, science, English, and religion. The students had little to do with the priest-principal or his assistant, except for cases of grave misconduct, of which there were few. The priests taught only one class—a senior, one-semester course in religion, more specifically, on marriage. I think few of us if any were struck by the incongruity of these celibate men instructing us in veiled terms of our future duties as Christian wives and mothers.

Although recruitment for the colleges staffed by some of the religious communities was zealous, even stronger was the rivalry among the sisters for candidates to their respective communities. Even as a sophomore I found myself told by a sharp-eyed, black-veiled sister that I had an appointment with her mother general on the following Sunday. Frightened by this unsolicited turn of events, I could only think of my mother's advice on more practical matters: "Don't sign anything before you think twice about it!" Was I being "signed up" for religious life before I had finished high school? It took all my courage to face the piercing eyes of the tiny figure before me and announce that I had not made up my mind about my future. I did not add that her particular habit was singularly unbecoming, but that probably played a part in my anxious but firm answer. The sister was more than a little displeased and scarcely spoke to me again until graduation day.

I was puzzled by the eagerness for new members so evident among the various sisterhoods. At the same time I felt curiosity and a kind of vague longing for the life most of these bright and lively women seemed to lead. I wondered how they had come so close to God. Who told them that they were chosen for the religious life? Little did I dream that the answers to questions such as these would become points of discussion during the most memorable and powerful events of my future life.

Although one of the Franciscan priests from my parish church had left his order, to the horror and endless gossip of the parish, to my knowledge no sister of my acquaintance had left her community. Such fidelity impressed me. Comparison of these women's lives with the permanence of the married state was inevitable in those days. Both religious life and marriage had attractive and frightening aspects for me.

But it was too early to make a decision, certainly in the sheltered life I led. Through my high school years I studied with persistence and arrived at graduation as valedictorian, with the choice of a college facing me. Somehow it was always a Catholic college that I thought of attending. I had been intrigued by my visit to Immaculate Heart College in the Hollywood hills. The sisters who taught there struck me as unique individuals, more so than the members of the same community I had met in high school. Something about the atmosphere delighted and challenged me.

Once enrolled and attending classes, I was not disappointed. The sisters at the college were few in number, but the staff was supplemented by part-time lay professors, including men, from nearby colleges and universities. The mix made for a rich and creative blend. The total enrollment was small in number; the Depression years meant that most young women were at work to help with family expenses. So the student body was called on for a variety of duties and given opportunities that would have been lost in a larger group. I remember being called upon to be sacristan of our tiny chapel, editing the *Tower Tattler*, our college newspaper, teaching class when Sister Eucharia Harney was ill, and seeing that there were enough doughnuts for First Friday breakfast.

I was inspired to academic achievement by the awesome Sister Margaret Mary, dean of studies, whose brilliance during a lecture left the blackboard filled with innumerable dates, places, causes, movements, names of kings and statesmen. It was said of her that once she had read some piece of information, she never forgot it, and we had no reason to believe otherwise. In literature there was Sister St. Paul, a graduate of Vassar and a convert to Catholicism, who had entered the convent at the age of fifty. Rumor had it that she had been a Shakespearean actress, and her readings in class seemed to bear out the story.

Of them all, my favorite was Sister Eucharia. Warm-hearted, generous with her time to the detriment of her health, her spirit made her the life of the college. She laughed at student pranks and thought up a few herself. She found funds when the student budget for a dance ran out. But before any dance was scheduled, she assembled the students for a lecture on the evils of "necking." I never dreamt that a nun could share our laughter and our tears so freely with us. I came to admire this woman for her warm and engaging personality, and soon became her good friend. It became clear to me that these sisters were genuinely human, while at the same time following their Rule. So convent life did not demand mystery, and it could be a source of expansive love and understanding.

Chapter 3

Background and Beginnings

Almost without my realizing it in my college years, I was growing closer to the Immaculate Heart Sisters, although I did not understand fully why I felt attracted to them. Looking back now, I can trace how they shared the thrust into the future, the exhilaration and optimism marking the rapidly growing city of Los Angeles. Like an omen of the future, above their motherhouse in the hills the gigantic sign "HOLLY-WOOD" was erected in the early twenties, a mark of the infant industry soon to flood the world with entertainment.

The sisters in their own way were a part of all the stir and growth around them. They were, when I first knew them, only nine years from the dramatic separation from their Spanish roots, only nine years into their new identity as the California Institute of the Sisters of the Most Holy and Immaculate Heart of the Blessed Virgin Mary. This long-desired independent status from their repressive Spanish origins was only one in a series of changes that were to mark the history of this attractive community.

Sisters of the Immaculate Heart were no strangers to change. Founded in Spain in 1848 in a semi-cloistered form, the community had for its mission at that time catechetical work for the poor. Within ten years the sisters were offering a broader range of subjects in their orphanages and schools in seven major cities in Spain. Soon they were invited, out of their small number, to send sisters to the rough-and-tumble California of gold rush days. Ten Spanish sisters volunteered for Los Angeles in 1871 and by a series of misadventures landed in northern California. They established themselves in various northern California cities, then decided to settle in the towns of Gilroy and San Juan Bautista. Since they did not know English very well, they established their first schools with assistance from English-speaking lay teachers. To earn a living, they taught music, art, and embroidery to the children of the wealthier Catholic families.

Well educated in Spain, those first members of the Immaculate Heart Sisters in California adapted to their new country and language quickly. Soon they offered a traditional academic curriculum, as the school records attest. Their pupils, attracted by these courageous nuns, included children of the first families of California. In 1886, with the encouragement of Bishop Francis Mora, bishop of Monterey–Los Angeles, and under the leadership of Mother Raimunda Cremadell, the sisters moved to teach in the new school on the grounds at St.Vibiana's Cathedral in Los Angeles. There they found a fitting challenge that established their reputation as superior educators.

Bishop Mora had a major concern. In two letters to Mother Raimunda he wrote that "the sisters who were sent there [to St. Vibiana's] would be academically well-equipped" and "only the finest teachers of the community [should] be entrusted with this important project."[1] The insistence on quality scholastic preparation, from this very first assignment, became an educational tradition for the community over the next six decades. This demanding principle of educational excellence was, in fact, one of the important issues that later shaped the conflict with Cardinal McIntyre of the Los Angeles Archdiocese.

Attracted by the courage and zeal for education of those early Immaculate Heart Sisters, American-born women joined the community. The number of venturesome[2] Americans grew gradually, and their leadership soon became apparent. The first American provincial, Mother Magdalen Murphy, for example, chose with considerable foresight the fourteen-acre site at Western and Franklin Avenues in Hollywood for the sisters' motherhouse and Immaculate Heart College. It was she who, from 1911 to 1924, was the greatest single influence during the first two decades of the century, overseeing the growth of community institutions.

The American recruits, along with some of the older Spanish sisters, saw the growing needs in the state of California. They realized that to

---

[1] For an account of the early years of the teaching apostolate of the Sisters of the Immaculate Heart of Mary, see Marian Sharples' fine history of the institute, entitled *All Things Remain in God* (Los Angeles: Unpublished work, 1963) 48.

[2] The story of Miss Ap-Jones demonstrates the adventuresome spirit of these mid-nineteenth-century women. Oral tradition has it that she came to enter the Immaculate Heart convent on horseback, realizing that a good horse was a valuable and necessary contribution to the community.

serve the Catholic population in the burgeoning West and to provide excellent schools, they had to adapt to the culture. The experience of rapid growth in California, the diverse population, and the need for flexibility in a traditionally rigid convent life created tensions. The IHM administration in Spain, which during this early period governed the California community, was unfamiliar with the challenges California posed to the sisters. Also, with the entrance of American women into the community, the attitudes of freedom of spirit, rugged individualism, and adaptation to life in California created a distance between the two groups. Delayed communication for minor requests, for instance, was difficult for those trying to work with Yankee efficiency. More grave was the imposition of Spanish authoritarianism over the sisters of the California province.[3]

It was not until 1924, however, that the sisters living in the California province felt that the restrictions were so unfavorable that they should seek separation from their Spanish origins. Both Mother Magdalen Murphy and Mother Genevieve Parker had been strong leaders in the California province. They had attempted unsuccessfully to gain the support of the successive bishops of the Los Angeles Diocese in their resolve to separate from the Spanish community. Nevertheless, the California sisters' work continued to prosper during the first two decades of the twentieth century. This prosperity was due to the individual sacrifices of many sisters who lived abstemious and austere lives. The strong administration of Mother Redempta Ward achieved financial stability for the California sisters even during the difficult years of the Great Depression. With the cultural assimilation of the Spanish nuns into the American way of life, and the security of financial viability, the sisters requested that Bishop John J. Cantwell petition the Vatican to establish an independent community in California. On November 29, 1922, the petition was sent to the Vatican.[4] Approval was granted on April 18, 1924.

[3] An example of the authoritarianism is found in the writings of Mother Augustina Coromina. As special visitor from the general administration in Gerona, Spain, to the California province, she was highly critical of the lives of several sisters. She remained in California for over two years (1921–23) and was asked to leave by both the sisters and Bishop Cantwell. For a very colorful description of her evaluation of the lifestyle of the California nuns, see Sharples, *All Things Remain*, 180–210.

[4] A vote was taken among all the members of the California province. Ninety-seven percent of the California nuns wanted to separate from their Spanish origins.

Ignoring Bishop Cantwell's desire to have juridical authority over the new community,[5] the Vatican granted the new institute pontifical status. This rank in Catholic orders of women historically has meant that the community designated "pontifical institute" was assigned a cardinal-protector in Rome to defend the sisters against possible encroachment of their rights by anyone, including the local hierarchy.[6] This new order was now to be called "The California Institute of the Sisters of the Most Holy and Immaculate Heart of the Blessed Virgin Mary," and its members were asked to modify their habit slightly to distinguish them from the original group. Their revised rule of life was written with the assistance of canon lawyers, as was the custom of the time. As with most orders, the constitutions (applications of the Rule) were unfortunately a code of laws rather than a simple testimony of a spirit and direction.

From 1924 onward the community steadily increased in numbers with a high of 600 members in 1963. More important, their firm determination and innovativeness matched that of larger communities of religious orders scattered across the country and serving much larger areas. By the Catholic standards of the day, both religious and lay, the Immaculate Heart Sisters had arrived: by 1967 the community staffed 51 parochial elementary schools and partially staffed 11 high schools, with a total full-time sister-teacher staff of 313 members. In the Archdiocese of Los Angeles alone, IHMs in 1967 had 125 sisters teaching in elementary schools and 72 sisters teaching in parochial high schools. In addition to its Los Angeles schools, the IHMs taught in six other Western dioceses in the United States and one in Canada, with a total student population of 23,600.[7]

Five sisters chose to return to the original community in Spain. Sharples, *All Things Remain,* 214.

[5] Sharples, *All Things Remain,* 105, 205, 208, 213, respectively; evidence from letters of Bishop Cantwell indicate that prior to his request to the Vatican, he wanted jurisdiction over the California IHM province.

[6] That such protection was sorely needed from time to time can be seen by reviewing the cases of the dozen or so other American institutes that looked for relief from diocesan constraints and even persecution in the nineteenth century. For these orders of religious women, "pontifical status provided the fullest and most secure route" to a measure of autonomy and self-determination. For the importance attached to this status, see Margaret Susan Thompson, "The Validation of Sisterhood: Canonical Status and Liberation in the History of American Nuns," in *A Leaf from the Great Tree of God: Essays in Honor of Ritamary Bradley, SFCC,* ed. Margot H. King (Toronto: Peregrina Publishing Co., 1994) 62–64.

[7] Sister Elizabeth Ann Flynn, "Background of the Ninth General Chapter's Decree on Education" (Los Angeles: Unpublished work, December 1, 1967). See

The sisters also had begun to teach not only in parish schools but to found their own institutions as well. As early as 1905 they had built a large motherhouse in Hollywood and established Immaculate Heart High School, the first Catholic school in southern California to obtain full accreditation from the University of California. By 1916 they also obtained a charter for and began work on Immaculate Heart College, the first standard Catholic college for women in southern California. By 1943 they had established a novitiate in Montecito, Santa Barbara County. On the same property they opened La Casa de Maria in 1955, the first retreat house in California for married couples. The eagerness to expand resulted in the opening and staffing of two hospitals—St. Mary Desert Valley Hospital in Apple Valley and Queen of the Valley Hospital in West Covina in 1956 and 1962 respectively.

As a community, the Sisters of the Immaculate Heart were not allied with any specific spiritual tradition, such as Benedictine, Franciscan, or Dominican. Their rule was that of Augustine, which was used by many orders as a guide to daily living. Ironically, their founder, Canon Joaquin Masmitja de Puig, a parish priest in Olot, Spain, had written devotional tracts that contrasted greatly with his progressive views about sisters' work and lifestyle.

Reverend Mother Eucharia (Elizabeth) Harney was a charismatic and dynamic influence in the community; she held office from 1939 to 1951. Unlike the stereotypical nun, portrayed as submissive and passive, "Mother E," as she was affectionately named, took an intuitive delight in the Christian intellectual tradition, with a fine disregard for the minute details of the Rule. She brought to all with whom she came in contact a reminder of the essential spirit of Christian love and of the perfection of charity rather than the letter of the law. It is perhaps in this characterization that is rooted the spirit of the IHM sisters' 1967 renewal decrees. She opened hearts by the warmth of her personality.

Appendix A, p. 225. As chair of the commission on apostolic works, Sister Elizabeth Ann headed the task force that documented the educational profile of the community. The profile provided statistical data that clearly demonstrated the herculean efforts and resources the community was using to provide teaching sisters for the archdiocese. It also proved the need to further educate the sisters prior to their entry into the classroom. Thus, this "Background" document was the factual basis on which we relied to write the decree on apostolic works. This decree on apostolic works of the Ninth General Chapter included the theological principles of our apostolate and the practical remedy for our situation of limited resources and under-prepared personnel. This decree became a major stumbling block for Cardinal McIntyre and a significant reason for his non-acceptance of our 1967 chapter acts.

She established during her tenure as mother general a unity and exuberance that was contagious. Her magnetic personality reached beyond the individual nun in the Immaculate Heart Community.

Prior to the Second Vatican Council, Mother Eucharia invited speakers from around the nation to Immaculate Heart College. It was not unusual to see celebrated Catholic speakers, such as Dorothy Day, Father Eugene Burke, C.P., Maisie Ward and Frank Sheed, Sister Madeleva Wolff, C.S.C., and Clare Booth Luce, on the college campus. In retrospect, the spirit of the Second Vatican Council was presaged by the spirit of Mother Eucharia. In the late fifties and early sixties, she created an environment unknown in traditional convent life.

Preceded by Mother Eucharia, Sister Regina (Josephine) McPartlin was elected mother general and held office from 1951 to 1963. Following Mother Eucharia's spirit of openness and promotion of excellence in education, Mother Regina continued the tradition of inviting Catholic and non-Catholic guest speakers for the sisters and college personnel. These guests represented an even broader political and cultural spectrum. The intellectual progressive thought was not due to the leadership of one person. Many IHM sisters studying for higher degrees would recommend lecturers they had heard, so that a collaborative spirit of renewal and change pervaded the community. In particular, Immaculate Heart College (IHC) became known as a progressive Catholic college, hosting theologians who promoted and explained the changes of the Second Vatican Council. These events were open to the public. Thus the college developed a national reputation for enlightened Catholicism and spiritual development not only for priests and nuns but for all Catholics.

It was during this time that Pat Reif, I.H.M., Ph.D., headed the program in Christian holiness, a post-Vatican II degree. The intent was to educate, as quickly as possible, those responsible for religious leadership and the formation of young nuns in the progressive reforms of the Second Vatican Council. This very successful program put the community and the college at the forefront of women's progressive (and for some detractors, radical) Catholic education. The IHMs were following in the tradition of their founders, who had insisted on the best preparation and education for their nuns.

The sisters read widely and attended lectures and retreats by speakers from a variety of backgrounds: the Canadian psychologist Noel Mailloux, O.P.; Jesuit activist Daniel Berrigan; well-known journalist and religion editor for the *New York Times,* John Cogley; and many theologians from the United States and abroad, including Hans Küng; Robert McAfee Brown; Gerard Sloyan; Avery Dulles, S.J.; Bernard Cooke; Eugene Kennedy; Bernard Häring, C.Ss.R.; Ladislaus Orsy, S.J.; Michael Novak; Gregory Baum; Martin Marty; and Adrian Van Kaam, C.S.Sp. These speakers and many others whose works were eagerly read, such as Karl Rahner and Cardinal Leon-Joseph Suenens, generated weekly informal discussions among the sisters in the motherhouse, many of them teachers at Immaculate Heart College, Immaculate Heart High School, and/or nearby parochial schools.

A new frankness became apparent in these discussions as sisters exchanged opinions on their identity as women and nuns. Once this honesty about their daily lives and their mission or goals began to develop, nothing could stop it. The young nuns were educated to articulate their views, to participate in public dialogues, and to present a reasoned argument. They engaged in sharp but kindly differences with sisters across lines of authority. Not for the first time but with a new urgency, many nuns struggled openly with the daily compromise between the service they sought to give and the rules based on Church law for women religious. Unfortunately, amid the philosophical and religious exchange, debate over the habit and secular dress held a weight disproportionate to their importance.

The dress or habit of most religious women of this time gave testimony to the customs of another day and tended to separate them from those they served, suggesting a kind of elite existence. Their daily, sacrosanct schedule had to be broken innumerable times to answer the needs of their students or patients. They were forbidden all but the most innocuous of radio or television programs and were allowed to attend motion pictures only in their own auditorium, and then only when it was a "religious" movie, such as *Going My Way* or *A Man for All Seasons*. Further, their reading was sharply curtailed—newspapers and news magazines were brought into convents only when a "liberal" superior so decreed. Conscientious teachers who wished to keep abreast of city, state, national, and international developments in order to be at least as well informed as their students and parents or their secular colleagues were at a distinct disadvantage. Their visits to parents were rare; to friends, even more sharply limited, thus further isolating them from the world around them and from channels of information. Decisions about teaching or nursing assignments and choice of the group with whom one lived under the rule of a superior were made remotely by the mother general of the order and her council. Only for a serious reason might an appeal to the mother general modify a sister's annual assignment.

These restrictions were designed originally to provide a kind of protective shield from a world viewed as replete with temptations that would distract a sister from her search for God. The effect, however, was to separate her from those she served and to foster a childlike mentality, since decisions about her own daily life were made completely by others.

The Second Vatican Council was convened by Pope John XXIII in 1962 to renew the character of the Church in the modern world. Invited scholars and Catholic theologians influenced by developments in theology, psychology, and sociology urged the council fathers to employ the modern understanding of the human person as a participatory and self-determining agent. The teaching of the council shifted the notion of virtue, so that the former unquestioning, passive obedience to ecclesiastical or religious authority gave way to the personal responsibility of adult, mature Christians.[8] Further, the Church was coming to be regarded less as an "institution" than as a "community." Also, authority, for all Catholics, was defined less as power over others than as service to them.

As Lora Ann Quiñonez, C.D.P., and Mary Daniel Turner, S.N.D. de N., point out, Vatican II was the first council to be called after the advent of the electronic mass media. "Its agenda was audacious. Quite simply it undertook to lay out the direction for the reform and renewal of the Catholic church *in the context of the contemporary conditions.*"[9] Vatican II called for change and at the same time reflected change already in progress.

Giving a clear rationale for reform, renewal, and change, Charles Curran wrote:

> The most significant changes occurred in ecclesiology itself. Vatican II accepted the notion of the church as always in need of reform. The principle of aggiornamento, or updating, included considering both the signs of the times and the historical sources. The church,

[8] Pastoral Constitution on the Church in the Modern World (*Gaudium et Spes*), in Austin Flannery, O.P., ed., *Vatican Council II: The Conciliar and Post Conciliar Documents* (Northport, N.Y.: Costello Publishing Co., 1981) 1:903–1001.

[9] Lora Ann Quiñonez, C.D.P., and Mary Daniel Turner, S.N.D. de N., *The Transformation of American Sisters* (Philadelphia: Temple University Press, 1992) 4.

then, is always in need of change, reform, renewal, since the church lives in the tension between the now and the future of the fullness of grace.[10]

For women religious, the most influential document of the council was *Perfectae Caritatis* (1965). Women in religious orders leading static, predictable, and regulated lives were given a mandate in this document to adapt, renew, and change. In hindsight, the two major themes of the document were somewhat contradictory. The first theme called for both a return to the Gospel as a source for living religious life and a return to the original inspiration of the founders. The second theme urged each community to update its lifestyle in order to be relevant to the modern world.

Central to *Perfectae Caritatis* was the concept that ultimate authority for renewal rested within the religious community itself. Any community engaged in the process of renewal could find in the document more specific guidance regarding decision-making and authority within religious communities. For example,

> . . . it is for the competent authorities, alone, and especially for general chapters, to establish the norms for appropriate renewal and to legislate for it, as also to provide for sufficient prudent experimentation. . . . Superiors, however, in matters which concern the destiny of the entire institute, should find appropriate means of consulting their subjects, and should listen to them.[11]

Thus, in the first place, the notion of experimentation, hitherto unspoken in the matter of the renewal of religious life, and in the second place, assent of an institute's members to the proposed direction of reform were regarded as essential to the renewal.

Rounding out this rather broad decree, a special enabling directive entitled "Norms for Implementing the Decree on the Up-to-Date Renewal of Religious Life[12] was issued by Pope Paul VI on August 6, 1966,

---

[10] Charles Curran, "What Can Catholic Ecclesiology Learn from Official Catholic Teaching?" in *A Democratic Catholic Church: The Reconstruction of Roman Catholicism*, ed. Eugene C. Bianchi and Rosemary Radford Ruether (New York: Crossroad, 1992) 98.

[11] Decree on the Up-to-Date Renewal of Religious Life *(Perfectae Caritatis),* in Flannery, *Vatican Council II*, 613, no. 4.

[12] *Ecclesiae Sanctae II*, in Flannery, *Vatican Council II*, 624–633.

to implement specific matters in religious life. It is a document clearly progressive with respect to the ways that might be used to effect real changes. Above all, it reinforced the religious order's own role in the renewal process, but added an important point. It called for a more clearly defined spirit of communal self-determination, with the participation of each community member.

Thus more flexibility than in the past was now encouraged in a structure whose immobility was once deemed its chief virtue. Not merely was experimentation to be encouraged, but immediate measures of renewal and adaptation were to be given an indefinite period of trial, ranging up to twelve or more years. Ample and free consultation of all members of religious orders was to be provided and the results made available to the sisters. Now at last, by virtue of these 1966 norms, the path seemed clear. The many sisters of other orders impatient for change, like ourselves, were at last coming to see the possibility of real change in their lives as religious.

Immediately following the issuance of the 1966 norms, we set up study commissions and elected delegates to the formal meeting known as the "Chapter of Renewal." It was clear to us that the highest Church authority—the Pope—had mandated a complete revision of the lifestyle and work of women's religious communities. We were unusually optimistic with regard to the renewal, because as a religious community of women we had the reputation of being the California nuns: progressive, liberal, and modern. Little did we know that this background would be the beginning of a conflict that would change our Catholic identity.

Chapter 4

Called to Be a Nun

Looking back, I cannot remember when it became clear to me that I felt "called" to religious life. I am sure that my friendship with Sister Eucharia was a strong influence in making the call a reality. My parents, especially my father, had ambitions of professional life for me. He really thought I could become a dentist specializing in children's orthodontics. Not even to please him could I have done that. What would he think of my becoming a sister?

Of course, the decision was not immediately firm. I was dating two young men during my junior and senior years of college. Both Ben and Jim talked about marriage and plans for a future family. And I cared for these men as friends. Ben, who was a little older than I, was a graduate of Loyola University and had become a young executive with Kodak Company. I went to noisy company picnics with Ben and to reunions of his college class and their special club, The Aristonians. Dances were sometimes sock hops at Loyola University and more formal evenings at the Coconut Grove. All this took place in a totally Catholic atmosphere replete with Jesuit chaperones.

Jim, on the other hand, preferred lectures at the Wilshire Ebell Theatre, concerts by the Los Angeles Philharmonic, and good movies. He was a graduate of Cal Tech doing experimental work in the discovery of new, worldwide oil fields, which he never grew tired of describing. But in spite of all this flattering attention, my deepest desire and attraction were for the convent, where I felt I might be able to teach, as well as to deepen my spiritual life. By June 1937 I had graduated from college. Gradually I knew that my vocation was to be a nun.

I applied for acceptance to the Sisters of the Immaculate Heart and was given a date for an entrance interview with Reverend Mother Redempta. She was stern-looking, but her twinkling eyes betrayed her sense of humor. On the appointed day I sat before her, awaiting her judgment. Was I a fit candidate for the Immaculate Heart Sisters? On the required form, in answer to the question "Why do you want to enter religious life?" I had written "To help others."

"Child," said reverend mother, disregarding my age, "what about your own soul? Didn't you think about that?"

I was nonplused, sure that somehow I had failed the test. But my letter of acceptance arrived soon after. Still a little uncertain, I investigated the local graduate schools. But I stopped smoking, "just in case." The feeling that I was somehow destined for religious life remained. And so, in September 1937, I entered the Sisters of the Immaculate Heart of Mary.

The most difficult part of my decision was leaving a home where the family ties were strong, so strong that they did not need verbal expression. While I felt some of the sorrow of parting before arriving at the convent, it was only after I officially stepped into the novitiate that I realized how, in those days, separation from family and friends was as complete as rules could make it. Frequent visits by family members and even letters from them were forbidden, and the short, black postulant's dress we wore made us feel apart from those we had known so intimately. But it was more than that.

For most people, good Catholic people, the "sisters" were a breed apart, and lay persons seemed to cherish that sense of having someone in the family or among acquaintances become a sister. For my part, the new remoteness from those I cherished brought an unexpected loneliness. Confinement to the limited space of our novitiate was another trial, for surrendering the car I had driven during college days meant giving up the freedom it had provided. But life as a postulant also had its reward for me in the classes I was unexpectedly told to teach at Immaculate Heart High School. I loved the classes; I loved the friendly students, and I know they cared for me. But the assigned tasks of washing dishes, dusting, polishing—all seemed to take precious time from reading, study, or even correcting my students' papers. Since we were not allowed to speak to the professed sisters, we were isolated with a small group of young aspirants, except for the novice mistress.

As the reception day neared, the day when we were to exchange a white wedding gown for the plain, blue serge habit of a novice, I began to reconsider my commitment. So far all was going quite well. But did I really want this dedicated life, shaped by the vows of poverty, chastity, and obedience, as a lifetime choice? Could I remain faithful to the promises I would make after a year as a novice? My whole family and educational background had formed in me a pattern of tenacious resolve to consider a promise once made as unbreakable. And this—a promise made to God? I clung anxiously to my earlier decision.

There seemed to be no joy of anticipation at the thought of my reception of the habit. I began to lose weight at an alarming rate, so that the gown, especially made for the reception ceremony, had to be altered several times. I was plagued at a level too deep to be articulated by the questions: What is the meaning of this life I am choosing? Does it mean an unending separation not only from those dear to me but also from the reality of suffering and struggle that much of the world had to endure?

Would it mean, too, that community prayers in a structure of time, place, and form were unchangeable? Where were the solitude and silence I had cherished and found even in my home, in the midst of family? And were we really somehow better, more pleasing to God, than our mothers and fathers, who visited us at the convent, humbly bringing permitted gifts to be shared by our sisters? Was this really a "more perfect" life, I wondered.[1] If only I could be certain. But I could not even voice my concerns. Rather, I chose to believe that these questions would somehow be answered during the coming novitiate year. And so reception day, preceded by a silent retreat of ten days, temporarily restored my peace of mind.

Only one other woman was received with me in May 1938. A veteran teacher from New Mexico, she had chosen religious life at an age beyond that of our novice mistress. We knelt at the altar together and received the blessed habit, and then exited to be stripped of our ceremonial wedding gowns and clothed in the habit of the community. We returned to the chapel to the inevitable accompaniment of tears from our relatives and friends.

The moment came for the presiding priest to address us by our religious names, an additional cloaking of the identity we were to shed as totally "hidden in Christ." My fellow novice received a variation of her baptismal name and was now known as Sister Francis Clare Baca. I

---

[1] For a lively discussion of this important question, as it came to be viewed by some theologians in the post-conciliar period, see Rev. John F. Mahoney, "Is Convent Life Fundamentally Unchristian?" *National Catholic Reporter* (March 6, 1968) 10–11, in which he argues that the value of the individual must not be sacrificed "on the gnostic altars of efficiency, church interests, or financial growth."

had hoped that my own baptismal name might be retained. But a far different name had been chosen by my mentor, Sister Eucharia: I was to be called Sister Mary Humiliata—a reminder of the humility I was encouraged to cultivate in honor of the Blessed Virgin. Audible gasps were heard in the chapel. Had the priest really read the name correctly? I soon lectured myself into accepting the name as a part of novitiate asceticism. I was determined to live the life wholeheartedly, and this was the first "humiliating" choice, to be laid aside only with the changes that the renewal would bring some thirty years later.

So what was this novitiate period? A full year during which all studies but theological ones were forbidden; a more strict prayer schedule was observed; our ability to lead a lifelong giving of self in terms of the three vows was scrutinized by religious authority; and a further withdrawal from the "outside world" was cultivated. We were fortunate in having as novice mistress Sister Enda Doherty, who had been snatched from an eighth-grade classroom, where her talents had flourished. As a teacher, she realized that our undue confinement and lack of physical activity could be harmful to her young charges. She provided us with recreational activities as custom allowed. Once a week we walked to Ferndell Park on Los Feliz Boulevard, where we sang old folksongs and munched on apples and cookies. Many afternoons, especially on weekends and holidays, we played basketball and tennis, and enjoyed a variety of other physical exercises. Each evening we engaged in conversation, told stories, and commented on the readings we had done that day, generally spiritual books like Tanquerey's work on the spiritual life or *The Catechism of the Vows*, which we had to memorize in the year before we were to take our first vows. But our novice mistress did not forget our future careers as teachers, and she glorified the role, telling us of her experiences in the classroom with a great deal of enthusiasm.

Our spiritual growth was limited by the nature of the library available to the novices and their mistress. The rich library of Christian tradition was closed to us, except for the rather dour writers of the nineteenth century who emphasized conformity, obedience, and the avoidance of what were called "particular friendships." Our schedule was fairly heavy. We learned to chant the Office of the Blessed Virgin in Latin, most of us not understanding the words. There was a plethora of recited vocal prayers, many bearing marks of our heritage of Spanish piety. Lectures by the aged chaplain centered on the series of predigested notes from his seminary days. After lengthy instruction, Father asked only two questions in our classes. One set answer was "hypostatic union," and the other was "transubstantiation." If one answer didn't fit the question, the other was sure to.

Sooner than I thought, I made a transition from my personal search for God to a regularized living of daily life. I seemed to have left behind my yearning for intimacy with God and settled for what I could sense of God's presence in the community.[2] The novitiate provided cozy companionship, although much of the time the novices, like the professed sisters, had to observe the practice of silence. And I soon learned how a world can shrink into delight over a box of sweets at recreation or into smothered laughter at a mispronounced word during spiritual reading at meals.

Then, with harsh unexpectedness, everything changed. It came with a call to the office of the novice mistress, where chiding for some infraction of the rules was ordinarily meted out. But this time it was different. The eyes of the novice mistress were soft with sympathy as she told me that my younger brother was very ill and that I might go that afternoon to see him in the hospital. I could hardly believe the message. Ten years old, bright, loving, healthy, and utterly beloved by me—Gilbert ill?

At the hospital, his eyes brightened as he surveyed my black veil, used by the novices when they had to leave the convent in emergencies. But his color was faded. When I bent to kiss him, the nurse forbade me, "We don't know what he has. Don't go near him!"

The whole next week was a nightmare. My intuition told me that I would never see him again. The following Saturday morning my novice mistress, her eyes filled with compassion, brought me that very message. I cried out in a pain I thought unendurable. I rebelled, I denied, I shut myself up in a desperate attempt not to believe the reality.

After the funeral, when the presence of the family was no longer a haven, I felt utterly alone again. How could that vivacious group of young novices understand the finality of this separation? I resolved not to inflict my private heartache on my novitiate companions.

[2] The term "community" is used throughout this book in place of "order" or "institute" to mean the groups of religious women united under the title Immaculate Heart of Mary. Later, in 1970, when the Immaculate Heart Sisters were obliged to separate into two groups, the first group, headed by Sister Eileen MacDonald, I.H.M., used the original canonical title "Institute," while the second, larger group, which I headed at that time, is referred to as "Immaculate Heart Community," a non-canonical lay group, a name by which we are still known today.

Nighttime in our curtained dormitory quarters made tears unthinkable. Where could I be alone and sob unnoticed and undisturbed? Uncontrolled sorrow at death was thought inappropriate for sisters. Their faith was supposed to teach them that reunion with family and friends in eternity awaited, and that was consolation enough. I had heard of one young sister whose tears at a family funeral were quieted by a sharp reprimand from an older sister-companion. I could not let anyone know that my sadness would last forever.

But there was a time and place at evening meditation in the semi-darkness of the chapel, and there, night after night, my face hidden by our heavy, white novitiate veils, I released my tears. As evening Angelus neared, I wiped away evidence of my sorrow, and by evening recreation I forced myself to remain under control as much as possible. I also resolved to introduce as much laughter as I could into the group, hiding my inner feelings. I suspect that at this time I found my deepest identity as a private person.

I had learned a bitter lesson. There had been other deaths in the larger family circle, but none could have done what Gilbert's death did to me or, I'm sure, to any of my siblings. For me certainly, Death had slid its long knife of separation into my heart, and I could not pull it out.

Chapter 5

Teacher, Professor, and Administrator

At the end of the year of novitiate, the ceremony of the first profession of vows was to be celebrated. These vows were called temporary, since they were made for one year, to be renewed one year at a time up to the final vows, three years later. We were told, however, that these first promises to God were in effect forever. And I believed it.

The custom was to send newly professed sisters from the novitiate directly into teaching assignments, whether or not they had completed their undergraduate degree. Then each sister was required to enroll in late afternoon, evening, or weekend college classes, completing her education as she went along. I was fortunate in that I had already completed my college degree and so received my first assignment as a teaching sister in 1939. I was "missioned," as it was called in the community, to teach at my own high school alma mater, Catholic Girls' High School. I would be close to my family, and in addition, my two younger sisters were attending the school, Marion as a sophomore; Beatrice, a senior. What fun!

But before I had packed up to change locations from the motherhouse to a parish convent near the school, a second white envelope was placed at my door. A change of mission! It was not to be Catholic Girls' High School after all, but St. Bernardine's High School, a small, undistinguished, coed, country secondary school taught by a handful of Immaculate Heart sisters. The building housed both grammar school and high school in a sometimes raucous mixture of bells, tramping feet, bouncing balls, and Latin conjugations recited in chorus. I wept.

In one of those turns that older sisters used to call "the blessing of obedience," St. Bernardine's came to be one of the most refreshing experiences of my life. The school desperately needed reaccreditation—that was our goal. So the five sisters, of whom I was the youngest, taught hard and well. The students were used to a slower pace than we set, but they responded. And we succeeded. Oratorical contests, science fairs, an annual concert, Latin, drama—students made their mark in what was then a small, backwater town.

We brought our best resource: a never-tiring ambition to make the students know that they had talent, to see their confidence grow, to see them off, a small army of athletes pitted against the gigantic "publics," and to cheer as they returned battered and bandaged but hailed as heroes. I volunteered as director of plays and rehearsed endlessly to keep the young people occupied during dreary weekends. I loved every minute of rehearsals; they brought me to life on otherwise interminable Saturdays and Sundays. I knew I had succeeded as drama teacher when my cast proposed a repeat staging of their senior play in the Los Angeles Coliseum!

But two years later, in 1941, a new summons came for me—graduate study for a master's degree at the University of Southern California. This meant living at the motherhouse in Hollywood. Although in my heart I never really left St. Bernardine's, the possibility of study opened another door. I found that my major in English at Immaculate Heart College stood me in good stead. I was well prepared and could enjoy the classes without the usual fears of failure or a C in any course. I soon felt at ease at the university. Even the habit we wore, which made the sisters on the USC campus conspicuous objects of curiosity, lent us a little amusement over the mild stir we created.

Normally the sisters in our community who were destined for teaching in college were sent to study for higher degrees as soon as they could be spared from teaching in elementary and high schools. In the choice of universities, there were varying opinions among community authorities. Some felt that a Catholic university, specifically the Catholic University of America in Washington, was the only proper place for the training of those who would be teaching at a Catholic college. Throughout the history of our training and in my years of leadership, the Immaculate Heart Community never felt restricted to this type of Catholic elitism, as though every thought or theory had to be baptized Catholic to be true. Choosing which sisters would be selected for advanced training was usually a matter of compromise between Immaculate Heart College department heads and authorities in the religious community itself. For both Sister Agnes Ann Green and myself, it was determined that the college needed two additional Ph.D.'s—one in science and the other in English—and so our lives took another turn.

After my venture into graduate studies at USC in 1942, I was, in an ironic change of mission, sent back to my first, aborted assignment at Catholic Girls' High. This was to be a year's interlude as a stopgap teaching duty due to the illness of a sister assigned there. The year was an extraordinary experience, bringing me into contact with a number of gifted young women, as I was given, among other classes, the honors' group. Released from the pressure of graduate work, I felt suddenly carefree, anxious to share with my students the literature I treasured.

At the end of this very satisfying year of teaching, I was given my next assignment—to complete my doctoral degree at Stanford University. So far north as to discourage visits from former students, even family for the most part, the location lent itself to long hours of solitude and study. I enjoyed the classes, the long hours in the library, and even the weekly papers, carefully typed for exacting professors.

Both Sister Agnes Ann and I were intellectually challenged in our graduate work, first at USC, and later at Stanford. Both of these institutions opened up new worlds for me, and after I had enlisted in the required number of units each semester, I signed up to audit additional classes. Regrettably there were some academic activities we could not engage in. We were not permitted, for instance, to go to drama performances on campus or to movies at theaters nearby, even though many of them would likely have added enrichment for a literature major. I filled many notebooks with subjects and aspects of subjects that I wanted to explore after the completion of my degree, such as the lyrics of Anglo-Norman literature, new theories of poetics, and studies in the French novelist François Mauriac. Although those desires were to remain unfulfilled, I have nevertheless always been grateful for the intellectual stimulation I experienced during those years. Only occasionally I was reminded by others of the anomaly of nuns in medieval garb engaged in rigorous twentieth-century scholarship in one of the world's foremost centers of learning.

Two minor incidents brought home this ironic juxtaposition, as the habit elicited from my teachers and students sometimes strange and awkward responses. One of my teachers at Stanford, Dr. Margery Bailey, a renowned (and redoubtable) professor of eighteenth-century literature, once met me walking through the famous Stanford Spanish-mission arches. It was a very windy day, and that part of the habit known as the "scapular," a black, hem-length panel that hung rather loosely down the front and back over the blue serge habit, not unlike a sandwich board, was flapping in the wind. Dr. Bailey remarked dryly in her inimitable manner, "You look just like a windmill."

The other incident occurred in class. A woman turned to me in Dr. Kennedy's seminar and said gleefully, "I would just like to scribble all over your white bib with my pen." Today I am not quite sure of the motivations of those responses, but I do know that the habit created a distance and mystery, even humor, on campus. But on the whole we felt comfortable in the academic milieu. Slowly Sister Agnes Ann and I were able to make friends with the students who were so curious about nuns attending the university, and thus partially to bridge the wide gap between lay people and ourselves created in part by the nun's habit.[1]

After receiving my doctoral degree in 1948, I was immediately assigned to the faculty of Immaculate Heart College, where in various capacities I was to spend some of the happiest years of my life. Teaching, writing, and speaking were all aimed at heightening the mission and reputation of our college. Almost at once I was appointed chair of the small English department. Two years later I continued in that position while adding that of dean of the newly formed graduate school at Immaculate Heart College.

Certainly the only course open to me was to learn by doing. I surely made my share of errors, but I was working with understanding and eager teachers in the graduate fields of music, education, and later religious education besides English, with other majors added in the next few years. Because the graduate school was very young with a modest enrollment, we as professors were able to lavish attention on the students. For that reason, perhaps, we could train young people, lay and religious, some of whom later made considerable contributions in education, to undertake further graduate study, writing, and speaking.

Ten years after I had come to the college, in 1958, following graduate school at Stanford, I was appointed college president by the mother general, Mother Regina McPartlin, and her council. Thought an honor, the position changed the scope and direction of my efforts at our college from teaching and research to administration, planning for the future, working with colleagues in other institutions, and certainly

---

[1] For discussions of the role of the habit in the efforts to renew religious life as a result of the Second Vatican Council, and as one of the main stumbling blocks in the Cardinal McIntyre's conflict with the Immaculate Heart of Mary Sisters, see Chapters 11 and 12.

fund-raising. But if the community of sisters, out of their own slender means and their faculty salaries, had not supplemented the college budget, Immaculate Heart College would have closed long before it did. The sisters on the faculty worked for room, board, and clothing; without them, the college would not have existed. As vowed religious, we considered it a privilege to be appointed to the faculty, and we accepted the situation in good spirit.

The late 1950s were marked by unprecedented growth and vitality among the faculty. Leading off in a flood of national publicity was the art department, with Sisters Corita Kent and Magdalen Mary Martin creating a new form of religious art. Music, with the Immaculate Heart Trio—Sister Mary Mark (pianist), Sister Denis (violinist), and Sister Anthony (cellist)—the Zeyen sisters—gained laurels for their fine artistry and recordings for Capitol Records. Less publicized but still finding growing audiences for performances was the drama department, headed by Sisters Marie Fleurette Keber and Ruth Marie Gibbons; their students were active in plays and on TV in the rapidly advancing theater world of Los Angeles.

Science was winning federally funded grants, the English department was publishing both as a department and individually, hosting nationally known guest speakers. Other departments were doing excellent work in teaching and preparing students for graduate studies. To work with such a dedicated group, both religious women and laity, was a challenge. As I look back, perhaps the greatest marvel was the cohesiveness and spirit of the college personnel, particularly the sisters, in the face of an endless barrage of criticism and admonition, and even demands for retraction and apology coming relentlessly from the Los Angeles chancery office.

Although there was certainly a growing tension between Cardinal McIntyre and the college—its faculty, its goals, its ideals—only once did I sense a fear that this tension might spell the end of my beloved Immaculate Heart College.

"Do you realize that your college is being criticized in the diocese as liberal?" the cardinal asked. I stood before his oversized desk like a prisoner in the dock. I was startled by the question and tried to think of what it might mean. This was in the late fifties, earlier than the confrontation with the cardinal in May 1965. Quite by chance I was in the archdiocesan chancery office, having accompanied Sister Marie Fleurette, who was in charge of the drama department. She was producing an Irish play directed by Ria Mooney from Dublin's Abbey Theater. She knew that Bishop Timothy Manning would enjoy the Irish play and had persuaded me to accompany her to the chancery to issue the invitation personally. Bishop Manning received us graciously as always; he promised to attend the performance and then, unexpectedly and somewhat hesitantly, stated that Cardinal McIntyre wished to see me. My companion was to remain in the waiting room outside his office. It was hard to tell if the bishop's natural pallor grew more noticeable as he saw my surprise at the unscheduled appointment with the cardinal. I had no hint of the purpose of the meeting. Was the cardinal upset with the play? With the drama department? But the charge was broader than that.

"Liberal"? I echoed his word, trying to understand its meaning as applied to the college. My immediate reply was, "I'm not sure, Your Eminence, what you mean by 'liberal.' We are liberal in the sense that Immaculate Heart College is a liberal arts college, but that's very different from being a liberal college."

"You should know what it means," was his response, in a remarkable bit of sophistry. "You are the ones being accused of it, so you are the ones who should give the answer to that."

The reply left me stunned. Where were we going from there? But His Eminence scarcely paused. He went on to explain that he was concerned particularly with the art department. Sister Corita's colorful new look of religious art was to him, as well as to some traditional Catholics, sacrilegious. All this the cardinal poured out to me in a vehement diatribe. But the art department was not the sole object of his wrath: "Your courses are too worldly; you are trying to imitate secular universities. How do you think of yourselves as a Catholic college when everything else comes before religion?"

When the cardinal stopped to take a breath, I drew examples from the curriculum to counter the objects of his displeasure. But clearly, "liberal" for the cardinal meant not merely modern but also not specifically Roman Catholic. Although I did not know it at the time, the word signaled a forbidden dimension, coming out of the historic "Oath Against Modernism" taken by Dunwoodie seminarians. The cardinal was one of those who had sworn the oath as part of the subdiaconate ceremony. In the cardinal's New York experience, the word "liberal" related to the modernist movement or even, in the fifties and sixties, to communism.[2]

---

[2] For a relevant incident of Cardinal McIntyre's treatment of Miss Frances Perkins, secretary of labor, see the memoir of Rev. George Barry Ford, *A Degree of Difference* (New York: Farrar, Straus & Giroux, 1969) 105.

The tension in the room became electric as the list of complaints went on. Did I consider myself an exemplary administrator of a Catholic college? And how did I classify Immaculate Heart? How could he recommend Catholic high school graduates to such an institution, seemingly more concerned with the modern world than with long-standing principles of religion?[3] How long could such a college expect to bear the name of a religious community?

As the minutes ticked on, the cardinal's face grew red with his failure to elicit a promise of change of policy from me. Suddenly he turned from me, apparently about to leave the room in disgust with no closure. Like a flaming fire, my own repressed feelings about the community, the college, and the cardinal flared. My thoughts of the sisters who worked long hours to make our small liberal arts college an effective and prestigious Christian influence; the community as a whole, which gave its hard-earned money (and never enough at that) and hidden hours of physical labor; the lay faculty, who believed in Immaculate Heart's progress—all flashed before me. In a spontaneous response I demanded that he return to his chair and listen to me. Not yet startled by my own brash action, I made my final defense of our desire to become an outstanding Catholic college in California.

But events had gone too far to convince him. The cardinal uttered some final words of rebuke, implying that "If this keeps up, the college will have to close." I was dismissed without the traditional episcopal blessing. Out in the waiting room, my now very anxious companion stood as I left the office. As we hurried down the exit stairs, she whispered, "I could hear every word he said through that thick oak door." All the way back to the motherhouse I was quiet, telling her intermittently of the scene that had just taken place, more to release my feelings than to inform her, since she had heard it all. On the verge of tears, I rushed to Reverend Mother Regina's office and abruptly interrupted her appointment. Abandoning any pretense at courtesy, I broke in.

"Reverend Mother, I must see you at once." One look at my distress and she dismissed the sister to whom she was speaking. I blurted out to her, "I think the college is in danger of being closed." She was calm and tried to calm me. But I knew that she shared my fears. It was the clearest threat we had yet experienced, one that touched the heart of

---

[3] The very charge leveled at Catholic intellectuals thought to be part of the modernist movement.

our work, the college, but also the very reputation of the Immaculate Heart Sisters of Los Angeles.

Episodes like this one, denying the academic freedom necessary to effectively operate a college, continued long after this encounter. In the early sixties the much publicized original Mary's Day of 1964 met with a volley of letters on its debut as well as on its use in the 1966 CBS film "Look Up and Live." A bit of history is enlightening. For years we had had a traditional Mary's Day, a day of prayer and procession dedicated to Mary as Mother of God. The program was fairly solemn, culminating in an evening procession winding up the college hill. Lastly, a crown of flowers was placed on the statue of Mary by a specially chosen student.

The repetition of this ceremony year after year left the students of the sixties cold. So Sister Corita Kent was asked by Sister Helen Kelley, then president of the college, to create a new Mary's Day, one celebrating the real woman of Nazareth. This time there would be colorful dress, not the solemnity of caps and gowns. Crepe-paper flowers, streamers, and banners fashioned by the students in the art department decorated the grounds, the visual representation of a new tradition honoring Mary. The bravest of the sisters even decorated their dark habits with bright garlands. Modern songs were adapted to fit the theme of the day, accompanied by guitars played by the students.

Word of these plans spread quickly. The curiosity of those students not immediately involved aroused excitement. To this were added rumors that the media would attend. The day was all that could be hoped for, and the enthusiasm of the participants and onlookers was captured by the press and TV.[4]

The cardinal was not pleased. At first there was no objection. But two years later, following another Mary's Day, it was not the college president who received a reprimand; rather, I, then mother general, was called to answer to the charges against Mary's Day. I received a letter from Auxiliary Bishop John J. Ward, in which he asked for an explanation concerning this festive celebration and the overzealous publicity it received.[5] His letter appeared restrained, and in fact was much more so than the cardinal's own criticism a few days later, upon

---

[4] For but one colorful account, including pictures of this day, see Lucia Pearce, "Sister Corita: Bringing Art into Learning," *National Catholic Reporter* (November 4, 1964) 5.

[5] Bishop John J. Ward. Letter to Mother M. Humiliata, I.H.M., May 6, 1966. Archives of the Immaculate Heart Community (hereafter cited as A/IHMCOM).

receiving my requested response. Since the successive letters are fairly typical of the chancery office's complaints in those years, I am including my correspondence following upon Bishop Ward's request.

My reply explaining Mary's Day, 1966, attempted to put things in perspective.

May 10, 1966

Most Reverend John J. Ward, D.D., J.C.L.
1531 West Ninth Street
Los Angeles, California 90015

Your Excellency:

I am happy to have this opportunity, Your Excellency, to reply to your letter of May 6. I should like very much to comment on the article regarding Mary's Day in the Los Angeles Times for Friday, May 6, which caused us as much dismay, I am sure, as it did the many people who called you. The day was in many ways as it was described—colorful, gay, truly joyous.What the article failed to convey was that the whole day, particularly the Mass, was altogether appropriate and reverent. The non-Catholic background of the reporter is exposed in such misreporting as the statement that during the Consecration Father Kent asked the names of those "asleep in Christ." This request took place at the Memento for the Dead. It was a quiet request (as you will know if you know Father Kent) and it was so quietly answered that those in the middle of the auditorium could not hear the replies. I was in the rear and failed to catch any of them. The Mass ended in silence, not as the report states, with the "Battle Hymn of the Republic." This was sung as a recessional sometime later with appropriately adapted words. Certainly the most unfortunate part of the reporting was in the headlines. The day as a whole was neither intended to be, nor did it turn out to be, a "party." The lunch on the lawn, with music and singing, could have been interpreted as a "party" but such is not the connotation borne of the article. I cannot say that I fully participated in this kind of celebration. From the reverent and full participation of the students in the Mass and in the procession and from their obvious delight in the close association of faculty and students throughout the day, however, I must attest that such a celebration speaks to the students in a very real way.

Since I realize that His Eminence was displeased at the manner of distribution of Holy Communion at Mary's Day last year, every effort was made this year to have all the liturgical regulations observed exactly. It was therefore with the utmost consternation that I read the *Times'* report on Friday.

I remained for the entire celebration so that I can witness to everything stated here by personal observation. I sincerely appreciate the fact, Your Excellency, that calls regarding this unfortunate report have been referred to us, as this has given us an opportunity to explain the inaccuracies in the article. I trust that these comments will clarify the matter. I shall be happy to discuss it further with you, should you so desire.

Respectfully and sincerely yours,

Mother M. Humiliata, I.H.M.
Mother General[6]

Within two days of the above letter, the cardinal himself responded, indicating that he did not accept the explanation provided.

May 12, 1966

Mother M. Humiliata
Immaculate Heart of Mary Sisters
5515 Franklin Avenue
Los Angeles, California 90028

My dear Mother Humiliata:

I write in acknowledgment of your letter of May 10th addressed to Bishop Ward. This concerns the article that appeared in the morning paper last week regarding the observance of Mary's Day at your college.

We have read your commentary with a great deal of interest and must frankly admit that the defense is not acceptable nor is the interpretation of the circumstances entirely accurate, according to other sources of information. The interpretation is far beyond the fact, and we can in no way agree with you that the Mass was "altogether appropriate and reverent."

As Ordinary, I wish to advise you officially that what pertains to the liturgy and to sacred art comes within my jurisdiction. Hereafter, any divergence from the prescribed liturgy of the Church where the interpretation of the Ordinary is prescribed may not, under any circumstances, be attempted. Variations must be submitted to the Chaplain, Father Martin, whom we shall hold responsible in these matters.[7]

---

[6] Mother M. Humiliata, I.H.M. Letter to Bishop John J. Ward, May 10, 1966. A/IHMCOM.

[7] Father Bernard Martin was the beloved chaplain at Immaculate Heart motherhouse for a number of years and was a loyal friend to the sisters during the entire time of their troubles. A seminary colleague of the cardinal's in New York, he had

May I say further, that we hereby request again that the activities of Sister Carita [sic] in religious art be confined to her classroom work and under your responsibility. You are reminded of the restrictions in this regard issued last year. Any other project that sister Carita [sic] may indulge in will have to be submitted to the Committee on Art composed of Monsignor Devlin, Monsignor Trower and Monsignor O'Flaherty, for approval.

In the light of the very unfavorable publicity which attended the fiesta last week, it is our suggestion that in the bulletin of the college that you send to the alumnae, a formal apology be inserted since many of the comments have come from the alumnae.

Faithfully yours in Christ,

James Francis McIntyre
Archbishop of Los Angeles[8]

In addition to his complaints about the activities of the art department, the cardinal was equally distressed by the atmosphere of liberalism that had crept into the Church in southern California at this time. Speakers suspected of "modernist" thought were not to be invited. Just as Chancellor McIntyre had required prior approval of speakers and refused permissions in the Archdiocese of New York, Cardinal McIntyre of Los Angeles now kept the same tight rein on churches and universities in the Los Angeles Archdiocese. Only now, during the period of the Second Vatican Council and its aftermath (1962–67), invitations to renowned speakers who had attended the council or who had guided the progress of this most momentous reform were especially sought after. Catholic laity and college faculty and students were anxious to learn not only of the decrees promulgated but the thinking that led to those decrees, sensing that after the long period of Catholic intellectual passivity, mighty changes were in the air.

But the chancery office was not sanguine about invitations to those philosophers, theologians, and political and social scientists. When the cardinal learned that the famous Swiss theologian Dr. Hans Küng had spoken to the Immaculate Heart College faculty and also to the

---

been invited to the archdiocese by the cardinal, even to share his episcopal residence with him. Father Martin chose the position of chaplain. It is a mark of his tact and diplomacy that he remained on friendly terms with the cardinal.

   [8] Cardinal James F. McIntyre. Letter to Mother M. Humiliata, I.H.M., May 12, 1966. A/IHMCOM.

Immaculate Heart young sisters when he lectured at the University of California, Santa Barbara, he was more than a little angry.[9] His reprimand on this occasion was written to me on November 4, 1966. The closing paragraph follows:

> You, of course, are acquainted with the fact that Father Hans Küng has come to Los Angeles and has appeared as a layman, and he has lectured at secular universities. He has not petitioned required permission for these appearances of the Ordinary of Los Angeles. In so doing, he has acted contrary to the provision of the decree "Exsul Familia" and has manifested a definite act of discourtesy to the Ordinary of the diocese and to regulations of the Church. I am, therefore, forced to construe your attitude in permitting his appearance before your faculty as likewise an act of discourtesy.[10]

[9] In a similar incident several years earlier that involved the Jesuit institution Loyola University of Los Angeles and the Swiss theologian Father Hans Küng, Cardinal McIntyre attempted to prohibit Küng from speaking. Eventually he reached a compromise with the Jesuits. Msgr. Francis J. Weber, *His Eminence of Los Angeles: James Francis Cardinal McIntyre*, 2 vols. (Mission Hills, Calif.: St. Francis Historical Society, 1997), explains Cardinal McIntyre's official rationale for this refusal. When the Jesuits of Loyola University (Los Angeles) invited Küng to give a public lecture after the conclusion of the Second Vatican Council's first momentous session, in January, 1963, the cardinal hesitated to give permission, fearing the effect on "impressionable students whose exposure to philosophy and theology was limited and far from mature" (2:572). A compromise was reached whereby Küng was allowed to speak to the university faculty at Loyola's Saint Robert Hall. Nearby universities, learning of Küng's availability, showed interest in having the famous theologian lecture. When UCLA invited Küng to join its distinguished speakers' program on "Positive Results of the First Session of the Second Vatican Council," almost four months later (April 3, 1963), Küng agreed, provided the cardinal would authorize it.

When Küng telephoned for verbal permission, he was reminded that according to official procedures, his request had to be in writing. Immediately, Küng sent a special delivery letter to the cardinal but was told by him in a letter of March 30, 1963, "'the extreme shortness of intervening time, which you mention, does not admit of our arranging for the necessary clearance in accordance with Canon 1341'" (Weber, *His Eminence*, 2:572–573). Furthermore, the cardinal wrote in a private memo that he doubted the "sincerity of officials at UCLA, noting that they 'had no interest whatsoever in religion and the only reason they would invite Fr. Küng is because it would stimulate controversy'" (Weber, 2:573). See also reference (Weber, 2:573–575; 606–608) to the article by A.V. Krebs, Jr., "A Church of Silence," *Commonweal* (July 10, 1964) 80:467–476.

[10] Cardinal McIntyre. Letter to Mother M. Humiliata, I.H.M., November 4, 1966. A/IHMCOM.

An apologetic note from my office followed. A specific complaint was lodged against Sister William (Helen Kelley) as president of the college for the expression of opinions in the publication *On the Move*.[11] All expressions of opinion for this journal were to be submitted to the chancery office for prior approval.

The names of prospective theology teachers had to be cleared with the chancery office. The same restrictions applied when IHM sisters were asked to speak at various universities and clubs not under Catholic auspices. Not only was academic freedom imperiled by the repetitious prohibitions but so was the very quality of opportunities for learning by our faculty and students.[12]

[11] Published by Immaculate Heart College and written by faculty and administration, *On the Move* was a periodic publication devoted to the exchange of ideas and opinions. A/IHMCOM.

[12] "Actions on the part of the Ordinary which have created difficulties for the Sisters of the Immaculate Heart." Unpublished photocopy not dated. This internal memo was compiled by a committee of sisters. There is no one author. The original intent of this memo was to document the chronology of difficulties we had with officials of the Catholic Church and to provide specific documentation in order to inform the total community of the obstructive and intrusive actions on the part of Church officials. It also served to demonstrate that the tension the IHMs experienced with Cardinal McIntyre pre-dated the adoption of the 1967 chapter acts. This is the first publication of this internal memo. Appendix B, p. 231.

Chapter 6

The Sixties and the
Sisters of the Immaculate Heart

While Immaculate Heart College was progressing steadily, despite the criticism of the chancery office, the community was looking at itself in a new way. The year 1963 was, without a doubt, a pivotal date in the history of the renewal of the Immaculate Heart Sisters. Certainly this perception is subjective and could be challenged. But for me and I think for many others, the date was decisive, marking a profound change in our lives and presenting evidence that something new was stirring at the heart of the community.

Thirty-five elected members of the community packed their bags for Montecito, California, where they would elect the new officers of the community by secret ballot, would take up matters of moment concerning the sisters' lives and work, would discuss in detail, evaluate, and make recommendations for the next six-year period, as delegates had done for nearly fifty years.

By this date, too, our constitutions and our book of customs (rules of the community), having undergone some revision at each succeeding chapter, were now being subjected to more strenuous criticism. Many sisters felt that there needed to be a more honest statement of our life as it could be lived in view of their Christian mission instead of a dry restatement of canon law. Some even saw that it could be a liberating document, one that challenged rather than subdued. All this stirring of thought, combined with a new method of electing the participants, made for both excitement and some apprehension regarding the outcome of the 1963 General Chapter (a meeting to adopt changes in the Rule and the election of officers for the community).

Montecito was a particularly lovely site for such a meeting, for it nestles peacefully at the foothills of the Santa Barbara mountains, just a mile inland from the Pacific Ocean, surrounded by giant oaks and cedars, with periwinkle lawns and orange and avocado trees. But on this occasion all was not serene, for the sisters were at a kind of crossroads. The conflict that was ultimately to split the community in 1967 appeared early in the 1963 spiritual retreat that prepared the sisters for the General Chapter. Even though silence was to prevail during this eight-day retreat, a shock wave went through the delegates and the General Council when each day, exactly at the noon meal, anonymous letters were distributed to everyone. The letters contained bitter criticism of the previous six-year regime and its progressive spirit. The purpose of these disturbing communications appeared to be the desire to halt the momentum of the new programs, ideas, and spirit that Reverend Mother Regina McPartlin embodied and to discredit those sisters thought most likely to be elected as the succeeding officers of the community.

Further, the delegates themselves were concerned about a number of things. Some freely and openly criticized the newer concepts, such as the changing role of authority; others were eager to consider these concepts. Some looked forward to the possibilities of a "new" religious life; others feared it. Some were questioning the old, irrelevant customs, even forms of prayer, while others affirmed them. Change and conflict were definitely in the air.

At the close of the retreat, but still in a solemn manner, the delegates assembled in chapel to await the cardinal archbishop of Los Angeles. He or his appointee was to preside at the election of the mother general, in keeping with canon law. All the delegates, sitting in prayerful anxiety, were relieved as they heard that Monsignor Edward Wade rather than Cardinal McIntyre was on his way to fulfill that duty. Those sisters who knew him as vicar for religious in the Los Angeles Archdiocese thought highly of him as a refined and caring prelate, honest and kind.

My own feelings were complex at this point. On the one hand, I felt a temporary respite in the cardinal's absence, for as president of the college, I was identified in his eyes with the "liberal" policies of that institution. The religion courses at the college were certainly based on the theology of Vatican II, to which, it will be recalled, His Eminence took exception. And I had invited speakers to the college lecture series who probably would not have been approved by the chancery office. I certainly had not lived up to the conservative standards His Eminence believed proper for a traditional Catholic college. I had, in fact, lived with the fear since the late 1950s that he might close the college if it proceeded on its "liberal" way. But now, learning that morning from the delegates who came up to me one by one that I might very well be elected mother general, I felt almost paralyzed. As I sat there in the chapter room, my mind went back to the early years of my religious life, weighing my own suitability for such a position.

I think I had been an obedient nun. In my home the gentle discipline of my parents was honored, and except for an occasional adolescent rebellion, I respected the few rules they laid down for their children. And my life in the convent had offered few occasions for disobedience. The hierarchy of command was clearly recognizable; further, it made for efficiency and an incredible productivity. Although my values were not always those of the governing body in the community, I had not usually, as a young nun, questioned the system. Occasionally, of course, I felt there to be an error in human judgment. It is interesting that when I look back to my first thoughts on this occasion, it was to my personal practice of the vow of obedience, to how well I fulfilled the will of superiors, the legalistic rules, rather than to anything more fundamental. I was still to some extent the devoted daughter of German Catholic upbringing.

But slowly, with a deeper understanding of human nature and of the freedom necessary to its full development, I was undergoing a change. The value of personal responsibility and of collegiality and the importance of appreciating the gifts and talents of each person were beginning to grow within me as well as in many members of the community. The hierarchical model, long respected in Church structure, as well as in the convent replica of that structure, was seen for what it too often easily becomes—a misuse of power that intimidates and cramps the human spirit.

The chapter of 1963 was to be a clear if not drastic manifestation of the change in priorities among the majority of the delegates, as they made clear that the whole idea of religious life was for them about to evolve, to change. The old lines between secular and sacred were being erased. Religious women had a new role to play in the modern world, and they were to be in touch with that world. So a radical change in the religious life of the IHMs was given strong impetus by the short but important chapter of 1963.

Then it happened. On the second ballot a majority made me the new mother general. There is little that can be said about my feelings that day. I do not believe that I had any ambitions for the highest office the community could bestow; rather, I feared for the community, I feared for myself. Surely I was not the cardinal's candidate. Although I had good reason to believe that at the time, I learned only at the end of that day that as Monsignor Wade got into his car for the drive back to Los Angeles, he shook his head and said sadly, "This was not, I'm afraid, the cardinal's choice." Although the election was not a compromise, I knew I was certainly not the unanimous choice of all the delegates. I wondered about the reaction of the entire community. What little courage I could summon up that day came from the smiling faces of the sisters at the chapter who looked to me for leadership in the immediate future.

The chapter moved on to the election of a General Council: Sister Elizabeth Ann Flynn, strong-minded champion of the education of the sisters; Mother Regina McPartlin, the former novice mistress, previous mother general, and our builder; Sister Charles Schaffer, beloved leader; Sister Gregory Lester, efficient secretary; and though not a formal member of the Council, Sister Eugenia Ward, who as treasurer was expected to be at council meetings. (Mother Eucharia Harney, a former mother general, had refused to be included in this advisory group.)

For the next two weeks the delegates together studied our Rule, which they saw as lacking inspiration and imagination. It was what rules were supposed to be in the nineteenth and early twentieth centuries—virtually a direct copy of canon law for religious, dealing for the most part with failures in obeying those rules rather than with the joys of a life of dedication.

In a way we were naïve American women who believed that law was normative, concerned with the attainable. To be dispensed from its observance was viewed as a concession to weakness that was to be avoided.[1] But the IHMs were not only American, they were generationally of the 1960s: they believed that one must "tell it like it is." The easy use of exceptions to the Rule seemed to us unworthy, something to be remedied at all cost.

This insistence on truth without nuance was not the only sign of the sixties among us. We had become suddenly engaged in the events taking place in the world around us. We had, in some measure, lived through the Second World War, had felt anxiety and fear as brothers, uncles, friends, and even students had gone into the maelstrom. But

---

[1] Joan D. Chittister, "Rome and the Religious Life," *The Ecumenist* (July–August 1985) 72–76.

this was different. Now we were sharing, not a sense of "continuous, lived history," but rather "a collage of fragments scooped together as if a whole decade took place in an instant."[2]

Gradually, in the sixties, we were opening up to the world around us, sometimes judiciously, sometimes spontaneously. I remember a scholarly nun of another order speaking to an audience of religious superiors, advocating that daily news columns be hung in our chapels as food for reflection, taking the place of statues of long-dead saints. The idea seemed shocking at the time.

Certainly the sixties were marked by a culture of youth—and youth highly critical of the times, scornful of the adult world, marking figures of authority as "proprietors without a cause." The world about to be inherited, thought the young, was "flimsy, phony, hypocritical."[3]

The student movement was fighting for recognition. The historical moment marked by "affluence, civil rights, the Cold War, Vietnam; Kennedy, Johnson, Nixon; the assassinations of Kennedy, Malcolm X, King, and another Kennedy; worldwide upheavals seeming to promise the founding of a new age in the ashes of the old."[4]

The sixties were just that: "years of hope and days of rage," as Todd Gitlin phrases it. And our place, southern California, had its kaleidoscopic changes in size and ethnic diversity that still continue thirty years later. There youth's private language, "rock and roll," "selected, produced, amplified, and channeled to the millions of teenagers looking for ways to declare who they were and were not,"[5] was the speech drowning out all other voices.

Some of this Zeitgeist certainly entered the doors of convents all over the United States and no less of our community after the 1963 chapter. The new officials of the community were both eager and fearful to meet the challenges of the sixties. At the same time we were conscious of the dangers of a too rapid change and of the inexperience and impatience of young IHMs.

As early as 1961 we as a community had been receiving assistance in helping us to cope with the rapidly evolving milieu by developing a healthy and spiritually rich community life. The first of these guides to

---

[2] Todd Gitlin, *The Sixties: Years of Hope, Days of Rage* (New York: Bantam Books, 1987) 3.

[3] Ibid., 31.

[4] Ibid., 5.

[5] Ibid., 41.

give us psychological understanding as well as direction in a life of dedication was Father Noel Mailloux, O.P., who had founded the department of psychology at the University of Montreal and was a professor there. He also acted as counselor for such groups as prisoners and delinquent youth. His theological foundation was in St. Thomas Aquinas. He was a most unusual retreat master for religious women. He preferred that the week with us be called an "ascetical workshop," and "the experience, a living experience, of spiritual life."[6] In non-technical language, he addressed the issues of anxieties, fears, change, passive aggression, and contemplation.

Not everyone heard those new teachings peacefully—Father Mailloux did not fit the mold. Indeed, one sister, whose interpretation of religious life was notably rigid, challenged the stout, white-robed Father Mailloux. "But Father, you have said nothing about grace, the sacraments, penance . . ."

Father Mailloux was unperturbed. Accompanying his words with a sweeping gesture, he announced in his strong French-Canadian, "We are coming to dat!" And he went on discussing how we renew ourselves, how a right self-love is the beginning of the capacity to love.[7]

To express ourselves, to discuss our experiences, to verbalize—these attitudes were to be encouraged in community life. We would learn more about all this in the years ahead as our psychological knowledge grew with other retreats, lectures, workshops, and readings. But our exposure to these basic theories underlying our struggle to become "good IHMs" left its mark not only on the thirty-some retreatants at Father Mailloux's workshop but on the whole community, to whom typescripts of his talks were circulated. That one could operate on sound psychological principles and be deeply devoted to the search for God, and that this might lead to a more fruitful apostolic life—all this was the beginning of a new understanding of religious life for us.

The retreat master to follow Mailloux in the sixties was the distinguished Father Adrian Van Kaam, C.S.Sp., whose influence on the Immaculate Heart Sisters was perhaps one of the most important in terms of helping them formulate religious goals for themselves. Father Van Kaam's background was that of the psychology of personality. This

---

[6] Noel Mailloux, O.P., "Ascetical Workshop for IHM Sisters" (March 24–April 2, 1961) 1. Unpublished photocopy, Archives of the Immaculate Heart Community, Los Angeles (hereafter cited as A/IHMCOM).

[7] Ibid., 115.

subject he studied both in Europe and in the United States, earning his doctorate from Western Reserve University. His most noteworthy volume on the integration of religion and psychology was *Religion and Personality,*[8] a religious interpretation of humanistic psychology addressing the theme of holiness in terms of reality. Much of his thought was assimilated by the Immaculate Heart Community from his books as well as from his retreats. Van Kaam's hope that the "present split between Church and culture"—his way of describing the unfortunate dichotomy between the sacred and the secular—might eventually be overcome by an enlightened humanity[9] became for the IHMs an important underlying philosophy in the formulation of their 1967 decrees. Other retreat masters and influential speakers followed these first two important guides, including Gregory Baum and Eugene Kennedy as well as Carl Rogers and his "encounter groups."[10]

Meanwhile, although more noteworthy changes in the daily lives of the sisters would be coming in the next four years, they were presaged by the minor but significant adaptations in the IHM lifestyle made by the 1963 General Chapter. Most significant among the decisions of the 1963 General Chapter was the recommendation that a long-range study of all IHM legislative documents—our constitutions, the book of customs, and the General Chapter decrees considered every six years—be undertaken, leading to revisions "guided by the spirit and decisions of the Second Vatican Council . . . revisions of Canon Law . . . and by the lived reality of the Institute."[11]

The first meetings of the new officers in 1963 were affected by the realization of the times and place in which we lived as well as by the excitement generated by the chapter just concluded. Although the new five-person General Council was composed of remarkably diverse personalities, we managed to persist in discussing matters with one another. Slowly but more and more clearly, we could see that the whole

[8] Adrian Van Kaam, C.S.Sp., *Religion and Personality* (Englewood Cliffs, N.J.: Prentice-Hall, 1964).

[9] Ibid., 83.

[10] Anita Caspary, I.H.M., "Psychological Influences on the IHMs." See Appendix C, p. 239.

[11] IHM General Chapter 1963, "Recommendation #52 of the 1963 General Chapter," unpublished photocopy. For a summary of the changes legislated in the Eighth General Chapter and implemented between 1963 and 1965, see also "Basis for Changes and Adaptations of Custom Made by the Sisters of the Immaculate Heart, 1963–65," unpublished photocopy. A/IHMCOM.

structure of religious life urgently needed redesign. So we began to formulate a Five-Year Plan for the renewal of the Sisters of the Immaculate
Heart. This plan consumed much of our time and energy in the first
year of our tenure. It was based on the principles identified by our own
delegates to the 1963 chapter, but it was far less bold than the later
document on religious life issued by the Second Vatican Council in
1965.

In the Five-Year Plan we wrote a new invitation, challenging each
sister to develop her fullest capacity as a person, to recognize her
unique contribution as a "woman living a life of dedicated and universal love," and to supplement her apostolic work in recognition of the
times, especially in the areas of contemporary culture and social problems. Significantly, the Five-Year Plan was even more specific in the
area of educational development. "The completion of [appropriate] degrees and credential programs for Sister-teachers currently in service"
on all levels and in all areas of work was deemed a basic requirement.[12]
This plan, while marking a stage of progress, was ultimately super-
seded, before its promulgation to the IHM sisters, by the publication of
two important documents from the Second Vatican Council recom-
mending the renewal of religious life.[13]

Meanwhile, my own duties as mother general and counselor came
to include an unusual number of requests for appointments from among
the sisters. As a tangible sign of the pressures placed upon them by the
sharply increased workloads due to higher enrollments and in many
cases a lack of adequate preparation, many sisters sought counsel from
religious or psychological sources. Each morning I opened my door, as
did other council members, to long lines of sisters of various ages,
some mildly downcast, some in obvious anxiety, some ready to acknowledge my hopeful smile of greeting. Each morning seemed to
bring a new revelation, and I braced myself for the long hours of
troubled queries and my own reactions, both physical and emotional.
Nevertheless, these hours of discussion and problem-solving made me
deeply conscious of the trust these women placed in me. I had come to
them from the academic world; I had never been a local superior; I had

---

[12] IHM General Council, "Community Objectives: Five Year Plan." Unpublished
photocopy. A/IHMCOM.

[13] The two documents to which I refer are *Perfectae Caritatis* and *Ecclesiae Sanctae II*,
in *Vatican Council II: The Conciliar and Post Conciliar Documents*, ed. Austin Flannery,
O.P. (Northport, N.Y.: Costello Publishing Co., 1981).

had little time or experience in their world of daily lessons and clamor-
ing children. Yet between us the fiber of a fearfully delicate bond was
spun. I wanted so to help to assuage in some marvelously efficient way
the doubts and fears of these sisters.

But soon, due in part to the ever present tension and long hours of
answering the urgent needs of the sisters, as well as to the ongoing disagreements with the cardinal, I became exhausted and ill. Almost exactly a year after my election, I was en route to the hospital for surgery.
The diagnosis of cancer meant less to me than the prospect of rest after
surgery. Only when I looked up from the hospital bed into the dis-
traught faces of my parents did I realize more fully the seriousness of
my diagnosis. But after a successful operation, a period of rest at a
mountain retreat gave me the leisure to think about the renewal of religious life.

It would be obvious to those in touch with the Immaculate Heart
Sisters that we would give enthusiastic reception to papal documents
that authorized wide consultation of members, the updating of our
Rule, and legitimate experimentation. And that was certainly the case.
Of course, we needed to do much more than merely "think" a new
form of religious life to bring about a hoped-for transformation. In
addition to the task itself, there was a new problem, for at this time the
General Council learned that a few of our members, in a distinct departure from the tradition of a community keeping its own counsel, were
alerting His Eminence to their fear of change. Anyone aware of our
past history of innovation and progressiveness, as well as of our difficult relationship with the cardinal, could predict a troubled future.

Chapter 7

Cardinal James F. McIntyre

In the story of the Immaculate Heart of Mary Sisters in the 1950s and 1960s, Cardinal James F. McIntyre, the first Roman Catholic cardinal of the Archdiocese of Los Angeles, played a singular and significant role. Despite his seventy-nine years at the climax of this story, he was a tall and stately, handsome man, commanding in almost dramatic style. He wore his ecclesiastical rank as he wore his clerical robes. And his manner, when his convictions were not challenged, could be soft-spoken, though often paternalistic and authoritarian.

This imposing person had an unusual and varied background for a cardinal of the Church. He was born June 25, 1886, in New York City of Irish parents of modest means. He lost his mother when he was only ten years old. He and his younger brother John were raised by his first cousin Mary Hannon Conley. After graduating from public high school, Francis went to work as a "runner" on Wall Street's Curb Exchange for three dollars an hour. He advanced quickly through the ranks from 1902 to 1915 to become office manager for the financial firm H. L. Horton & Co., where he had a bright future.[1]

After his invalid father died, Francis decided to return to school at City College and for one year at Cathedral College. Then, having decided to become a priest, he attended St. Joseph's Seminary at Dunwoodie, New York, for the next six years. The seminary was a training institution whose director thought of it as a kind of Catholic Annapolis, with the virtues one might expect to see emphasized at a military institution: "courage, heroism, patriotism, discipline, obedience, and

---

[1] Msgr. Francis J Weber, *His Eminence of Los Angeles: James Francis Cardinal McIntyre* (Mission Hills, Calif.: St. Francis Historical Society, 1997) 6–7.

loyalty to the 'corps.'"[2] Dunwoodie was fairly typical of American Catholic seminaries from the turn of the century up to the 1960s. Intellectual pursuit of the important issues of the day, knowledge of a wide variety of subjects, respect for research and investigation and even, or perhaps especially, for biblical or ecclesial matters were not only discouraged but frowned upon.

Pope Pius X had issued a papal encyclical in 1907 whose purpose was to combat the perceived unorthodoxy of the modernist movement in Catholic intellectual circles, including the Church's seminaries and its schools of higher learning.[3] This all-out attack reverberated for decades.[4] By today's standards, one of the key ideas of the Catholic modernist movement would seem to be vital to the intellectual and spiritual development of students and seminarians alike: modernists desired to bring the Church abreast of the latest research and scholarship in all branches of knowledge, including, among other subjects, the Bible, and to rethink the exclusive emphasis on Scholastic philosophy and theology in educating young people. It is also true that many modernists, particularly in Europe, seemed to be subverting traditional Christianity and the Church by propounding that "the essence of Christianity lay not in intellectual propositions nor in creeds, but in the very processes of life."[5]

While there were virtually no American modernists,[6] the papal encyclical condemning modernism affected the whole American Church for decades to come. To guard against the modernist "heresy" and its alleged "unregulated curiosity and excessive pride," draconian steps had to be taken. Pius X, therefore, advised all bishops to set up "committees of vigilance" in their dioceses and to discharge immediately any professor or director sympathetic to modernist thought. Religious matters in books, periodicals, and newspapers were to be scrutinized and censored if need be. Formal gatherings of priests, in congresses for

---

[2] Michael V. Gannon, "Before and After Modernism: The Intellectual Isolation of the American Priest," in *The Catholic Priest in the United States: Historical Investigations,* ed. John Tracy Ellis (Collegeville, Minn.: St. John's University Press, 1971) 356.

[3] The encyclical *Pascendi Dominici Gregis* was issued by the Vatican's Holy Office on September 8, 1907. See John Tracy Ellis, "The Formation of the American Priest: An Historical Perspective," in *The Catholic Priest in the United States: Historical Investigations* (Collegeville, Minn.: St. John's University Press, 1971) 61.

[4] Ibid.

[5] Gannon, "Before and After Modernism," 336.

[6] Ibid., 338–339. Gannon can identify only three in the entire country at that time.

example, were prohibited in general. Priests were not allowed to study at secular universities if Catholic universities offered the same courses.[7] And as if these measures were not sufficient to quash intellectual curiosity and scholarship in universities and seminaries, the Oath Against Modernism (1910) was required of all priest-candidates "for ordination to the subdiaconate, and of priests before assuming certain offices, especially the episcopacy."[8]

Even by 1930 the pall cast over Catholic intellectual endeavors still weighed heavily, prompting the Catholic chaplain of the University of Illinois, Father John O'Brien, to urge his fellow priests to "build bridges to the American intellectual community." Keenly aware of the newer advances in psychology, biblical criticism, historical sociology, physics, astronomy, anthropology, comparative anatomy, paleontology, and archaeology, Father O'Brien foresaw the "need of familiarity not merely with the thought of the thirteenth century, but with the thought of the modern world. . . ."[9] Drawing on the thought of the great sixteenth-century Christian reformer and Renaissance figure Erasmus, O'Brien borrowed a quotation to describe the Church's predicament: "By identifying the new learning with heresy, you make orthodoxy synonymous with ignorance."[10] But his was a voice crying in the wilderness.

Despite this challenge, interviews conducted by Father Philip J. Murnion in 1969 "with fifty New York priests ordained from St. Joseph's Seminary, Dunwoodie, in the years 1915 to 1929 reveal that the typical Dunwoodie product of that period felt secure in the assumption that he had passed through a superior regimen of intellectual formation."[11]

Monsignor Michael Gannon provides a bleak description of the seminary. He wrote, ". . . the course work required little or no reading outside the textbooks and some notes; no papers to do; a library open to students only two hours on Sunday and Wednesday mornings; and an institutionalized four hours and forty minutes of study in the horarium."[12]

There were few books to read and little free time to do so, although some testified to the variety of popular magazines available. There was conversation about current events—sports, personages, etc.—but little

---

[7] Ibid., 336–337.
[8] Ibid., 337.
[9] As quoted in Gannon, ibid., 350–351.
[10] Ibid.
[11] Ibid., 355.
[12] Ibid.

discussion of the lectures or notes of the day. The daily schedule, or horarium, was to be strictly observed; it covered virtually every minute of the seminarian's day and was inflexible. Furthermore, the seminary budget under then Archbishop Patrick Hayes was minuscule—five hundred dollars for buying, processing, and maintaining books. An expanded budget could have updated and improved the library collection, since the publication date for virtually all books was 1907 or earlier. But neither Cardinal Hayes (he was elevated to cardinal in 1924) nor the rectors he appointed had strong academic interests; one rector was reported to have had "no academic experience."[13]

It was during this period that James Francis McIntyre entered Dunwoodie, in October 1916. It is not surprising, therefore, that the historian of this seminary was of the opinion that McIntyre and his contemporaries "were shortchanged intellectually and spiritually. . . ."[14] History records the negative implications the Dunwoodie seminary education had for later Church life. The lack of a broad curriculum of study and research, but one narrowly focused and without academic depth, had a stultifying effect on later Church policies, particularly for the hierarchy.

Father George Barry Ford, a critic years later of New York's archdiocesan authoritarianism, commenting on James Francis McIntyre's need for the scrutiny of speakers in New York parishes, wrote: "The narrow channels into which local officials of the Church attempted to force the thought of the clergy had their origin in the absence of scholarly attainments among the episcopacy. . . . [The result was] their unceasing attempt to restrain the expression of scholarly thought. . . ."[15]

James Francis McIntyre was ordained in 1921 at the age of thirty-five. His quick mind and experience in finance soon led to his appointment, two years later, as assistant to the chancellor of the New York Archdiocese and to the position of chancellor in 1934. It was in his capacity as chancellor that he was especially valuable in the Depression years, when he was able to refinance the debts of the many New York parishes, thereby saving them from defaulting on their loans. He was a competent administrator over the archdiocese's two thousand priests; and even in the role Monsignor Weber calls the archdiocesan "hatchet-

---

[13] Ibid.

[14] Rev. Thomas J. Shelley, *Dunwoodie: The History of St. Joseph's Seminary* (Westminster, Md.: Christian Classics, 1993) 195.

[15] Rev. George Barry Ford, *A Degree of Difference* (New York: Farrar, Straus & Giroux, 1969) 131. Although there were exceptions among bishops and cardinals, most, Ford notes, lived in the nineteenth century.

man," they found him honest and equitable in his business dealings.[16] However, this competence did not transfer to other areas of Church life. Shelley describes the cardinal, considered one of Dunwoodie's most prominent alumni, as "a pragmatic man not noted for the range of his intellectual interests or sympathies."[17]

But it was as chancellor, too, and later as bishop in New York that he came to be seen by many clerics and laity as close-minded in dealing with those whose sympathies were not as conservative as his own, a harbinger of things to come in his later appointment as archbishop of the Los Angeles Archdiocese.

Because of his critical role in the Immaculate Heart story, an examination of some other facets of Cardinal McIntyre's life is worthwhile. John Cooney, the biographer of Cardinal McIntyre's mentor, Cardinal Francis Spellman, reports that many in New York, including his priests, found Chancellor McIntyre to be authoritarian, even harsh, in dealing with his subordinates, no doubt in part due to the role assigned to him by his superior, Cardinal Spellman. His enemies, as with Cardinal Spellman's, were those who might be called "liberal," whether in the political, social, artistic, philosophical, or theological sense. Thus priests who publicly supported certain civil rights proposals, who were pro-labor or pro-union, who assumed legal responsibilities vis-à-vis persons or events not in favor with the cardinal, who supported ecumenism or who formed friendships with non-Catholic ministers or clerics, who anticipated certain liturgical changes in their churches (later approved by the Second Vatican Council), or who were connected in some way with more modern or progressive developments in the arts and education found themselves in disfavor. Those priests often received letters of disapproval demanding changes or withdrawal from such activities or memberships, and could be harassed or passed over for noteworthy positions in their careers.[18]

One such cleric who was criticized for "transgressions" in nearly all these areas was the charismatic Father George Barry Ford, pastor of Corpus Christi Parish and chaplain to Catholic students in New York City. Father Ford's memoirs record the events in the life of a parish

---

[16] Weber, *His Eminence*, 1:51.

[17] Shelley, *Dunwoodie*, 213.

[18] John Cooney, *The American Pope: The Life and Times of Francis Cardinal Spellman* (New York: Times Books, 1984) 78, 88–90. According to priests interviewed by Cooney, "Cardinal McIntyre, for example, never hid his prejudice and priests asked him in private not to make racial slurs" (283). See also Ford, *A Degree of Difference,* 99.

priest in the New York Archdiocese, first under the benign Cardinal Hayes, then from 1923 to 1948 under the chancellorship of Bishop McIntyre, and finally under Cardinal Spellman until his own retirement in 1958. His is one of the very few such priest-autobiographies of the period, and one that reveals in dramatic detail the nature of Cardinal McIntyre's preferences and antagonisms, with ironic parallels a decade or two later, to the conflicts experienced by the Immaculate Heart Sisters.

Father Ford summarizes the policies under Bishop McIntyre, and to a lesser extent under Cardinal Spellman, as overriding "all personal and pastoral rights stipulated in canon law," and substituting "an oppressive usurpation of authority, a centralized control comparable to the tactics of the Gestapo."[19] Strong words from a gentle man, and one whom the cardinal later described as "a thorough gentleman, splendid chaplain, and an excellent pastor," despite what he regarded as Father Ford's antics.[20]

According to Father Ford, Cardinal McIntyre seemed to have had the same misgivings about secular expertise in the academic forum when he was chancellor of the New York Archdiocese. When the Newman Club, holding its annual weekend featuring a renowned speaker on a subject of special academic interest, invited Miss Frances Perkins, secretary of labor under President Roosevelt, Chancellor McIntyre was especially disturbed, "not so much because she was Episcopalian as because of the liberality of her views, which, to him, meant that she must be a Communist."[21] Furthermore, it was believed that the Perkins invitation prompted the chancellor in the early forties to "require the approval of any speaker before inviting [him] to address any public gathering under Catholic auspices."[22] The chancellor's denial of a speaker like Miss Perkins could also be understood as a failure to recognize the role of women in administrative positions, large or small. Similarly, when Father Ford desired to "appoint a woman as one of the two lay trustees" in his parish—an innovation at the time—his request was again denied by the chancellor.[23]

Because Father Ford was a man of good will, understanding, humor, and charm, he was often invited to be a member of various high-level

[19] Ford, *A Degree of Difference*, 99–100.
[20] "A Christian Gentleman," *Newsweek* (January 19, 1970) 85–86.
[21] Ford, *A Degree of Difference*, 105.
[22] Ibid.
[23] Ibid., 107–108.

interfaith groups, such as the Bureau for Intercultural Relations and the National Committee to Combat Anti-Semitism. But Chancellor McIntyre disliked such affiliations, and on September 8 and again on September 16, 1944, he wrote to Father Ford that he should withdraw his name from the sponsorship of the latter organization. Evidently Bishop McIntyre disliked some of the sponsors, although no clear reason was given. Father Ford's reply was a long and considered one, lamenting that the Church appears to be leaving the fight for social justice to others and commenting that association with colleagues of different persuasions does not mean identification with their point of view, any more than the Pope's recognition of the German representative at the Vatican meant that he subscribed to totalitarianism. Ford followed his reply reluctantly with his resignation as pastor of Corpus Christi and chaplain at Columbia University,[24] but his resignation was

---

[24] Ibid., 108–113. Because Father George Barry Ford's experience was similar in so many ways to the experiences of the Immaculate Heart Sisters, often in the same areas of innovation and apostolic work, it seems appropriate to provide some additional background from his life. Ford was a priest with considerable integrity and courage, who tried to act in accordance with his conscience as a Christian. He was a pioneer in parochial school education, supplementing the solid diocesan curriculum with enrichment studies in art, music, and dramatics. He required that the nun-teachers at his parish school, Corpus Christi, located near the Columbia University campus, have quality higher education and degrees, even from secular institutions. He was particularly concerned about training in the art of teaching, which at that time was not always a regular course offering at many religious colleges. To instill a sense of independence and responsibility, he required students at every grade level to assume some schoolwide responsibility, for example, the morning milk distribution, the school store, the school bank, the school newspaper, etc.

The same sense of pride in participation was to be found among Corpus Christi's parishioners, who were invited to share fully, intelligibly, and in English (some thirty years before the vernacular was mandated by the Vatican) with the priest in liturgical functions. It was apparent that both Father Ford's school and his parish, although successful, were nonetheless a thorn in the side of Chancellor McIntyre. Further, Father Ford's quest for the essentials in religion, for a renewed spirituality, led him not only to seek the good in others, regardless of their religious affiliation, but to call attention to the central teachings of his own faith. When asked by some students, for example, about certain "popular devotions," he observed that these were "diverting Catholics from the essentials of divine worship, and often were directed merely toward asking favors instead of bestowing them in love . . . [thus] increasing superstition and giving the impression that religion was magic instead of living" [Ibid., 100–101]. On this occasion Bishop McIntyre requested a copy of his words and subsequently relieved him of the chaplaincy of the Newman Clubs in the metropolitan colleges and universities.

reversed by McIntyre's superior, Cardinal Spellman, upon the latter's return to the archdiocese.

Cardinal McIntyre's general opposition to change and what might be called progressiveness in the Church is perhaps best illustrated by his views expressed at the Second Vatican Council, particularly by his famous "intervention"[25] on the continued use of the Latin language as opposed to English in the Mass. His argument for the continuance of Latin went beyond the advantages of keeping a long-standing tradition. Discussion of the laity's "active participation [through the responses at Mass] is receiving more consideration than needed," he complained, especially when practiced by those whose "whole intellectual capacity is not great. Furthermore, active participation is frequently a distraction."[26]

The historian Thomas Shelley gives a vivid account of Archbishop Paul J. Hallinan's opinion of Cardinal McIntyre and his resistance to the liturgical renewal. Drawing on the personal diary of Hallinan,[27] Shelley writes, "Even earlier Archbishop Paul J. Hallinan of Atlanta, the only American member of the conciliar liturgical commission, summed up his impression of McIntyre in two words: "'Absolutely stupid!'"[28]

Needless to say, the cardinal's objection to active participation presented in his intervention was at odds with the spirit of the entire constitution on the liturgy. The document states, ". . . full and active participation [in the sacred liturgy] by all the people is the aim to be considered before all else."[29] Few doubted that full participation by the

---

[25] Interventions were the formal addresses or proposals on council schemas, conducted in Latin, either in oral or written form. American prelates presented five percent of the council's total interventions. See *American Participation in the Second Vatican Council,* ed. Msgr. Vincent A. Yzermans (New York: Sheed and Ward, 1967) 11. One cannot help wondering what role Cardinal McIntyre's well-known difficulties with the Latin language played in his understanding of debates and issues during the Second Vatican Council. See also Weber, *His Eminence,* 1:11, for McIntyre's lifelong difficulty with Latin.

[26] Yzermans, *American Participation,* 153–154. See also Shelley, *Dunwoodie,* 238.

[27] "Hallinan recorded his comment in his diary on October 16, 1962. The Hallinan diaries are in the possession of His Eminence, Joseph Cardinal Bernardin, Archbishop of Chicago. I am grateful to Cardinal Bernardin for allowing me to use them." Shelley, *Dunwoodie,* 393, note 26.

[28] Shelley, *Dunwoodie,* 238.

[29] The Constitution on the Sacred Liturgy *(Sacrosanctum Concilium),* in *Vatican II: The Conciliar and Post Conciliar Documents,* ed. Austin Flannery, O.P. (Northport, N.Y.: Costello Publishing Co., 1981) 8, no.14.

laity could be better accomplished through the use of each nation's vernacular. It is fair to say that the cardinal's stance at those sessions he attended (chiefly the first two in 1962 and 1963) was similar to that of his mentor, Cardinal Spellman, who was reported to have vowed to his aides in a burst of hyperbole as he left for the opening session, "'No change will get past the Statue of Liberty.'"[30]

Cardinal McIntyre seemed to harbor a distrust of theological and philosophical expertise, which inevitably brought new ideas, new understandings, into the arena; hence his scornful remark concerning those invited consultants who served the council as "periti" when Vatican II's schema on ecumenism was being considered in August 1963. On this notable occasion he accused "some modern periti" of being "so-called periti." And he added, "'Neither have I accepted from them all the new things which are taught by some modern Catholic theologians.'"[31]

The sessions of the Second Vatican Council on ecumenism were apparently not much to Cardinal McIntyre's liking, as he often found himself in the opposing small minority on some schemas. And not un- expectedly so, since the agenda of both Pope John XXIII and Pope Paul VI was one of reform and change. When the third session of Vatican Council opened with a Mass in September 1964, the cardinal collapsed and had to be carried out—some accounts said from the heat. His auxiliary bishop, Bishop John Ward, blamed the long, non-stop flight from Los Angeles to Rome, but others speculated that the cause was anxiety at the new direction the council was taking. At any rate, the doctors found nothing wrong with him, and about two weeks later he was received by Pope Paul.[32]

Cardinal McIntyre spent long hours in fervent prayer and was admirably dedicated to his responsibilities, according to priests in the dioceses he administered. However, Cooney writes: "To many priests, McIntyre was an enigma. He spent long stretches on his knees obviously

---

[30] Cooney, *The American Pope*, 276. There was one significant liturgical change, however, that both Spellman and McIntyre had no difficulty supporting, namely, the use of English for clergymen in the recitation of the Divine Office, prompting one Italian cardinal to exclaim, "Ah! Questi Americani! Now, they want the priest to pray in English and the people to pray in Latin!" See Xavier Rynne, *Letters from Vatican City* (New York: Farrar, Straus & Co., 1963) 125.

[31] Yzermans, *American Participation*, 294. The quotations from the council sessions have been translated from Latin into English by Monsignor Yzermans.

[32] "Pope Sees Cardinal McIntyre," *New York Times* (October 1964) 25, col. 6.

praying fervently, but when he stood up, the grace he had tried to summon drained out of him. He was a mean-spirited, vindictive man who rationalized his conduct as always being for the good of the Church."[33]

Perhaps it is not surprising, then, that when he was appointed archbishop of the Los Angeles Archdiocese, there were many in New York who praised the "freedom train" that carried him westward.[34]

After the death of Los Angeles Archbishop John J. Cantwell in 1947, the Vatican was looking for an able administrator and financier who would oversee the projected rapid growth of the Southwestern diocese, not only for its more than a million new parishioners but for the new churches and schools it would need. It was widely believed that Cardinal Spellman, a friend of Pope Pius XII, favored the appointment of another New Yorker and his chancellor, James Francis McIntyre, for the Los Angeles vacancy. The appointment came in March 1948. He would earn the name "the brick and mortar priest" (an epithet applied to many pastors in the United States before him), as Los Angeles underwent the greatest expansion of any metropolis in the nation at that time.

After World War II was over, one million parishioners came to California from many parts of the country as well as from other parts of the world, chiefly Mexico, Eastern Europe, Italy, Cuba, and the Far East, necessitating the building of churches and schools. The number of parishes in the Los Angeles Archdiocese increased from 221 to 318 and parochial schools from 159 to 351 during Cardinal McIntyre's administration.[35] Many pastors responsible for the building of their parish churches and schools were hard at work raising money in their parishes, while the archdiocese aided through numerous diocesan-wide drives and helped to secure more favorable building loans and contracts. Cardinal McIntyre also was responsible for creating a revolving fund, the "X account." To this account wealthier parishes that had a surplus in their bank accounts contributed in order to provide monies needed to reduce the indebtedness of poorer parishes, particularly with respect to mortgages.

As one writer summarized the McIntyre era, the cardinal represented a different Church tradition—that of "the old Irish Catholic priest—stubborn, paternalistic, authoritative, frugal, and puritanical

---

[33] Cooney, *The American Pope*, 78.
[34] Ford, *A Degree of Difference*, 158.
[35] Weber, *His Eminence*, 2:328–343, 649.

on moral behavior. But he was also a dedicated, hard-working church-man who left monuments in his archdiocese in brick and mortar, solidly financed."[36] Others, like John Cogley, religion editor for the *New York Times*, remarked that in an era of great religious ferment, he was described as "the most reactionary prelate in the church, bar none—not even those of the Curia," a tribute to his unbending brand of conservatism.[37] He believed in exerting his power and authority for what he deemed to be the good of the Church; but seldom if ever did he listen to the spokesmen of new directions or change, let alone to the women of the Church.

[36] Gladwin Hill, "Cardinal McIntyre of Los Angeles, Retired Archbishop, Is Dead at 93," *New York Times* (Biographical Services, July 17, 1979) 950.

[37] Ibid. See also "A Cardinal Conservative," *Newsweek* (June 24, 1968) 65.

Chapter 8

The Archdiocesan Visitations

In early November 1965, energized by the spirit of hope and excitement marking this period of the Church, the Immaculate Heart General Council decided that it would be wise for those engaged in renewal to send a representative to Rome, where the Second Vatican Council was still in session. They chose me to go. I was delighted by the opportunity, for it was a thrilling and never-to-be-forgotten time in the Eternal City. There I visited the very special house called "Villa Miani," founded and financed by Cardinal Leon-Joseph Suenens, the great forerunner of sisters' renewal. The cardinal's purpose was to bring together representatives of certain religious women's communities and engage them in discussions and study of the latest trends in modern theology. The IHMs had been invited to send a sister to the villa. Sister John Baptist Wallace (Ruth Wallace) was chosen to attend. The work going on there I found to be both lively and informative, and I was pleased to be asked to address the group.

It was also exciting for me to attend the press conferences at which experts in Church law, theology, or Church history daily briefed journalists of all ages and talents, while listeners, sisters, priests, and lay people gathered eagerly. My stay in Rome was planned to be a short one, so the days were packed with informal gatherings at which great theologians from all over the world, in a multiplicity of languages, met for lively discussions and pleasant camaraderie. The richness of these occasions made me hopeful for the future of the IHMs.

But all too soon the joy ended. A phone call came for me from the United States. Our vicar-general, Sister Elizabeth Ann Flynn, informed me that all was not well. She had been told by the chancery office that all the Immaculate Heart Sisters in the Archdiocese of Los Angeles were to have an official visitation from priests of the archdiocese and that, according to the vicar for religious, Monsignor Edward Wade, ours was the only religious community to be visited in this manner. This move, coming as it did from the cardinal's office, certainly had as its purpose to inquire about the state of the sisters' religious life. Immediately it carried for both Sister Elizabeth Ann and myself the implication of disfavor and penalty.

Although visitations in general were prescribed by Church law for religious orders, their frequency was limited to five-year intervals except under very special circumstances, such as evidence of injustice occurring in a particular religious house or lack of responsiveness to the needs of sisters under a local superior. Generally, too, a visitation was a pious chat with a priest appointed for the purpose. In this case, however, the five-year interval between visitations had not yet elapsed, the latest one having been a "special canonical visitation" conducted by Cardinal McIntyre himself only six months earlier. Furthermore, prior to this time a visitation was generally conducted by a single priest; now, we learned, the cardinal had requested an entire team of diocesan priests to act as visitators. Hearing of this, I was overwhelmed by a sense of foreboding.

The stimulation I was experiencing in the atmosphere of the Second Vatican Council suddenly dwindled as I pondered the meaning of this latest episode with His Eminence. Although Sister Elizabeth Ann had protested to the cardinal over the timing of the visitation in my absence, it was to no avail. In fact, more than likely, it was thought, the timing was calculated. And there were even some in the chancery office who interpreted the unusual move as "a form of persecution of the community."[1]

Promptly I made arrangements to return to Los Angeles, but before I left, I went to visit the crypt where Pope Pius XII and Pope John XXIII were entombed in the customary marble sepulchers. The miniature chapel where Pope Pius rested held a single vase with long-stemmed roses; not far away, the tomb of Pope John was surrounded by jars holding field flowers. Groups of people were praying there, bent as if in mourning. I knelt at both memorials, one Pope remaining in my memory as an aristocrat, a prince, with whom I had had my first encounter with the great tradition of the papal audience; the other, a man overflowing with love for all people, simple though learned, who

[1] Minutes of the IHM General Council, November 12, 1965. Archives of the Immaculate Heart Community (hereafter cited as A/IHMCOM).

suited the need of our times. It was a pilgrimage I hoped I could repeat someday. I bought my plane ticket and left for Los Angeles, restless and apprehensive on the long journey.

Once home, with a sense of helplessness I heard from the sisters of the humiliating interrogations by the visiting priests. The fear the sisters felt soon gave way to honest indignation as each one faced questions designed, it would appear, to undermine their faith in the renewal process by questioning the present practices of the Immaculate Heart Sisters and many other matters mostly unrelated to the modest experimental changes proposed at the 1963 chapter.

After the interrogations, conducted by two priests, a number of sisters wrote down the questions they had been asked and the interview methods used by the priests. The questions have been kept on file in the community archives but have never been disclosed up to this time, nor have they been studied in order that we might all gain a fuller understanding of this entire period. As the sisters noted in case after case, the priests did not take notes in the process. Some of the questions were direct, some related to the proposed changes, but a number were highly personal, having an unhealthy cast.

"Do you think the Sisters' sex life is affected by reading novels?"

"Do you think sisters should take so many secular subjects in college?"

"Don't you think it will take too much time to fix your hair if you were to change your habit?"

"What do you think about contact with seculars?"

"Don't you think some of the new ideas in catechetics are not real doctrine but merely 'topping'?"

"Do you have any books by non-Catholics in your library?"

"You don't have any books on existentialism, do you?"

"Do you approve of the changes since your 1963 General Chapter?"

"Do you feel they are in keeping with the spirit of your institute?"

"Do you want to look like a little girl?"

"Do you want to look like a floozie on Hollywood Boulevard?"

"Would you like to look like a Social Service Sister?"

"Do you have freedom of place with regard to meditation?"

"Are there any means in use for checking as to whether or not each person was fulfilling her obligations?"

"Do all the sisters avail themselves of the privilege of the sacrament of penance regularly?"

"Who is your regular confessor?"

"Do you feel that adequate retreat masters are available to you?"

"Do you have hootenanny Masses?"

"Do you like saying the Rosary?"

"Do you think Holy Hour, as presently conducted, is meaningful?"

"During the past two years, your community has been applying many variances in practice and discipline 'ad experimentum.' What is your reaction to the experiments?"

"Do you read and approve of the diocesan paper [*The Tidings*]?"

"What do you think of *Ramparts* magazine? Why did Sister Mary Jean write for it?"

"What did you think of a course on James Joyce taught a couple of years ago at your college? Do you know how pornographic *Ulysses* is?"

"Do you want to get out in society? Religious shouldn't work that much with people—look what came out of the French Worker Priest movement."

"Do you know why your community is being investigated?"[2]

These and many other questions were addressed by two priests confronting each sister in an atmosphere clouded by suspicion and disapproval. Although no official summary or report of the priests' interrogations was ever made public, a letter from His Eminence purporting to represent the consensus of the visitators would soon be forthcoming. The fact that the visiting clerics so obviously failed to understand where the sisters were in their theological and social thought proved quite disconcerting, even disillusioning, to the great majority of the sisters. They had hoped against hope that the Roman Catholic clergy would be eager for, or at least accepting of, the changes approved by the Second Vatican Council sessions and its documents.

It was after my hurried return from Rome that November and my briefing by the sisters that the vicar-general, Sister Elizabeth Ann, and I were summoned to the chancery office for a meeting with the cardinal

---

[2] Excerpts from IHM Community members' notes. A/IHMCOM.

and his staff—Bishop Timothy Manning, Bishop John J. Ward, and Monsignor Edward Wade, vicar for religious. The cardinal was armed with some statements from a minority in the community by whom change was either sincerely opposed or generally resisted, because it represented new ideas. In that meeting of December 27, 1965, His Eminence accused the Sisters of the Immaculate Heart of disobedience to the Ordinary (the cardinal himself), failure to cooperate with the archdiocese, and of the adoption of regulations and customs at variance with the views of the archdiocese on what was proper for religious communities. The cardinal then announced to the two of us that our General Council was being allowed sixty days to respond to him; the response should indicate whether or not the sisters would conform to traditional religious life as defined by the Ordinary. In addition, His Eminence stated, all decrees and decisions regarding community customs would have to be approved by him before being promulgated.

Sister Elizabeth Ann and I responded as best we could to the cardinal's demands as we faced him in this interview. We indicated that as we understood the rules of the community and Church law, we could not agree to his demands. First, the charges made against the community concerned matters decreed by the sisters' General Chapter of 1963. According to our Rule, decrees voted on at the General Chapters had the force of law; only the Sacred Congregation for Religious could reverse them. Secondly, the customs objected to were internal to the community and thus not subject to the local Ordinary. Once again, the fact that we were a pontifical institute was the basis of our argument.

His Eminence then announced that if the IHM General Council refused to conform to his views, all moral support and help of the archdiocese would be withdrawn from the sisters. This threat was intimidating. A series of questions rushed through my mind. What kind of support did he believe he now gave? Would the sisters' monthly stipend for teaching in parochial schools be reduced or even withheld altogether? What all this might mean we could not imagine.

As a final note concluding the interview, I stated in as firm a voice as I could manage, but with no little trepidation for the community:

> In all that concerns public worship or the works of the archdiocese, we will submit in loyalty and obedience to the Ordinary and consult with him. However, in those things which have to do with the internal life of the community, especially the decrees of the general chapters, we do not feel that we must consult the Ordinary. By rule

and according to canon law, we do not believe that we should submit these matters to the direct authority and approbation of the Ordinary.[3]

In so stating, I had had the assurance of several theologians and canon lawyers who were consulted earlier in anticipation of this unfortunate situation. Further, I requested that my statement be recorded in the minutes of the meeting. Abandoning my usual deference to clergy, I also asked that all persons present consider themselves as witnesses to the statements of His Eminence regarding his approval or disapproval of chapter decrees and General Council decisions and the necessity of his approval before promulgation of such proposals.

Sister Elizabeth Ann and I left the chancery office that late December day with sinking hearts. We knew now that all our efforts at renewal, as long as they were of any consequence, would meet with opposition. Shaken by our encounter, we discussed our plight with other members of the council. They agreed that we must appeal immediately to the Sacred Congregation for Religious, the Church body delegated to assist religious in just such conflicts with the local hierarchy. The congregation had as its head Cardinal Hildebrand Antoniutti.

Fortunately for us, we knew little at the time of Cardinal Antoniutti's personality and methods of dealing with problematic situations. He was a native of the mountainous Italian region of Friuli near the Yugoslav border. He was said to be "as strict and hard" as the Udine seminary located there. He was variously described as "straightforward" and having "a sense of absolute justice." He was somewhat ambivalently known as "soft-spoken and diplomatic" as well as "intrinsically dictatorial."[4]

But even as Sister Elizabeth Ann and I were preparing to go immediately to the Vatican to ask for assistance from Cardinal Antoniutti, we knew nothing of all this background, nor did we have any presentiment of the outcome. We had not yet started our journey when we received a letter from Cardinal McIntyre dated December 28, 1965, the day following our meeting with him and his staff. In this letter he again made his recommendations for restoring our former way of life before any changes were enacted. This advice was purportedly based on the

[3] Minutes of the meeting of Sister Elizabeth Ann and Mother Humiliata with Cardinal McIntyre, December 27, 1965. A/IHMCOM.

[4] Desmond O'Grady, "Ildebrando Antoniutti: IHM Case Figure 'Gets What He Wants,'" *National Catholic Reporter* (June 19, 1968) 2.

findings of "unrest, uncertainty and dissatisfaction"[5] among the sisters who had been interrogated by the priest-visitators.

The letter began with a surprising admission from His Eminence to the effect that he had received the priests' visitation "report" only a few minutes before the previous day's meeting with Sister Elizabeth Ann and myself. He acknowledged that he "had not yet digested it" when he had met with us. What this suggested to us, of course, was that he had already made up his mind about the outcome of the visitation, indeed had probably sent the visitators on their mission to bring back the "evidence" that would prove the negative views he held.

The recommendations contained in Cardinal McIntyre's letter demonstrate his negative attitude toward the sisters' experimental changes. His militaristic and dictatorial demands are listed here to show the extent of the cardinal's desired involvement in our lives. Some of these conservative mandates even went beyond our own original Book of Customs dating back some forty years.

1. The traditional practice of a fixed rule applicable to all should be resumed. Deviation from this rule should be by special permission. A general privilege of optional compliance should not prevail with regard to rules of action. Nor should any members of the community indulge in considering their own opinion and conscience above the rule and regulations of the community.

   The seeming discontent prevailing in the community appears to be attributable to the policy invoked in recent years wherein experimental changes in practice have been inaugurated and indulged in. These without consultation with the Ordinary or the Vicar for Religious or their knowledge *[sic]*. Such a procedure was contrary to canonical practice.

2. The rule should be observed by all. It is recommended that there be a community Mass every morning at which all should attend, except those excused for legitimate reasons.

3. It is observed that silence is required only during what is usually sleeping hours.

   It would be recommended that you find some way of emphasizing in a practical way, the value and the virtue of a short period of silence daily.

[5] Cardinal McIntyre. Letter to Mother M. Humiliata, December 28, 1965. A/IHMCOM.

4. Retiring time should be observed universally. The exception of night studies, etc., should be discouraged; the rule of the house should be predominant.

5. The Holy Hour seems to be a serious point of disagreement. Our recommendation is that the traditional practice be followed in your community. Traditionally, a Holy Hour consists of a full period being devoted to the Adoration of Our Lord exposed in the Blessed Sacrament in the Chapel. This is the primary purpose of the Holy Hour. Accompanying devotions might be taken from any or all of the following:

> Ten or fifteen minutes of silent meditation
>
> Benediction Homilies, prayers and litanies in common
>
> Recitation of the Rosary
>
> Public reading of meditations by one of the community
>
> Hymns

During the Holy Hour, the Holy Scriptures may be enthroned in the sanctuary. This type of Holy Hour should be held once a week.

6. The names of retreat masters should be submitted for approval to the Vicar for Religious before an invitation is extended.

Confessions should be heard regularly every week.

Where a retreat master introduces any novelties with regard to the procedure for confessions, the matter should be reported promptly to the Chancery Office.

Any form of general absolution should not be permitted.

You will note that the practice of saying the Act of Contrition necessary for confession should be at the time of the confession and in the Confessional, not prior or after.

7. In the celebration of Mass and the distribution of Holy Communion, variations should not be adopted beyond those formally approved by the Ordinary of the Archdiocese.

8. A few minutes at a specified time should be allotted each day for the recitation of the Rosary by each member of your community. This is to be in common or in private, but an exercise to be conducted at the same time by all.[6]

[6] Ibid.

At the end of these recommendations, the cardinal reminded us that he was acting in his capacity as Ordinary, adding ominously that "a visitation [another?] is within the judgment of an Ordinary under any given circumstances." He expected cooperation, he said, and all this was "for the good of religion in general."[7]

In sum, then, His Eminence had merely repeated his verbal admonitions of the meeting of December 27 in the chancery that the "fixed rule" applicable to all should be resumed. It made no difference to him that we were an active order, our days filled with teaching and nursing responsibilities to a public having its own time concerns. Our legitimate experimentation, authorized by our 1963 General Chapter and under evaluation by our own sisters, was basically denied, to be replaced by the old, minute, and uniform specifications as to time, place, and type of prayer. Clearly this change from absolute uniformity led to the undeserved suspicion that much or all prayer was being eliminated. That was not the case. The sisters merely sought flexibility of time and place for prayer in their active apostolate.

From the cardinal's side, what was desired, even demanded, was absolute fidelity to the past and unquestioning obedience to the hierarchy—this in spite of the fact that the community as a pontifical institute was exempt from the local hierarchy's special directives except in public matters that might prove scandalous. Ironically, the cardinal's own insistence was on local control, while the community stood firm in its pontifical affiliation.

In addition to the letter of December 28, 1965, a memorandum was sent to us following our visit to the chancery confirming the fact that the cardinal was particularly concerned about local authority in each convent. Part of the note from him read: "We deplore the limitation of house superiors, and would wish a sister to be in charge of each house and responsible for the maintenance of the occupants. The Superior should know at all times the whereabouts and practices of the members of the house."[8]

Meanwhile Sister Elizabeth Ann and I, appalled by the scope and severity of the cardinal's recommendations, arrived in Rome in early January 1966. We were accompanied to the office of Cardinal Antoniutti

[7] Ibid.

[8] The memorandum from Cardinal McIntyre's office is undated and appears to be late December 1965 or early 1966. This is another example of the frequent and intrusive nature of his communication with the IHM Community. A/IHMCOM.

by a member of his staff, who happened to be a sympathetic advocate, a Holy Cross priest, Father Bernard E. Ransing. We found ourselves received by the prefect of the Sacred Congregation for Religious with polite formality. Cardinal Antoniutti was a tall, imposing figure. He explained that we had not violated our rights and even assisted us in writing a dignified and courteous response to Cardinal McIntyre. It seems ironic to me now, remembering that first, highly formal, gracious reception and contrasting it with later letters of reprobation from the same congregation. At that time I was somewhat naïve about the impregnable hierarchical structure of male authority; no doubt a bond stronger than I could imagine existed among all the ecclesiastical male authority figures who were central to our story.

Cardinal Antoniutti's solution to the dilemma that faced us was to suggest that a letter be written by the IHM General Council declaring our proven loyalty to the hierarchy of Los Angeles. The text suggested by Antoniutti for the letter was both ingenious and gracious. First, he urged us to assure Cardinal McIntyre of our intention to remain obedient to him in matters under his jurisdiction. Then, in a secondary position in the letter, he suggested that we gently remind Cardinal McIntyre that in matters of community government, we were of course subject to the Holy See as a pontifical institute. Thirdly, Cardinal Antoniutti deftly proposed that we borrow a neat bit of *romanita* that is engraved in my memory. He suggested that a statement like the following inserted in the letter would assure the cardinal of our commitment: "We would be deeply grieved if you thought that we as religious women were other than loyal to Holy Mother Church."[9] Accompanying this suggestion was a surprising final proposal: "In spite of these and other efforts to serve the Church in the Archdiocese, it would seem that we have been a continued source of embarrassment to you. Such has never been our intent. Yet, perhaps Your Eminence would prefer that other communities replace our sisters in your schools. If so, we will acquiesce to your wishes for surely we do not desire to be burdensome to you."[10]

[9] Personal notes of Mother Mary Humiliata, I.H.M.

[10] Undelivered letter of February 1, 1966, from Mother M. Humiliata to Cardinal McIntyre. With the advice of the IHM General Council, I composed a letter that included the four suggestions of Cardinal Antoniutti. However, after discussion and reflection, I never sent this letter to Cardinal McIntyre. I include part of it here to demonstrate the type of advice we received from Cardinal Antoniutti and our desire to find some means (and an advocate) to negotiate with Cardinal McIntyre. A/IHMCOM.

It is ironic to think, in retrospect, that a proposed threat on our part, even one of Vatican origin, became a reality with our dismissal from the Catholic schools in such a short time. But at that time our visit to the Vatican had encouraged us by urging us to be confident in our thinking. We thought that we had gained the understanding and sympathy of Cardinal Antoniutti, and so we felt that our visit had not been a waste of time.

With the proposed text in hand, Sister Elizabeth Ann and I returned to discuss the matter with the General Council. Instead of the letter suggested by Antoniutti, we decided to send instead a polite missive assuring Cardinal McIntyre of our cooperation but omitting any reference to the schools. We felt that a hasty and angry response to a veiled threat might actually precipitate matters and plunge us into a situation with which we were not prepared to deal. We were anticipating the preparations for our 1967 Chapter of Renewal. The possibility of withdrawal from our schools was a risk we felt unable to take. So Cardinal Antoniutti's suggested letter remained unused in the IHM files.

My letter of February 7, 1966, attempted both to respond to Cardinal McIntyre's recommendations of December 28, 1965, indicating our good intentions, and to restore some harmony following the meeting of December 27, while maintaining our rights as a pontifical institute. It is quoted in full below.

Your Eminence,

I regret very much, Your Eminence, the circumstances of our last meeting and I assure you that the Sisters of the Immaculate Heart wish to cooperate zealously and diligently with Your Eminence for the good of the Church here in the Archdiocese of Los Angeles. Along with the many Religious in your jurisdiction, we wish to be of ever increasing assistance to you, as members of your diocesan family.

The recommendations made to us in your letter of December 28 have been discussed by the General Council. We are in agreement that these recommendations should be followed. The first recommendation—that there should be traditional practice of a fixed rule—is a part of the life of our sisters. We have such a rule from which deviation is granted only by special permission. Our sisters are not free to do as they please, but are required to conform to this series of regulations, a copy of which is enclosed.

The other recommendations meet with our complete cooperation likewise, except for the fact that our Chapter Decree Number 10, issued in 1963, states: "The Rosary may be said privately at a time chosen by each Sister." Our Customs' change from the same year (1963) at our

General Chapter states: "The Mother General shall conduct an experiment in which the time of evening retirement is left to the discretion of each Sister. Upon completion of the experiment, the Mother General may delete Article 161 of Customs if she deems it advisable. If the experiment of evening retirement is unsuccessful, Article 161 shall be changed to read: "The lights shall be out at 11:00 [p.m.] unless a Sister has permission from the superior to keep them on later." The vote on this was 458 yes and 43 no. Thus the time of retirement is, by Chapter decree, left to each Sister's discretion. A copy of our Chapter decrees is enclosed.

With regard to the Holy Hour, we have read your recommendation carefully. We would like to continue our practice in the Motherhouse of following the period of Bible readings with Holy Mass on Sunday. We have Benediction in the convent chapel as often as permission is granted. If you wish, we might very well have a Holy Hour with Exposition of the Blessed Sacrament at another time during the week. Actually all 148 of us are extremely crowded in our small chapel when we have Holy Hour at one time. For the same reason, there are scheduled two community Masses in the Motherhouse.

Again, Your Eminence, please be assured that the Sisters of the Immaculate Heart pledge their heartfelt loyalty. We wish not only to cooperate but to enjoy a close coordination of all apostolic works and activities. A concerted effort will, I am sure, foster a union of policy and discipline, as well as a harmonious and fruitful relation for the good of souls in this Archdiocese. We feel privileged to serve Christ and His Church as devoted religious in Los Angeles, under your guidance as its Chief Shepherd.

With every best wish, I have the honor to be, Your Eminence,

Respectfully in Mary,

Mother M. Humiliata, I.H.M.
Mother General[11]

Interestingly enough, on the very same date as the letter above, two letters came to me from the cardinal, both dated February 7, 1966. One expressed the gratitude of His Eminence for relieving him of anxiety regarding the Immaculate Heart Sisters. Mentioned in the first letter are "various reports, complaints and observed circumstances of the past few years," placing the administration of the archdiocese in the "unwelcome position of finding it necessary to request an explicit con-

[11] Mother M. Humiliata. Letter to Cardinal McIntyre, February 7, 1966. A/IHMCOM.

firmation of . . . conformity to . . . Canon Law."[12] This letter concluded by stating that such confirmation had been given by me and that the anxiety of His Eminence was thereby relieved. The tone of this letter indicated that it was written in response to my letter; perhaps its date was in error.

But the reassurance of this first letter was strangely contradicted by the second letter of the same date discussing specific practices that varied from the past. His Eminence suggested that some of his criticisms of the community were due to his lack of knowledge of the rules of the Immaculate Heart Sisters, which had not been given to him since 1960–61. The lengthy remainder of the second letter commented unfavorably on various revisions in the practices of the community, especially regarding prayer. Basically, this second letter had significance for its expression of the cardinal's displeasure at the term "experimentation." He was distrustful of a trial-and-error period in the renewal of religious life. There is no doubt that this conviction recurred in his later disapproval of our 1967 decrees.[13]

Meanwhile, for almost a year all seemed peaceful in the archdiocese, and the sisters went about their daily tasks, teaching, praying, and looking forward to the once-in-a-lifetime special Chapter of Renewal that was to take place in the summer of 1967. Suddenly, however, in March 1967 yet another canonical visitation, less than two years after the previous one, was announced in a letter from the cardinal. The visitation was to be confined to "the Motherhouse, the College and the Novitiate."[14] The ostensible reason for the extraordinary visit was explained by the cardinal but was no doubt inspired by the imminence of the Chapter of Renewal just four months away. The following excerpt from the cardinal's letter indicates that this visitation was to act as a complement to the earlier visitation.

> My dear Mother Humiliata,
>
> You are aware that this office receives a multitude of reports in all areas which concern the Church. It is incumbent upon the Ordinary to prudently evaluate the truthfulness of these allegations made spontaneously by many persons. Accordingly, the visitation is the vehicle which

---

[12] Cardinal McIntyre. Letter to Mother M. Humiliata, February 7, 1966 (a). A/IHMCOM.

[13] Cardinal McIntyre. Letter to Mother M. Humiliata, February 7, 1966 (b). A/IHMCOM.

[14] Cardinal McIntyre. Letter to Mother M. Humiliata, March 23, 1967. A/IHMCOM.

the Ordinary has to make an accurate finding of facts by hearing truly competent witness. . . .

[Signed James Francis Cardinal McIntyre]

The interrogation of the sisters was to cover the following points:

a) whether discipline is maintained conformably to the Constitution;

b) whether sacred doctrine and good morals have suffered in any way;

c) whether there have been offenses against the law of enclosure (lay persons allowed in dining or recreational areas formerly forbidden to anyone besides sisters);

d) whether the reception of the Sacraments is regular and frequent.[15]

For this visitation two monsignors and a diocesan priest were assigned to conduct the interrogation. The letter cited above stated that a suitable place outside the "enclosure" should be provided for the visitation.

The encouraging letter of February 7, 1966, with its puzzling second letter of the same date, were not referred to in this new announcement. The motives for the visitation and its legality were no longer the issues. The new ground for visitation had apparently shifted to the reaction of the general (Catholic) public to any experimentation pertaining to renewal or change. As might be supposed, by this time the patience of the majority of sisters had worn thin. Nerves were on edge, and each convent suffered from questioning by the Catholic public regarding the problems of the community, as lay people sensed the disapproval of the cardinal and of some diocesan clerics, and wondered about the propriety of the sisters' lives, even though they saw little evidence for concern.

Yet, this latest visitation was taken with as much aplomb as possible, as the sisters, young and old, answered the negatively cast interrogations. Inevitably, their responses were colored by the ideas emerging from Vatican II, now so much a part of our thinking and feeling. In fact, the sister accompanying one of the visitators to the front door of the motherhouse after a long day of questioning heard the priest-visitator say, with a shake of his head as she closed the door behind him, "The trouble with the Immaculate Heart Sisters is they're all hung up on Vatican II."[16]

[15] Ibid.

[16] This comment has become part of our IHM oral tradition. Years ago our first reaction was one of shock and distaste; as the years pass, we now humorously repeat these words as a badge of honor we gladly wear.

On May 15, 1967, an official report was sent to me by Bishop John J. Ward, the vicar for religious, regarding the March canonical visitation. Among his recommendations was an observation that the visitators found a "fair segment of those interviewed . . . quite willing for change but did not wish it to be so rapid or radical. This group seemed to think that the religious and spiritual character of the community was suffering as a result of the present pace of change."[17] This letter drew real indignation, hurt, and the inability of the sisters, especially those teaching in college, to keep silence. Nearly a hundred of them wrote a strong letter, without my knowledge, addressed to Cardinal McIntyre, indicating that they felt no damage had been done to their spiritual lives by the changes or their pace and that the progress toward renewal was not a hindrance but a help in their dedicated lives. Because one seldom has the opportunity of seeing a spontaneous response from the grassroots of an organization, so that we can understand their feelings and their virtual unanimity, I am quoting the letter in its entirety here. My first reading of it was made through tears as I was touched by the loyalty of the sisters and their understanding of the principles of renewal.

April 2, 1967

His Eminence, James Francis Cardinal McIntyre
1531 W. Ninth Street
Los Angeles, California

Your Eminence:

Since we realize your great concern for our spiritual welfare and since we know it is difficult for you to ascertain the thoughts and feelings of all the members of our Institute, we would like to make the following statement in order to assure you of our collective thinking as far as the most important aspects of our spiritual life are concerned:

1) The community, in accord with the recommendations of the Conciliar document on Appropriate Renewal of Religious Life together with the *Motu Proprio,* both of which urge the necessity of experimentation in order that the apostolate may be carried out with greater effectiveness, has chosen to follow the injunction of the Council that "The manner of living, praying, and working should be suitably adapted to the physical and psychological conditions of today's religious" (*P.C.* Decree, No. 3). In

---

[17] Bishop John J. Ward. Letter to Mother M. Humiliata, May 15, 1967. A/IHMCOM.

order to do this we have not discarded our Rule or relaxed our pursuit of holiness. Rather, we are examining our Rule in order to see which regulations are outmoded and inappropriate as far as the life of the Church is concerned.

2) No sister has been coerced or asked to subscribe to any kind of limitation as far as her prayer life is concerned. On the contrary, each of us is encouraged to pray daily at the time best suited to our individual needs. This kind of personal freedom obviously allows more time for mental prayer, spiritual reading, study of the Scriptures, etc., than our former mode of life which minutely regulated, in terms of a fixed schedule, our attempt to grow spiritually.

3) Our higher superiors, women of profound spirituality and intellectual acumen, are much concerned that we observe religious obedience in a way that, in the words of the Document, "[the dignity of the human person will not be diminished] but will rather lead it to maturity in consequence of that enlarged freedom which belongs to the sons of God" (*P.C.*, No. 11).

4) Our higher superiors also constantly urge us to obey the directions of the Ordinary and by their own example encourage us to do so.

5) For many years now, our community has been doing what the Decree on Renewal points out as being of the utmost importance, that "religious should be properly instructed, according to the intellectual gifts and personal endowments of each, in the prevailing manners of contemporary social life and in its characteristic ways of thinking and feeling" (*P.C.*, No. 18). It is by doing this, we are convinced, that we have been able in the past and are able at the present time to make our contribution to the various aspects of the apostolate in which you are so vitally interested.

6) Lastly, Your Eminence, since our lives as Sisters of the Immaculate Heart are totally dedicated to the service of the Church, we wish to assure you that all experimentation has been undertaken in an effort to discover and to reformulate a manner of life most appropriate to our dedication. Experimentation so oriented, we believe to be a most effective means of avoiding mistakes and confirming values in our final decisions regarding religious renewal.

Sincerely in Christ,

There followed the signatures of each sister, young and old, giving the proud date of each one's religious profession.[18]

---

[18] Members of the Sisters of the Immaculate Heart. Letter to Cardinal McIntyre, April 2, 1967. A/IHMCOM.

My own reply to Cardinal McIntyre commenting on this most recent visitation was an attempt once more to point out that the legislation of the chapter of 1963 had rescinded earlier rules. Only another chapter could reinstate these rules if the members so desired. The charge of His Eminence that he was unaware of the 1963 changes to our Rule met with my reminder to him that copies of any new legislation were immediately sent to him. I pointed out that in spite of this action, the second group of visitators were still under the impression that older regulations prevailed, although letters of His Eminence clearly showed that he withdrew much of his criticism after reading the regulations of 1963. As to the presence of the entire community at one Mass, that was impossible because of the size of our chapel. Building regulations already limited the number of persons present at any one time to fewer than the number living in the motherhouse. However, the sisters attended daily Mass—most in the motherhouse chapel and the overflow in the college chapel—a fact that seemed never to be understood, since His Eminence returned to this point again and again.

We now knew that we were dealing with contradictions, and our explanations were disregarded. We could foresee that the Chapter of Renewal was meeting with some internal disapproval from a few sisters; no matter how small the number, this fact was strongly affecting the attitudes of the cardinal. Yet we could not, even if we had wanted to, stop the growing tide of renewal that had caught the imagination of the majority of sisters.

Chapter 9

The 1967 Chapter of Renewal:
Creating the Vision

Although the IHM sisters living in the Archdiocese of Los Angeles had already experienced the intimidations of several canonical visitations, we now felt that the recent recommendations of the Second Vatican Council on religious life gave us the assurance of papal authorization—that of Pope Paul VI. The document stressed the importance of renewal by the religious institutes themselves if the "adaptation of their way of life and of their discipline" were to reach fruition.[1]

Further, the Pope exhorted institutes to "study carefully the Dogmatic Constitution *Lumen Gentium* . . . and the Decree *Perfectae Caritatis* . . . and they should endeavor to put the Council's teaching and directives into effect."[2] It seemed less a polite invitation to renew than a command to work seriously for renewal. The central passages emphasized below are the Vatican norms for the implementation of *Perfectae Caritatis*, the Decree on the Up-to-Date Renewal of Religious Life. These were the ecclesial directives used by the Immaculate Heart Sisters in their process of renewal. They also were the principles found to be unacceptable by Cardinal McIntyre of the Archdiocese of Los Angeles after their adoption by the 1967 Chapter of Renewal.

1. Empowerment of those responsible for renewal:

It is the institutes themselves which have the main responsibility for renewal and adaptation. They shall accomplish this especially by means of

---

[1] Pope Paul VI, *Ecclesiae Sanctae II*, in *Vatican Council II: The Conciliar and Post Conciliar Documents*, ed. Austin Flannery, O.P. (Northport, N.Y.: Costello Publishing Co., 1981) 624.

[2] Ibid. Italics in items 1 through 5 are added.

general chapters. . . . The task of general chapters is not limited to making laws; they should also foster spiritual and apostolic vitality.[3]

2. Encouragement of cooperation on the part of all superiors and subjects:

   The cooperation of all superiors and subjects is necessary for the renewal of their own religious lives, for the preparation of the spirit which should animate the chapters, for the accomplishment of their task, and for the faithful observance of the laws and norms laid down by the chapters.[4]

3. Establishment of specific timing for renewal chapters:

   In each institute, in order to put renewal and adaptation into effect, a special general chapter is to be summoned within two or, at most, three years. This can be the ordinary general chapter, or an extraordinary one.[5]

4. Establishment of the means by which material to be considered for chapter decisions should be gathered:

   In preparation for this chapter, the general council must arrange, by some suitable means, for an *ample and free consultation of all the subjects*. The results of this consultation should be made available in good time so as to guide and assist the work of the chapter. The consultation may be done at the level of conventual or provincial chapters, by setting up commissions, by sending out questionnaires, etc.[6]

5. Establishment of the extent of powers of each chapter:

   This general chapter has the right to alter, temporarily, certain prescriptions of the constitutions . . . by way of experiment, provided that the purpose, nature and character of the institute are safeguarded. *Experiments which run counter to common law*—and they should be embarked on with prudence—*will be readily authorized by the Holy See as the need arises.*

   Such experiments may be continued until the next ordinary *general chapter, which will be empowered to grant a further prolongation* but not beyond the date of the subsequent chapter.[7]

---

[3] Ibid., 624–625, no. 1.
[4] Ibid., 625, no. 2.
[5] Ibid., no. 3.
[6] Ibid., no. 4.
[7] Ibid., no. 6.

Thus this directive could theoretically allow for up to twelve years of experimentation, since general chapters occur every six years.

What is particularly striking about these instructions, we believed, was the emphasis upon experimentation. A scientific term with the aura of legitimacy, it lent a new respectability to the concept of change, especially for those in religious life whose chief impetus was a devout faith. For some still, the term was bound to stir up fears that the changeless face of the Church was being challenged. So to justify the concept of experimentation, an explanation was thought to be necessary. If the Church was to renew itself, it had to gather, and gather widely, new information about the best ways to renew.

> It is evident that no new clear and definite legislation can be formulated except on the basis of experiments carried out on a sufficiently vast scale and over a sufficiently long period of time to make it possible to arrive at an objective judgment based on facts. This is most true since the complexity of situations, their variations according to localities and the rapidity of the changes which affect them make it impossible for those charged with the formation of the youth of today to an authentic religious life to determine *a priori* which solutions might be best.
>
> This is why this Sacred Congregation for Religious and for Secular Institutes, after careful examination of the proposals submitted regarding the different phases of religious formation, has deemed it opportune to broaden the canonical rules now in force in order to permit these necessary experiments.[8]

Because of these numerous provisions emanating from the highest authority and expressed in the sincerest desire to enhance our mutual spirituality, the Sisters of the Immaculate Heart of Mary were eager to follow the papal exhortation to renew their spiritual lives. With interest high, the General Council had called for a special meeting of all community members on October 31, 1966, to initiate plans for a special Chapter of Renewal. This special meeting followed hard on the address of Pope Paul VI to the United Nations with its clarion call, "The hour has struck indeed . . . for personal renewal."[9]

[8] *Renovationis Causam*, in *Vatican Council II: The Conciliar and Post Conciliar Documents*, ed. Austin Flannery, O.P. (Northport, N.Y.: Costello Publishing Co., 1981) 636.

[9] Pope Paul VI, "Address to the General Assembly of the United Nations," October 4, 1965, pars. 19, 23, in *The Gospel of Peace and Justice*, ed. Joseph Gremillion (Maryknoll, N.Y.: Orbis Books, 1979) 383–384.

These words became the theme of my speech announcing our special Chapter of Renewal, urging the sisters to give full and gracious response to the papal exhortation. Fortunately, I felt, the wealth of talent among our community members matched this challenge. Even so, the call for renewal was an intimidating duty for me. My sources were authoritative; it was my task to bring them into focus for the members of the community in the here and now.

The major points of renewal, I suggested, were taken from Pope Paul VI's document on the subject of renewal for those living the religious life. In spite of some blurred distinctions, the document was clear on the basic issues of renewal. These were, in brief: (1) an orientation to Scripture; (2) an orientation to liturgy; (3) an adaptation of the concept of authority as service; (4) a new understanding of the ecumenical movement; (5) a deepening awareness of contemporary life and our situation in it; (6) the development of a social conscience; (7) abandonment of a narrow legalism in favor of the guidance of the Holy Spirit.

My ideal for the development of religious life was a statement that for the world the religious becomes witness to a kind of last-stand testament that life and love are greater than death and boredom.

To answer the question, Does a religious life described in terms of being a part of the modern world constitute release from all regulation? Not at all. In fact, "this new freedom, this concept of the community 'without walls' demands far more highly disciplined sisters than ever before. . . . It demands a life that does not make sense if God does not exist."[10]

I concluded: "As Sisters of the Immaculate Heart, we must be aware of the charism, the gift that is ours. We must develop it fully and confidently, rejoicing and blessing the Lord who has let us live to see this great day in His Church."[11]

Again, all these thoughts were not received with the same enthusiasm by all the sisters. As has been noted, some certainly were satisfied with the old and familiar, and for them the new insights seemed perhaps too academic, too remote, and too frightening. Some of those objecting were unhappy even about the dictum of Pope Pius XII, who years earlier had said: "Far from drawing you within yourselves and

---

[10] Mother Mary Humiliata, I.H.M., October 31, 1966. Unpublished speech to IHM sisters. Photocopy, Archives of the Immaculate Heart Community (hereafter referred to as A/IHMCOM).

[11] Ibid.

behind the walls of your convents, your union with God broadens your mind and heart according to the dimensions of the world."[12]

There is no doubt that such openness would bring new and challenging awareness to the religious life. Responsibility and concern for civic, national, and international problems must be faced. But some sisters, trained to think of themselves as removed from these problems through the security of prayer, were peaceful and satisfied with their lives and did not want to hear about the realities now about to touch them personally.

As the meeting broke up, I met new hope and enthusiastic response in the eyes of most of the sisters. But I could already sense that there were small groups that were dismayed, disturbed, or openly opposed to the notion of a renewal of their lives. Following this meeting, the larger number of community members formed ongoing study commissions on the chief issues as requested; and this time, with the involvement of the total community, these issues that would be the concern of the upcoming Chapter of Renewal were discussed in earnest. After this late October general meeting, the volunteer committees and commissions, working steadily and for long hours, were able to announce in December that they could present their agenda for a General Chapter. The date for this chapter was fixed for the summer of 1967.

It was not long, however, before the cardinal was informed by the disapproving community members of the impending renewal program. Leadership within this group was beginning to emerge. Soon it was evident that the initiative was headed by Sister Eileen MacDonald, a well-educated, personable sister, who had administrative background as former dean of Immaculate Heart College. She had assisted Cardinal McIntyre in setting up the curriculum of the major seminary for the Los Angeles Archdiocese at Camarillo. She also had won the approval of the cardinal in her passionate defense of women's education in separate institutions.

Interest in our Chapter of Renewal had now spread beyond the Immaculate Heart Community. Catholics who knew the IHM sisters from years past were beginning to watch the developments with unusual attention, the more so, perhaps, because they had had virtually no preparation or information from the archdiocese concerning the

---

[12] Msgr. Vincent A. Yzermans, ed., *The Unwearied Advocate: Public Addresses of Pope Pius XII*, 2 vols. (St. Cloud, Minn.: St. Cloud Bookshop, 1956) 1:195.

new recommendations for the renewal of the Church. Elected chapter members were themselves beginning to be both fearful and expectant—fearful of the responsibility placed upon them and expectant of the new directions they felt the community was about to take.

The chapter members sensed, too, that they were becoming the controversial, innermost center of a series of concentric circles: close to the core, an inner circle of sisters within the community who did not wish change under any form; next to this a small circle of local hierarchy who had already made the community the subject of several canonical visitations; a circle of friends of the sisters, their former students, and the parents of the students they were presently teaching, all of whom were influenced not only by the community members they knew but by their previous idea of religious life. The sisters felt the growing concern of the general public, Catholic as well as non-Catholic. The latter were showing a remarkable interest in the actions of this small group of women who were developing a deeper faith in themselves. And on the outer edge, the world of the interested—priests, theologians, religious leaders of several faiths, and the Vatican itself.

One cannot think of this period of time without remembering especially the women (and men, too) of the hundreds of other religious communities. Many of these had been active in the Sister Formation Conference, which drew membership from all over the country and included representatives from numerous religious women's groups. So important was this wide group of religious women that it has been called "without question, the single most critical ground for the radical transformative process following World War II."[13] A number of the orders and their members were impatient for change, and while in many instances they did not share our specific ideas, they felt the need for some progress following the exhortation of Pope Paul VI. They watched with varying degrees of apprehension our "bold" steps, unhalted even after word of the reprimands and visitations of the cardinal archbishop and his associates became public.

Although these women's conferences had begun in 1953, well before the feminist movement in religion was underway and long before Vatican Council II convened in 1962, the sisters' movement had been preceded by an urgent call by Pope Pius XII for educational advancement for sisters in the teaching ministry. On September 13, 1951, this

---

[13] Lora Ann Quiñonez, C.D.P., and Mary Daniel Turner, S.N.D. de N., *The Transformation of American Catholic Sisters* (Philadelphia: Temple University Press, 1992) 6.

call resulted in the First International Congress of Teaching Sisters. A year later a second conference, entitled Participants in the International Congress of Superiors General of Orders and Congregations of Women: On Religious Vocations, was held and was attended by the reverend mother of the Immaculate Heart of Mary Sisters, among seven hundred others. Its agenda was that sisters should be as prepared as their secular colleagues for their educational apostolate.[14] And although Pius XII's plea focused immediately upon proper teacher preparation, he also urged the updating of the customs, dress, and approaches to the modern world by religious women. Both of these ideas were deemed important in their own right but were also considered by Pius XII as critical to the worldwide problem of the loss of religious women's vocations:

> We have a most special reason for speaking to you in this manner. You know that the Orders of women are passing through a very serious crisis: We refer to the decrease in the number of vocations. . . . In some places, where twenty years ago women's religious life was in full flower, the number of vocations has been reduced by half.[15]

Pope Pius XII's recommendation for addressing this worldwide problem in the early 1950s was forthright, pointing to the need for modernization of orders of religious women, as much for the sake of the applicants themselves as for the work of the Church:

> In this crisis of vocations, take care that the customs, the kind of life or the growth of your religious families do not constitute a barrier or a cause of failure. We refer to certain usages which, if at one time, they had meaning in another cultural frame, no longer have it today, and in which a truly good and courageous girl would find nothing but obstacles to her own vocation.[16]

---

[14] Ibid., 12.

[15] Yzermans, *The Unwearied Advocate*, 1:195.

[16] Ibid. This concern of the Holy Father, as far as anyone could tell, was not shared by Cardinal McIntyre. His Holiness continued in the same vein, showing a concern for the effect of unpreparedness upon a teaching sister. "And here, show no narrowness, but be broad of vision. Whether it be a matter of education, pedagogy, care of the sick, of artistic activity or something else, the sister must have this feeling. my superior gives me a training which places me on a level of equality with my

Such openness, consultation with all the sisters, and the lack of inhibition in the face of differing opinions created a totally different climate with regard to the coming IHM chapter. Suddenly what had been secretive in previous chapters was on the table, so to speak, and the formerly disguised polarization of the "progressives" and those who did not wish any change became more evident each day. The compilation of written proposals to be submitted for vote made non-participants realize that they might eventually have no voice in a new set of regulations through their own non-involvement. Hence many more than would otherwise have participated now joined in the discussions.

A kind of shock of recognition that the old order might well exist no more really struck us all, but especially those who had thought of renewal as a kind of dream never to be realized. It seemed even clearer that the static, institutional, enclosed convent might slowly and with painful steps find a new place in the modern world. Because of the chapter's chief priority, namely, laying the philosophical and theological bases for any changes advanced, the proposals were permeated with the acknowledgment of each person's responsibility for herself and for helping to build community. Since the proposals inevitably involved the wider group, the term "community" was no longer to be seen as a society organized to accomplish an assigned work that would glory in its tradition and consistency with the past. Nor was it to mean a kind of organization in which uniformity of thought and action pre-

---

colleagues in the world. Give them also the possibility of keeping their professional capacities up-to-date. We developed this aspect, too, last year [in the September 15, 1951, congress], but we repeat it for the purpose of underlining the importance of this need to the internal peace and activity of your sisters." Yzermans, *The Unwearied Advocate*, 195–196.

Pope Pius XII's promotion of the education for religious women was a precursor of Vatican Council II. Thus for all religious women two goals were inextricably bound together: for teachers or health or social workers, better professional preparation; for religious women, the modernization and renewal of their apostolic and spiritual lives. The Sister Formation Conference had in fact come together out of a common need to realize this twin goal: to work toward a more just approach to sister-teachers and their pupils by first "providing their teachers with the basic academic work required of all [certified] instructors" and giving them the "foundational intellectual and spiritual preparation for a mature religious life." Elizabeth Carroll, Ph.D., "Reaping the Fruits of Redemption," *Midwives of the Future*, ed. Ann Patrick Ware (Kansas City: Leaven Press, 1985) 58.

dominated. The old conformity in living conditions, horarium, prayers, and dress seemed more and more irrelevant. Instead, "community" now meant loving, living relationships based on both the recognition of Christ in every person and of the diversity of qualities in one another.

Moreover, the newer concept of authority was moving toward its enunciation following the writings of the Vatican Council. Whereas authority had once meant absolute power residing in religious hierarchy, and thus an order to be unquestioningly obeyed, the new governing group was to be dedicated to service. For Christ said, "The first shall be last, and the last first," giving an unforgettable example of the most fruitful use of authority in the washing of feet. Advice, encouragement, consultation—all these were the true work of governing officers, so that the simple vertical relationship of governor and governed no longer existed.

At the same time, the growing consciousness of one's dignity as a person required the individual to assume responsibility for her actions. She then had to freely and willingly bring these into correspondence with others. Here the idea of community was expanded upon in the new thinking. This concept of interrelationship and the concept of personal responsibility were clearly ones that would stimulate much discussion. Measured by the older theory of adherence to the will of authority as the will of God, the new acceptance of responsible freedom was a challenge.

It was about this time that I began to share my own personal view of the burden of the formal structure of authority within a religious order. From the perspective of a mother general of an order with some 600 religious members, with 450 teaching sisters, the burden of this highly structured mother-child relationship with its parental control over dedicated, adult women, many of whom were much older—and wiser—than I, seemed at times insupportable. In a speech I gave in October, 1968, entitled "What Happened to Mother Superior?" I tried to give the feel of the onerous details of a life of a "general" and a "dispenser of permissions," a task that I shared with every superior from the inner-city convents to the smallest outpost in British Columbia.

> I have lost my place at the head of the table, my office of leading community prayers, of never wearing the worn-out or faded habit so that sisters could be proud of me, the almost unbearable burden of being asked my will, my pleasure, about everything from the time a trip would be taken to the appropriateness of table settings,

the relevance of new work, the ability of nuns to publish, to paint, to speak in innumerable and varied situations.[17]

And after presenting this picture of the superior exercising control over such minutiae, I considered the more serious harm that such a system can do to an individual personality. "How much of the human personality with its needs for expression of diversity and its need for making free personal choices," I asked, "can be subjected to managerial demands? Does such a situation honestly make for the glory of God who has made us what we are?" I noted also that by 1967 sisters were maturing in their relationship with the world around them and becoming a new generation of women.

As we discussed the concept of authority, we felt that we could no longer ask our superiors to play the role of all-wise mothers to what amounted to, in psychological terms, a group of children—the sisters. Such a relationship tended to force peers into a familial mother-daughter pattern and often was resented by sisters who considered themselves adults. The best of our superiors were unhappy with it too. Such a structure placed a barrier between the superior and the sisters, a barrier that made for false relationships, sometimes based on fear, sometimes on currying favor, seldom completely honest and without pressure.[18]

New proposals with regard to assuming personal responsibility in financial areas was another shock to sisters who had been taught "she who has a penny isn't worth a penny." Several proposals were made concerning the sisters' financial support of the community: (1) voluntary contribution of a set amount; (2) either a specific amount with the option of an added personal donation; or (3) a clear percentage of any salary earned, with the option of a donation left free. The older practice of all earned funds being contributed to a general coffer, with dispensation in case of need or according to the judgment of the superior or her representative, changed among the sisters.

It was clear to almost everyone that the task of taking up important issues, of weeding through less important ones, of preparing proposals, of studying alternatives for such an important chapter, and of keeping

[17] Mother M. Humiliata, I.H.M. Speech given October 31, 1968, in the Christian Culture Lectures, sponsored by the Paulist Fathers, Boston, Mass. Unpublished photocopy, A/IHMCOM.

[18] Anita M. Caspary, I.H.M., "The Making of 'Servant Community,'" speech delivered at Tacoma, Wash., on June 14, 1973. Unpublished photocopy, A/IHMCOM.

faith with the spirit of Vatican II was almost overwhelming. And therefore in preparing ourselves for the 1967 Chapter of Renewal, it seemed incumbent upon us to organize it as carefully as possible, to be sure that it allowed free expression by all the sisters while having some perceptible structure so that the agenda could progress logically. Most importantly, the basic reasons for change had to be articulated and understood so that they could either be accepted or rejected before anything else was done. The General Council and I were well aware that efficiency and clarity are more easily obtained when a small, closely knit authority structure simply issues an order, but we were most eager that this chapter be as far as possible broadly representative of the sisters' needs, desires, and hopes for their own future and that of the community.

Our method of organization—attempting to combine structure and the general participation of as many sisters as possible—was simple yet apparently satisfying to most members. The position of general chairperson of the chapter was assigned to the vicar-general, Sister Elizabeth Ann Flynn, instead of the mother general. This move was intended to provide a somewhat more democratic environment for the delegates. Sister Elizabeth Ann was a fortunate choice. Her organizational skills were of a high order, and she was passionate in her desire to improve our educational program. Assisting her were four sisters on the steering committee, who were to be in charge of the agenda, working through meetings before and during the chapter. Closely associated with this top organizational group was a series of chairpersons, each in charge of an area already noted as being of high interest to the community. These areas, at first numerous, were reduced to the following: religious life, apostolic spirituality, apostolic works, education of sisters, government of the community. Each area then elected a chairperson, a vice-chairperson, and a secretary.

The sisters joined the committee of their choice, held open discussions, and formulated proposals for action by the chapter. Each proposal was to be prefaced by a rationale, making clear the reasons for action and the relationship of the proposal to the whole purpose of the renewal. The volume that was finally typed and collected was sizable indeed and was open to the entire community for reading. Further, the formation of counterproposals for the chapter was encouraged to provide for full discussion.

Of the highest priority for the sisters who had dedicated their lives to the educational apostolate was the improvement of the conditions under which they worked, in order that they might offer quality education. In preparing the proposal called "Apostolic Work" for the following summer's special chapter, they addressed some basics: the need for fully credentialed teachers, for a limited number of students in the classroom, and for an administrator free not only from a full day's teaching load but also from simultaneous administration in the convent as superior. On this course most of the community seemed unified, anxious to better the situation.

At first glance our demands for improvement in the schools might have seemed abrupt and precipitous. Actually, the call for better teacher preparation had a very long history in the order, beginning in the nineteenth century with Bishop Francis Mora's earnest request of the Immaculate Heart Sisters that the first cathedral school in Los Angeles be staffed with high-quality teachers. Hardly more than a quarter century later, the IHMs themselves, realizing the need to have their sister-teachers well prepared for their work, built and staffed the first women's college in southern California. And in addition to Pius XII's insistence on higher standards of preparation and the steady drumbeat from the Sister Formation Conference, there was now the encouragement of Pope Paul VI urging new ways to meet the challenges of the modern world. Thus the IHMs, long aware of this respected tradition, had made faithful and often heroic attempts to better the Catholic schools in California, where the largest number of them were employed.

But what made it increasingly difficult to meet higher standards was the explosion of the Catholic population in southern California after World War II. And in the Archdiocese of Los Angeles, where the majority of parishes operated by the IHMs were located, Archbishop, then Cardinal, McIntyre encouraged the building of parochial elementary schools (which more than doubled in the 1950s and 1960s) and to a lesser extent parochial high schools throughout the archdiocese, all of which required staffing.

As a result of this phenomenal growth, pastors and archdiocesan school officials besieged the offices of the IHM Community government (and doubtless other orders as well), asking for sisters to staff the schools. The offer of a new convent and a new school building was often regarded by pastors as a plum to the religious order invited to work there.

Meanwhile the plight of the uninitiated sister, thrust into a crowded classroom after taking her first vows, only grew worse. Although aware of the injustice to young teachers and kept informed by Sister Elizabeth Ann, our vicar general and one of our representatives to the

Sister Formation Conference, our community found itself unable to deal with the painful refusal of requests from pastors for still more sister-teachers. And from the standpoint of the pastors and the chancery office, the staffing by dedicated nuns was something of a bargain. To be sure, lay teachers in their schools earned the minimum, but nuns working long hours and asking few questions of their employers were low-cost labor for schools they taught in. According to one study, in 1966 the average nun's salary in Catholic elementary grades was about one hundred dollars per month, with no health or retirement benefits.[19] The priests in many dioceses often fared better, as in the Los Angeles Archdiocese, arguably the most advantaged, according to Cardinal McIntyre's biographer; they had a car, insurance, and social security, all paid for by the chancery office.[20] Needless to say, the IHM sisters' proposals never involved individual salaries.

Throughout the tenure of at least two mothers general, the IHM General Councils sought other solutions to the problem of demand and insufficiently prepared sisters. One such plan was the proposal at the General Chapter of 1957 to establish a "scholasticate" (or juniorate) for newly professed nuns to provide them with a more adequate preparation for college.

When this plan could be only partially implemented due to the usual shortages of personnel, the next IHM meeting in 1963 advocated a revised plan entitled the Teaching Apprenticeship, which was meant to provide at least minimal preparation for teaching by assigning one experienced teacher to every two beginning teachers. By 1966 this plan, too, failed because of the assignment of all sisters to separate classrooms upon their religious profession.

In another, quite ingenious attempt at a solution, a "Service Corps" was initiated in 1965, designed by Sister Richard (Patricia Reif) to appeal to the generosity of graduates of Immaculate Heart College. Volunteers were asked to give a year of service to Catholic education, taking the place of sisters who had not yet completed their studies.

---

[19] Joan D. Chittister, O.S.B., "No Time for Tying Cats," in *Midwives of the Future*, ed. Ann Patrick Ware (Kansas City: Leaven Press, 1985) 16.

[20] Msgr. Francis J. Weber, *His Eminence of Los Angeles: James Francis Cardinal McIntyre*, 2 vols. (Mission Hills, Calif.: St. Francis Historical Society, 1997) 2:522–523. Concerning Monsignor Weber's statement that "many Sisters complained that they were not adequately compensated for their work," the IHM sisters were not among them. However, if a comparison of the salaries had been made, there would have been cause for complaint.

And while a number of graduates did in fact donate their time to this worthy program, the overall need proved greater than the number of volunteers available.

Other measures were designed to shrink the large gap between supply and demand. The decision was made by the IHM government not to replace sisters who had left the community or who were ill. A close examination of staffing at each school was undertaken, with a consequent reduction of non-teaching personnel. Each sister's extracurricular responsibilities, such as choir director, organist, athletic coach, etc., all of which took hours away from a sister's teaching duties, were reviewed and pastors were notified of the elimination of these additional roles. Nevertheless, despite all these attempted remedies, the problem remained and, in fact, was further exacerbated by still other factors.

Sisters teaching the primary grades, for example, faced continually spiraling enrollments, with the result that many teachers had to teach back-to-back sessions or classes with excessively large numbers of children. The need to teach effectively under these overflow conditions was greatly increased both by the growing sophistication of Catholic parents and tighter state education accreditation standards. To meet these challenges, the sisters had for years taken evening classes during the week, Saturday classes throughout the semester at Immaculate Heart College, and summer school courses. Nevertheless, in spite of these measures, by 1967 some seventy teaching sisters out of the order's 450 members were still without their baccalaureate degrees. Thirty-five of these had been professed for ten years or more.

To say that those sisters who struggled on year after year with their college courses, leading hopefully to the baccalaureate, often felt great discouragement is an understatement. One former Immaculate Heart member recently recalled those days when, after much soul-searching and pain, she left the community in 1967, along with many others who suffered similarly:

> What made it so pressing for IHMs, I think, was the widespread angst within the community because of the crunch in the L.A. schools over those post war years—when overcrowded classrooms were staffed by undertrained nuns. People were sick and tired of business as usual and were [in effect] "striking" for better working conditions. It was basically a labor issue. Even those of us better off in the 60's had terrible memories that impelled us to push for change. During the chapter preparations [in 1966–67] my own traumatic first years were always at the front of my mind. At 19 I'd

had 72 third and fourth graders in a classroom with 60 nailed-down desks and was taking calculus and "Critical Analysis of the Pentateuch" on Saturday. If it hadn't been for [Sister] Corita helping me with my lesson plans on Saturday, I probably would have left then. I grew to 170 lbs., from 118 in the novitiate, had nose bleeds every morning and threw up frequently. And unfortunately my story was not unusual.[21]

In preparing for the special general meeting of 1967, the IHM commission on education, under the able leadership of Sister Elizabeth Ann, gathered important background information for the anticipated statement and decision.[22] Her doctorate from USC was in the field of education, she had long worked on the problem of inadequate teacher preparation among the IHMs, and as has been noted, she had made several proposals to help solve the problem, always striving to secure a higher percentage of baccalaureates and credentials for the sisters. The commission now developed an important background report that detailed the steps already tried, the statistics that pointed up the problem, and the rationale for a more radical solution to increase the number of properly prepared teachers in the Los Angeles archdiocesan schools. Her commission presented the hard fact that fewer sisters had obtained bachelor's degrees in the mid 1960s (only 54.9%) than in the late 1940s (70%), because the younger sisters had to begin teaching in parochial schools upon their first profession. In recalling that difficult period, Agnes E. Flynn (Sister Elizabeth Ann), interviewed on tape May 15, 1988, spoke with great sadness:

> By the fall of 1965 I was made painfully aware that something had to give. We had too many Sisters without degrees and credentials, still trying to complete their education in what was informally, but not very joyfully, known as the twenty-year plan: 1) too many people in wrong assignments because there was no other way to spread the available people; 2) too many Sisters trying to teach in classrooms of 50 and 60; 3) too many young Superiors and principals without adequate preparation of studies and experience; 4) too many Sisters in need of psychological help [because of the stressful situation in education]; 5) too many who should not be

---

[21] Dorothy Dunn-Smith. Letter to Anita M. Caspary, I.H.M., June 21, 1997, 1.

[22] Sister Elizabeth Ann Flynn, "Background on the Ninth General Chapter's Decree on Education" (Los Angeles: Unpublished work, December 1, 1967). See Appendix A, p. 225.

teaching or in hospital work because their talents lay in other fields. Many should never have entered [religious life] but some could possibly have accommodated under other circumstances. Then as was the case in religious communities across the nation there was a steady flow of Sisters applying for dispensation.[23]

The recommendations advanced by Sister Elizabeth Ann's commission to support the 1967 document were based on data gathered by the committee on education. A representative portion of that data is supplied below.

"The figures listed (below) indicate that the percentage of sisters holding degrees decreased markedly between 1947 and 1963. In the meantime, commitments were made to staff 34 additional schools. Contributing, however, to the decision to accept schools was the fact that novitiate groups between the years 1945 and 1962 were very much larger than at any other period before or afterwards."[24]

(1) Number of Schools Staffed by the Community in Proportion to Sisters Holding Baccalaureate Degrees.

Year	Number of Elementary Schools	Number of High Schools	Percent of Total with BA/BS Degrees
1947–48	21	6	70.0%
1950–51	31	6	69.0%
1955–56	39	9	62.0%
1957–58	41	10	60.0%
1963–64	50	11	54.9%

In May 1967 an up-to-date analysis of sister-teachers still without degree or credential was as follows:

[23] Agnes E. Flynn, I.H.M. Interview by Doris Murphy, I.H.M. Audio-cassette recording, May 15, 1988. This project undertaken by Doris Murphy is an excellent example of a collective oral history of a religious community.

[24] "Background of the Ninth General Chapter's Decree on Education." See Appendix A, p. 225. The statistics in the report were made available to diocesan educational authorities, to pastors, and to IHM Community committee members prior to the 1967 Chapter of Renewal.

	Elementary School	High School
Percent of IHM sisters teaching full-time without credentials	43%	37%
Percent included above, who have neither degree nor credentials	39%	9%
Percent of IHM principals without certification for principalship	82%	50%

Furthermore, in preparation for the new decree on education (entitled "Apostolic Works"), the sisters visited the superintendents and pastors in every diocese to discuss with them the projected 20% reduction that would have to be realized in the number of sisters assigned to each school. At the same time, the IHM school principals accepted the hardships brought on by a reduction of staff.[25]

Although there are no hard and fast figures tracing the loss of members in teaching communities to this particular problem, namely, that of stress due to lack of proper teacher training and degrees, it is felt by community administrators to have been one of the most important causes in those communities' not insisting on a preliminary degree and/or credential requirement. It should be recalled that as early as 1951, Pope Pius XII had called for appropriate sister preparation, which, he said, would then enable teaching nuns to gain "internal

---

[25] See Appendix A, p. 225. The chancery office claimed not to have received notice of the possible changes for the coming school year. Lengthy discussions had occurred between the Immaculate Heart Community supervisors and archdiocesan authorities prior to the adoption of the decree on education and other Chapter of Renewal proposals. See note 23 above. Monsignor Francis J. Weber, in *His Eminence,* 2:420, also repeats the error that archdiocesan officials were not consulted. Archival evidence verifies that the IHM sisters were willing to develop a plan with each diocese. IHM sisters visited each Catholic school district superintendent in California: on October 30, 1967, with Father John Dickie, the San Diego diocesan superintendent; on October 31, 1967, with Father Bernard Cummins, San Francisco diocesan superintendent; on November 2, 1967, with Monsignor James Poole, Sacramento superintendent; on November 3, 1967, with Father Patrick Hannon, Fresno diocesan superintendent; and on November 17, 1967, with Monsignor Donald Montrose, Monsignor James Clyne, and Father John Mihan, of the Los Angeles archdiocesan department of education. A meeting with Monsignor Pearse Donovan, superintendent of the Oakland diocese, was set up by appointment, but when the sisters arrived, they were told he was out of town. A/IHMCOM.

peace."[26] Certainly the statistics concerning vocational losses in general among U.S. religious communities are revealing: according to the *Official Catholic Directory* for 1970, the number of sisters decreased from a high of 179,954 in 1965 to 160,931 in 1970, a drop of nearly 20,000 in a five-year period. And the decline in the number of the sisters in the country was to continue dramatically. The period from 1965 to 1990 saw a 43% decrease in religious communities of women.[27]

These statements are eloquent in themselves, but to them should be added the silent testimony of disappointment, illness, and discouragement of the sisters who had kept on teaching without having yet earned their college degrees. Earlier, as college president, I had been aware, of course, of this problem and had felt the anguish of these teachers. But once in the position of mother general, I found my office besieged by sisters whose physical health and mental well-being were being endangered by their situation. As a teacher, I was incensed by the destruction of the self-confidence of these sisters. As an administrator, I could see that there would soon be a widening gap between the "elite," those sisters chosen to obtain higher degrees at a university, and the still noncredentialed sisters who taught in the elementary and high schools we staffed. Because of all this, the deep concern over the possible relief of the situation through the chapter decrees was quite understandable.

Most eagerly read by the sisters were the proposals on education, the boldest of which stated the absolute need for credentialed teachers, the importance of classrooms properly limited in size, and the necessity for full-time administrators. The freedom of sisters to choose other areas besides teaching was also proposed and generally well received.

These were the main thrusts of the new community proposals on education, although more proposals were reserved for the chapter meetings themselves. Each proposal placed in the final volume comprising some two hundred pages of questionnaires, proposals, and rationales had been approved by the preparatory committees.

In the spring of 1967 the chapter started with a retreat for all the delegates. The opening Mass on June 26, 1967, set a tone of solemnity and intensity that pervaded the sessions during the chapter. Each delegate had become aware that in some way this chapter was to be written

[26] Yzermans, *The Unwearied Advocate*, 1:195–96.

[27] Helen Rose Fuchs Ebaugh, *Women in the Vanishing Cloister: Organizational Decline in Catholic Religious Orders in the United States* (New Brunswick, N.J.: Rutgers University Press, 1993) 47.

in the community annals not only as unprecedented but also as a post-script to the history of the post-Vatican II Church. We began to understand our vision, and our conflict with ecclesiastical authorities as part of the women's struggle for equal status in the mid-twentieth century. This sense of the historic moment of faith and freedom was heightened by the interest of the wider public. Even before the chapter began, reporters were asking for interviews or permission to observe proceedings, unprecedented requests. The unsought notoriety made us even more apprehensive. Needless to say, all such requests were refused.

Sister-delegates sat day by day for six weeks in the chapter hall debating the chapter proposals and decrees, but most important, working out a new way of living the religious life. They understood that this "new way" had necessarily to be experimental and inconclusive; they came to see that the process of reevaluation would henceforth be constant, taking account of time and place.

But all that was to come later. At first the discussions proceeded slowly, clinging fairly closely to the text of the rationales and proposals already worked out. It was gradually perceived that change could not be made in units, by single steps, through single proposals indicating progress and regression in contradiction. Rather, a new theology of the life itself, a pattern of themes, had to be established out of which the desired changes would organically grow. And this basic theology of the life known to the official Church as religious life had to emerge from the about-face the Church had made at the Second Vatican Council, whether or not this fact had yet been acknowledged. Religious life of the past, we felt certain, had to develop into new forms.[28]

After the opening sessions of the chapter, a holiday was declared for the Fourth of July, a well-deserved break from the hours of serious thought and discussions. But the General Council met during the day, and the thought of Cardinal McIntyre's words burned in their minds: "You will suffer for this!" Was it fair to allow the discussions to proceed and proposals to pass without the chapter members' knowledge of how thoroughly His Eminence disapproved of change in religious life? For those chapter members who did not live in the motherhouse or in Los Angeles convents, the whole question of disapproval by the local hierarchy or any hierarchy seemed remote and academic.

---

[28] For personal accounts of this period in a wide variety of religious communities, see Kathleen W. Fitzgerald, Ph.D., and Claire Breault, M.A., *Whatever Happened to the Good Sisters?* (Lake Forest, Ill.: Whales' Tale Press, 1992); Ursula Vils, "An Experimental Religious Community," *Los Angeles Times* (July 9, 1974) 4.1.

That day the General Council decided that the facts of the cardinal's strong disapproval of the Immaculate Heart Sisters must be laid before the chapter delegates and a decision made as to whether to proceed with such complete renewal. Further, the possibilities of recrimination that the entire community might suffer from our actions had to be honestly examined. Then we could decide whether we should go on or conclude the chapter rapidly.

We hastily sent out word to the chapter members, some of whom had gone for the holiday, that by evening the already announced celebration party would be followed by a short chapter meeting. Unaware of the solemnity of the occasion, many chapter members, I am sure, groaned at the thought of an evening session and wondered at its urgency. Independence Day! How the term seemed to mock me as we sat in the great, high-ceilinged study at Montecito, after the songs and refreshments, to listen to the account by us, the General Council, of the cardinal's special canonical visitation in May 1965.

The faces of the chapter members reflected the grave concern and worry we had passed on to them. Suppose the chapter were to make superficial changes and close, awaiting a more favorable time, we asked. There was an almost unanimous "No" from the chapter members, for they were full of hopeful joy that their ideal community, formed from their dreams, might at least be given a foundation at this chapter.

What if the changes we pictured were actually made? What then? What powers did canon law give the cardinal over a pontifical community such as ours? Our cardinal-protector in Rome, Cardinal Joseph Pizzardo, appointed to this office in 1945 by Pope Pius XII, was now quite elderly and most likely out of touch with a conflict that promised to be of such magnitude. We had, however, received on July 13, 1967, a formal greeting on Cardinal Pizzardo's ninetieth birthday, which said, "I prayed for you, dear Sisters of the Immaculate Heart of Mary. . . ."[29] But there was not a hint of encouragement concerning the reforms recommended by the Second Vatican Council, which had ended just two years earlier. And although we did not know it at the time, the custom of having cardinal-protectors, which had begun with St. Francis of Assisi in the thirteenth century, had only recently been ended by Pope Paul VI, and the positions were not filled when the current hold-

[29] Cardinal Joseph Pizzardo. Letter to the Sisters of the Immaculate Heart, July 13, 1967. A/IHMCOM.

ers died.[30] The real channel for any appeals to the Vatican was to be the Sacred Congregation for Religious, whose head was Cardinal Hildebrand Antoniutti. Had we known of this development in the following year or two, we might surely have been even more discouraged at gaining a hearing at the Vatican. Later, when we learned of the termination of this office, we realized that Cardinal McIntyre seemed never to have been aware of this change of the protector's role, for he never referred to it.[31]

But there were many other questions affecting our future, practical ones. How did canon law relate to civil law? Could our properties or our institutions be taken from us? Could we be asked to leave the diocese? Certainly we could never be asked to disband our community. Or could that happen?

Furthermore, we realized that a small band of sisters who were making their views heard both in the motherhouse and in the chancery office were opposed to the changes as a matter of conscience. Were they, then, to become the "real" Sisters of the Immaculate Heart?

Persons with vivid imaginations could picture us as a large group of sisters assembling at the corner of Franklin and Western Avenues, where our motherhouse stood, with our suitcases and bundles in hand, setting out to find a place to live. In such a case, exaggerated though it might be, how many sisters, accustomed to security and care, would be able to withstand the psychological shock of alienation from the local Church hierarchy, separation from relatives and friends, and loss of work, to face an unknown and uncertain future? Was excommunication—unthinkable as a personal possibility heretofore—to be thrust upon us?

The discussion was called to a halt, and a vote about proceeding with changes was postponed until the morning meeting. The General Council tried to leave the room, but we were surrounded at every point by sisters filled with questions, worry, even tears. I wondered what it all might mean; I would have to face a deadening halt to all our plans. Finally all were gone and the lights were out. But the morning's assembly told of what the night had brought—in the white faces and dark-circled eyes

---

[30] Robert C. Dory, "Ban on Cremation Is Relaxed by Pope," *New York Times* (June 6, 1964), sec. 1:3. The papal decision to end the custom of having cardinals as protectors is reported in this article.

[31] Cardinal Pizzardo died in 1970, ironically the same year that we formed the non-canonical IHM Community. He would have been ninety-three years old.

of the chapter members. Now they faced a reality they could hardly comprehend.

After roll call I simply called for a vote. Should we hold a chapter, making only the preliminary changes and putting off the larger questions until later? A firm "No" was the response. Should we continue to restructure, rebuild, renew the community? A clear "Yes" was heard as the roll call revealed unanimous agreement for immediate and complete renewal. A great storm of applause that heralded our unanimity filled the assembly hall. And the agenda, the discussions, the exhilaration following the discouraging evening was such that the air seemed charged with electricity—or was it with the Spirit of God, who, we daily prayed, might be with us. With diligence and care the work went on. I was torn between joy and the anticipation of the route ahead.

Perhaps this all appears to indicate that the group was absolutely sure of its direction. Such was not the case. There were dark moments when sentiment and deep feeling for certain prayers, customs, the apostolate, and its relationship to religious women worked their painful way through to a more open view. Then those whose whole lives had been built on these feelings or on a cloistered flight from the tawdriness of the world or on a military precision by which time could be exactly scheduled and work accomplished efficiently—those, few as they were, felt keen apprehension as cloister, cherished devotional life, and adherence to order evolved into a new form of religious life.

There were other, lighter moments of at least ironic humor when, for example, a letter arrived on July 11, 1967, solemnly hand-delivered to me by a frightened-looking seminarian. The letter from Bishop John J. Ward, the vicar for religious, informed the chapter that an anonymous communication had been received at the chancery office stating that those sisters experimenting with their religious habits in locations outside Los Angeles were given undue sums of money to carry out this expenditure. Bishop Ward also protested that he had not been notified of the chapter's opening nor given the chapter agenda and a list of delegates.

Since the chapter was in session and was therefore the highest authority in the community, I read the letter to the chapter members, and was instructed to reply that the credence given an anonymous letter was puzzling to us, as was the intention of the writer in making disturbing statements about expenditures. Concerning the substance of the letter, we had no knowledge.

In our reply to Bishop Ward, we reminded him that he had, in fact, celebrated the opening Mass of the chapter by our invitation. Further, we stated that there was no precedent for submitting a list of chapter delegates or the agenda to the chancery office.[32]

The chapter ended with the completion of both rationales and practical applications for a new religious life in early August 1967. But hard work was not ended at this time: the next phase was one of shaping the results of the chapter into a coherent whole. A writing committee was appointed to place the decrees and decisions in final form. Copies would be circulated to the chapter members for amendment before promulgation to the community, planned for October. No notice regarding the close of the chapter was sent to the chancery office, nor were inquiries made by that office after our explanatory letter to Bishop Ward.

After the final writing of the decrees, I was asked by the chapter members to call on various canon lawyers and theologians to obtain their opinions of the decrees before the hundreds of copies would be made in preparation for our "Promulgation Day" in October and before presenting Cardinal McIntyre with a copy. The interviews and opinions gathered from the experts in canon law and theology would reflect, I knew, a spectrum of views unmatched for variety. There was to be a worldwide conference of Vatican II experts in Toronto in late August, making it possible to solicit their opinions and analyses firsthand, prior to any response the cardinal might give. I would therefore gain not only intellectual and spiritual advice but perhaps tactical help as well. I set out for Toronto in August 1967.

---

[32] Mother M. Humiliata, I.H.M. Letter to Bishop John J. Ward, July 18, 1967. It states: "We are puzzled by the comment that no formal notification of this chapter was received. We are enclosing such a notification together with a photostat of the letter of invitation to you, Your Excellency, and one of your gracious reply. We were happy that you celebrated the opening Mass. . . ." A/IHMCOM.

Chapter 10

Embracing the Vision

Between August 17 and September 11, 1967, at the request of the chapter delegates, I was in Toronto to gather comments on the decrees we had enacted at our special Chapter of Renewal during the summer. These conversations, in addition to written commentary, yielded a plethora of ideas. The first comments from theologians and scholars stressed the excellent command the IHMs had of understanding the purpose and vision of the Vatican II documents pertaining to religious life. Other comments were of necessity tactical. Many foresaw conflict in view of the conservative bent of the local hierarchy. Some advised us regarding potential disagreement with the cardinal. Others provided support and suggestions for the diplomacy and steps that would allow the IHMs to evade a major, possibly disastrous turn of events.[1]

Cardinal Suenens, the Belgian prelate who had early on championed the work and renewal of women religious, advised us that a certain amount of give-and-take might be needed. This remark was clearly designed to slow down what is often regarded as typically American: too much spontaneity and demand for haste in settling matters. Further, he expressed the idea that the freedom from restrictions our decrees sought must be seen as desirable for the apostolic and ecumenical thrust of the community. In a private conversation, his last word to me

---

[1] This is a partial list of theologians who advised us during this period: Gregory Baum, O.S.A., Centre for Ecumenical Studies, Toronto; Dennis Burke, University of San Francisco; Thomas E. Clarke, S.J., Woodstock College; Joseph H. Fichter, S.J., Harvard University; Bernard Häring, C.Ss.R.; Dr. Martin E. Marty; Norbert J. Rigali, S.J.; Rosemary Ruether, Ph.D.; John Schuette, S.V.D.

was to consider disbanding as a community. This last-resort option would certainly be considered a threat. As I pondered this conversation and the many ideas circulating at the time, I see that Cardinal Suenens spoke with a prophetic wisdom. Known for his pastoral as well as diplomatic acumen, Cardinal Suenens, the quintessential archbishop-pastor, could not imagine a fellow prelate choosing to participate in the dissolution of a religious community of women without attempting various avenues of compromise.

Cardinal Suenens honored and respected women religious. He understood their prophetic role in the history of the Church and promoted the advancement of women in the Church. I had a deep sense that he foresaw that the service of women religious, traditionally in the fields of education, health, and direct service, had to move beyond these vocational (employment) areas for the Church to expand and evangelize a broken world.

At this same time the IHM decrees were given to Father Bernard Häring, the German Redemptorist priest known to be very progressive. In our conversations it was clear to me that he understood our situation and the implications for the Church. Father Häring quickly went to the heart of the sisters' commitment by saying that the sacrifice of self is necessary in religious life. He asked, "Are the sisters prepared for the life described in your decrees?" At another time, another question: "Are your women strong enough to follow this proposed life?" In addition, Father Häring pointed out the necessity of a deeply scriptural orientation: that the communal life we described should be lived in accordance with the Beatitudes. In a tactical aside, he suggested that the decrees might be sent at this point to the Sacred Congregation for Religious so that the first impressions of that body would not be from an adversary of the Second Vatican Council; no doubt he had in mind our local hierarchy.

Father Häring's advice and support extended from minute word changes in the decrees to public support before the media. In 1967 he wrote:

> On several occasions during the past two weeks I spoke publicly on your matter, for instance at the Symposium on the Association of Chicago Priests, before several groups of religious in the areas of Washington and Philadelphia and in my lectures at Temple [University]. I know that several personalities wrote to Archbishop Dearden expressing their full solidarity with your congregation. I

am absolutely disposed to speak out before any forum if I am approached by the mass media since it is a matter which concerns the whole Church. I hope that you brave sisters will preserve peace of mind and look forward courageously.[2]

In Rome it was through the good offices of Father Vincent O'Keefe, S.J., formerly president of Fordham University and at this time assistant to Father Pedro Arrupe, S.J., that I was able to meet the kindly and revered general of the worldwide Jesuit order. He, in turn, contacted Father G. B. Andretta, consultant to the Sacred Congregation for Religious. Father Andretta's commentary on the IHM decrees was given completely from the viewpoint of his position as consultant to the congregation, an important perspective to have. He saw religious life as regulated by the horarium, the rule, novitiate formation, uniformity of clothing, the need for mortification, engagement in community works, etc. Because of these entrenched ideas, he advised us that we seem destined to become a secular institute. However, he saw a possible problem in the fact that secular institutes at this point were subject to the Sacred Congregation for Religious.

Archbishop Giovanni Benelli was consulted in 1967 as a member of the Secretariat of State. Ironically, as head of that office he was to hear our final plea in 1969. His words were strong and clear, his advice eminently tactical: we must agree to give and take, learn to wait, not wish to cut off the heads of those who disagreed, not move too quickly to become a vanguard with no followers. At the same time, he remarked, the community should not become discouraged. All this seemed strangely out of character when I visited him two years later.

Many other prelates knowledgeable in canon law and theology, both at the Toronto post-Vatican conference and in Rome, were shown copies of our decrees. Since it is not possible to present all of them, a few of the more significant ones have been selected, and the remainder are summarized here. Some felt, not unexpectedly, that we had gone far beyond the original meaning of the Pope's pronouncement on renewal and should revise or revoke our decrees immediately before further trouble ensued. Some commented only on the change to secular dress, which was now permitted, and focused entirely on the subject of uniformity in clothing as protective of poverty and celibacy. Some were

---

[2] Bernard Häring, C.Ss.R. Letter to Anita Caspary, I.H.M., November 28, 1967. Archives of Immaculate Heart Community (hereafter referred to as A/IHMCOM).

delighted with the thrust of the decrees but felt that the freedom to choose one's own work might lead to the dissolution of our own institutions. Some felt that our attempt to allow a wide range of freedom to persons who had been subject to obedience would lead to imprudent action and to the loss of the reputation of the Immaculate Heart Sisters. Others mentioned the lack of specific discussion of spirituality in the decrees, not understanding our hoped-for integration of the secular and the spiritual urged by the documents of Vatican II. Still others were unreservedly enthusiastic, thinking that if these decrees were lived out, there would emerge new hope for the revival of religious life, which appeared to be dying from the loss of vocations. Meantime, the community at home was waiting to hear the decrees that were to shape their future.

It was an autumn Saturday afternoon, October 14, 1967, when the entire Immaculate Heart Community assembled at the motherhouse in a spirit of anticipation, waiting to hear the outcome of the Chapter of Renewal. "Promulgation Day," as we called it, held the promise of new patterns of life and work for an eager audience. That there would be a chilly Monday morning to follow was on the minds of some of us as the sisters from all parts of California gathered, laughing and talking.

I opened with a short talk on the significance of the six-week Chapter of Renewal. I tried to stress the temporary, experimental nature of most of the decrees. I wanted to reassure our sisters with my own conviction, as well as that of the General Chapter, that our commitment to the religious life was the same as always. I tried to allay the inevitable uncertainty and fears, reminding the sisters that the preparation for the chapter had been longer and more tedious than any we had known, that there had been nothing of "change for the sake of change," a cliché often used by critics of renewal.

Since one of our chief problems in the chapter had been the new understanding of "community" as something different from organization or voluntary association, I wanted to restate the theme that a person can fully develop only in and through community. For this reason I quoted a passage from the prologue written by Sister William (Helen Kelley), college president, one of our chapter members. The passage was often to be quoted by journalists later as a kind of epitome of our aims and goals:

> What the world desperately needs is bridges, individuals and groups who, like Christ Himself, put an end to all the distances

which divide men *[sic]* and which hinder their access to truth, dignity and full human development. This is another way of saying that the world needs community; it needs models of community to convince it that the diverse and warring elements in the human family can be reconciled.[3]

I rounded off my address with an affirmation of our desire to answer the real needs of today's world. We would seek only to serve in the name of Christ. That would mean constant review of our ability to continue in certain works as well as attention to the gifts of the individual. A sister would no longer be assigned her work by the reverend mother or her council but would be free to choose the field in which she could use her talents best. Further, she might elect to serve in a Church-related institution, in one not so related, or in one without specific institutional commitment. Since previously the sisters all had work assignments, mostly as teachers, the repercussions of this statement would be heard far and wide. When the opening talk concluded, there was applause. Then silence.

Now came the real moment of heightened anticipation and insatiable curiosity. Chapter members had been enjoined to keep silent at the close of the Chapter of Renewal so that the community's reaction would not be influenced. The planning committee for the meeting had decided that the decrees would be given to the sisters one at a time. Time would be allowed for reading the decree, and then a panel of chapter members would explain the decree and its implications, followed by a question-and-answer period. Thus attention could be focused on one matter at a time.

Because of the high interest in the subject, the first decree to be distributed was that on "apostolic works," that is, teaching and education. After nearly a year of study, meetings, proposals, and revisions, the

[3] Decrees of the Ninth General Chapter of the Sisters of the Immaculate Heart of Mary (Los Angeles: Unpublished, October, 1967). This document is a summary of the theological and philosophical principles on which the Immaculate Heart Community was established. Commissioned by the chapter delegates, a small committee of members wrote the decrees, which were later affirmed by the chapter delegates. These decrees continue to be the operating principles out of which we live our lives. Of course, amendments to various practical applications of these principles are an ongoing part of our community life and are made by the total community rather than by delegates. See Appendix D, pp. 243 and 246.

community's decree on apostolic works was found to be a happy cul-
mination of the sisters' hopes: this decree proposed a thorough plan to
help them in their teaching apostolate. True, a temporary hardship would
be imposed both on the diocesan schools and on the community; yet
these difficulties seemed healthier than the interminable series of unsuccessful remedial steps that we had attempted over a period of years.[4]

As a separate section of the decree on apostolic works, the hoped-
for freedom was given for sisters to work not only in their present
fields (teaching or nursing) but in others as well. Further, the decree
granted wider fields of action, recognizing that not everyone was
gifted as a teacher and that there were those whose gifts enabled them
to work in a variety of other occupations. Those sisters could become
involved in temporal affairs of many kinds, including political institutions, international relations, the arts, and economic affairs.[5]

After the cheers and sighs of relief from the assembled sisters as the
decree on apostolic works was read, the Promulgation Day program
continued. The balance in the next decree, the decree on person and
community, emphasized the "sacredness of the human person and his
[sic] fulfillment within community."[6] Community was described in this
decree as "a quality of relationships based in part on the mutual recognition of shared personal needs for affection, inclusion, privacy, inner
discipline, and external limits."[7] This decree was a carefully made

---

[4] Ibid., 247.

[5] Meanwhile, and unknown to us, earlier that same year Cardinal Hildebrand
Antoniutti, prefect of the Sacred Congregation for Religious in Rome, had already
stated his view of some applications of *Perfectae Caritatis* and was critical of the involvement by religious women in social justice issues. In his position as prefect, his
would be the final voice of approval or disapproval of our decrees when they would
eventually be sent to the Vatican. In a speech to the major superiors of Italian institutes, the cardinal said, "And if some superficial writer wishes to see the Sisters on
the scene of every sort of human event and foolishly calls the sacred walls which
protect them, relics of the past, many, very many people are praying that the
Spouses of Christ may not be unfaithful to the vows. . . ." Further, he stated, "It
must be remembered that the Special Chapter [referred to in *Perfectae Caritatis*] may
not modify the nature of the apostolate for which the Institute was founded and approved. . . ." Cardinal Hildebrand Antoniutti, "Religious Life in the Post-Conciliar
Period" (January 1967) 18, 22. Paper presented in Rome at the Extraordinary Assembly of the Union of Major Superioresses of Italy. This paper was distributed by
the chancery office of the Archdiocese of Los Angeles. Cardinal McIntyre never referred to this essay in his dealings with our community.

[6] Appendix D, p. 251.

[7] Ibid., 252.

tapestry, weaving together the corresponding themes of the person's fulfillment in community and the responsibility of the person to the community. In terms of practical applications, the decree authorized no particular form or structure. ". . . [C]ommunity is not simply an historical legacy. It is an ongoing creation enjoined upon all its members."[8]

With regard to the next decree, there was an expected curiosity among the sisters. Would the decree on apostolic spirituality significantly alter the present practice, or would this renewal chapter merely repeat the pattern designed to develop holiness in previous times? How could a new approach that no longer separated the sacred from the secular be justified in terms of religious life?

Again, the importance of full human development was emphasized in this decree. Much of the text was devoted to prayer, viewed not as an isolated activity but rather as openness to the Holy Spirit that enters into "the total rhythm of our lives. . . ."[9] Prayer, both liturgical and personal, the decree stated, is the revelation of God and inspires "a response of faith."[10] Scripture is seen as providing nourishment for prayer. Both the ongoing nature of our relationship to God and the need for a willingness to deal with reality were given note. Thus: "We are women on pilgrimage who recognize our need, personally and communally, for conversion of mind and heart. The greater openness to reality in conversion often entails pain."[11]

A hint of the ecumenical nature of the community-to-be was found in the conclusion of this decree, where the unity of all humankind in prayer, regardless of the diverse forms that prayer might take, was proclaimed.

All this was true to our feelings and thoughts on the meaning of prayer, but what of practical application? How often was community prayer scheduled? What were the required forms of prayer? What of Holy Office? The rosary? The novenas? Holy Hour? Preparation for Death prayers? The decree established new flexibility while maintaining the importance of prayer.

There was to be continued experimentation by which (a) each sister was allowed to decide the kind, time, and duration of her formal prayer; (b) sisters who lived together would make provision for some form of

[8] Ibid., 253.
[9] Ibid., 254.
[10] Ibid., 254.
[11] Ibid., 255.

communal prayer, the manner and extent of which were to be determined by the group.[12]

The decree on authority and government began the process of collegial decision-making, a process that would take some years to develop. It connected the themes of community with authority and obedience. It claimed that "while authority is our share in the mission and power of Christ, obedience is our active response to the demands placed upon us by that participation."[13] The consequences of this view of authority were a distancing from the sociologist's "total scope institution," in which "internal motherhood" and an almost military-style organization prevailed. Formerly the superior (usually not elected by those she would govern) had to be sought out for every kind of permission, from a trip to the dentist to staying a few minutes beyond retiring time to finish paperwork for the next day's teaching assignment—surely an intolerable burden not only for adult nuns but also for the superior.

The decree on preparation for life in community addressed the program planned for candidates who would join the community during the next few years. The former "uniform pattern of induction," with its "closed and isolated environment, constant supervision and control, and discipline aimed at behavioral conformity," was to be replaced by a more flexible period in which each potential member would be guided by the newly formed committee on community membership. A program would be specifically delineated for each candidate, taking into account each one's spiritual and professional experiences and needs.[14]

Finally, the prologue and the epilogue were read to the assembled sisters, both emphasizing the freedom of women to choose the mode of Christian service they might best respond to while bonding ever closer in the supportive ties of community.[15]

When the last paragraphs of the decrees were read to the sisters, those of us who were chapter delegates were deeply moved and pleased by the standing ovation our work received. Joyously and spontaneously the entire assembly broke into a resounding "Mine eyes have seen the glory of the coming of the Lord . . ."

---

[12] Ibid., 255.
[13] Ibid., 256.
[14] Ibid., 259.
[15] Ibid., 261.

While all this was going on, His Eminence Cardinal McIntyre was receiving at his residence a hand-delivered copy of these same decrees. By Monday the General Council would face an unforgettable morning.

Chapter 11

The Cardinal's Response to Renewal

It was a predictably chilly, smoggy morning when the members of the IHM General Council arrived at the chancery office to hear Cardinal McIntyre's opinion of our renewal decrees. We had been notified of the time and place of our appointment only the day before the meeting. With it, the memory of the generous and heartening response of the sisters at Saturday's promulgation meeting was beginning to fade.

So, on Monday, October 16, 1967, praying silently as we ascended the marble staircase to the conference room at the Los Angeles Archdiocese chancery office, we prepared to meet the criticism that was inevitable. The scene was set for a drama incomparable in tension and pent-up emotion to any I had ever seen. The five General Council members—Sister Elizabeth Ann Flynn, vicar general; Mother Regina McPartlin, former mother general; Sister Charles Schaffer; Sister Gregory Lester; and myself, along with the general treasurer, Sister Eugenia Ward—were asked to be seated facing the cardinal's empty chair. The room was very narrow and long. As we took our seats at the table, there was barely enough room to pass behind us. Indeed, the walls seemed to close in on us. The air was electric with anticipation.

Then the door to the cardinal's inner office opened. His staff entered: Bishops John J. Ward and Timothy Manning; Monsignor Benjamin Hawkes, the cardinal's chancellor; along with Monsignor Donald Montrose, the superintendent of high schools; Monsignor James B. Clyne, the superintendent of elementary schools; and Father John Mihan, the assistant superintendent of elementary education. As we rose, Cardinal McIntyre entered, with his copy of the IHM decrees in hand. There was a low murmur of greetings around the room, and we all took our seats. The cardinal opened the meeting with a short prayer. He glanced quickly around the room and dropped the decrees on the table.

His opening salvo was a reprimand that he was unable to read the IHM decrees thoroughly because they had arrived only a few days prior to the meeting. However, he continued, his brief review of the decrees left him shocked and angered at the possibility that the sisters might not be wearing habits but rather "street clothes" in archdiocesan classrooms the following September (1968).[1] The cardinal fixed his attention on me to ascertain the accuracy of his interpretation. My response was an attempt to calm the situation, "Yes, Your Eminence, but it is only experimental." The cardinal immediately challenged this by emphasizing the compulsory canon law on the subject of the habit. Again I started to explain the nature of our renewal as mandated by the documents of the Second Vatican Council. But I was cut short. His response was simply to stand up and declare in an angry voice that the meeting was over. He stated firmly and very loudly that he would not have any IHM sisters in archdiocesan schools without religious habits. Everyone was shocked into silence. There was no hesitancy in his announcement that the Immaculate Heart Sisters would not be teaching in any archdiocesan school the following fall. I could not believe that after decades of serving the Catholic Church of Los Angeles we were being fired over the issue of women's clothing! Suddenly a deep physical pain wrenched my stomach as though someone had struck me.

As the cardinal picked up his papers, a member of his staff pulled firmly at the cardinal's sleeve, saying, "Surely, Your Eminence, we need to talk more about this." For a few seconds it was not at all certain what would happen next. But finally the cleric's plea prevailed and the cardinal resumed his seat, his face flushed with anger.[2]

In an interview twenty-five years later, Bishop John J. Ward's recollections of that momentous day were similarly etched in his memory. Ward stated:

> . . . one of the points in it and this was the ignition point, was in [the chapter documents] September of the following year that they would no longer wear the habit. I was sitting here, Cardinal Manning

[1] According to the 1967 Chapter of Renewal, the choice of clothing was at the discretion of the individual sister. During the time of this meeting we had sisters choosing either contemporary clothing or retaining the religious habit.

[2] Years after this eventful day I was approached by an auxiliary bishop in California who told me of his experience of being the young seminarian on duty as receptionist during this meeting. He stated that from a considerable distance he could hear the cardinal's voice reprimanding us. Others had similar experiences of wit-

was sitting here, Mother Humiliata was really anxious, "Mother," he [McIntyre] said, "there is just one point here, you know we just got this Saturday at 10:30, and I haven't been able to read it all, but Bishop Manning and Bishop Ward have . . ., but there is just one point: [it says in the document that] in the schools where your nuns are that you will be in secular dress." She said "Yes." He said, "Is that what you mean, that you will no longer wear your habit as the Code of Canon Law says everyone must?" She said, "Yes." He stood up, "Mother, I will not have your sisters in my schools in secular dress." . . . The cardinal stood up and said "Well, Mother, I must be prepared then, to accept the fact that your sisters will not be with us." Then he said "Thank you very much" and the thing was over. . . . I said, "Well your Eminence is that official?" He said, "Well, what else is there? I will not have the women religious in my schools in secular dress."[3]

After the cardinal sat down, he began a series of rapid-fire questions to me: When were these decrees written? Why was I not consulted on the decisions made in these decrees? Don't they need to be presented to the Sacred Congregation for Religious? His Eminence was clearly upset, hostile to the entire matter before him. I knew at this point that we could not have a thoughtful or reasonable discussion, but we were there and had somehow to make an attempt.

Ignoring the earlier questions, I turned at once to the question on the Sacred Congregation for Religious. Equipped with my consultations with theologians, canon lawyers, and advisors to the Sacred Congregation itself, I replied that the regulations for the renewal of religious life promoted by the Second Vatican Council indicated that submission of experimentation to the Sacred Congregation was not required at this point. Fearing that the cardinal was not familiar with this recent papal document, particularly because it gave legitimacy to the procedures of experimentation, I asked Bishop Ward, the vicar for religious, if he

nessing the anger of Cardinal McIntyre. See Jim Naughton, "James Shannon: A Former Bishop," *Washington Post* (September 17, 1987) C, 1–3.

[3] Bishop John J. Ward. Interview by Marshal H. Mercer. Audio-cassette transcript, 31–35, December 10, 1992, Los Angeles. Bishop Ward confirms the centrality of the abandonment of the habit and the adoption of secular dress as a critical issue in the dismissal (firing) of the IHM sisters from the archdiocesan schools by Cardinal McIntyre. See Marshal H. Mercer, "'You People Don't Pray Right': A Study of Organizational Power and Superordinate Goal Conflict." Unpublished dissertation, Claremont, Calif., 1994.

would explain to those present the provisions of the Church document that inspired our decrees. But, probably sensing the cardinal's opposition to the document, he politely declined.

However, much to my surprise, Bishop Ward then indicated agreement with me. His Eminence brushed this aside: "I have a letter from Rome," he countered, without revealing more about the contents or his source, implying that Rome supported his views. With this he widened the attack. "The practices of the community during the past year have been contrary, in fact, in direct violation of canon law," he charged.

I asked to what practices he was referring. "I did not call this meeting to discuss details," was his curt reply.

At this point every word uttered seemed to be a land mine about to explode. Then, more quickly than I thought possible, the central point of the meeting was reached. The cardinal was clearly angry at what he had already heard about our decree concerning teaching and education.[4] We had anticipated that he would probably be opposed to the determination of our 1967 chapter requiring professional standards for teacher preparation, among other recommendations, because it would directly affect staffing and budgeting in archdiocesan schools. We had stated unambiguously in the decrees that beginning in June 1968,

- a carefully prepared annual agreement should be drafted with the aid of legal counsel and signed by all of the parties concerned.

- the . . . Sisters will agree to assign to such schools only those members of the Community who are duly qualified to engage in such an important work for the Church.

- if the Community is to be a party to the agreement, the terms must be accepted by a committee on which representatives of the diocese and of the Sisters . . . shall sit.

- the Community will withdraw from schools for which such agreements cannot be made.[5]

---

[4] The eminent historian Monsignor John Tracy Ellis, while admitting Cardinal McIntyre's charity toward the poor, describes him as "'notoriously short-tempered and often prone to outbursts about matters on which he was less than well informed.'" Msgr. Francis J. Weber, *His Eminence of Los Angeles: James Francis Cardinal McIntyre* (Mission Hills, Calif.: St. Francis Historical Society, 1997) 2:571.

[5] These specific proposals were adopted by the IHM chapter delegates in July 1967. Archives of the Immaculate Heart Community (hereafter referred to as A/IHMCOM). The decrees found in Appendix D (p. 243) are an abbreviated version

Still, I thought, even though our fate seemed sealed, we must try to win his understanding on certain key points so that we might better serve the Church through better preparation of our sisters.

"Your Eminence," I began again, "in section two of the decrees, we have tried to provide for some badly needed teacher preparation, and we've suggested working in committees with each of the pastors and the school superintendents, so that we can reach some agreement . . .," but I was not allowed to finish.

"You dare to threaten me with withdrawal from my schools unless I agree to your conditions?" Evidently the cardinal had been alerted by his bishops or his school superintendents of the last clause above, namely, that if we should fail to reach an agreement, the community would have to withdraw. We had seen no other way to initiate the necessary teacher certification program, since all other attempts through the years had failed. We hoped that our firm statement would serve to open a negotiating process.

Now, however, both the community members and, I think, the cardinal's staff were taken aback by the words "threaten" and "withdrawal," as though our proposals were an ultimatum. Speaking almost all at once, we hastened to assure him that no such ultimatum was implied, that time lines regarding the needed improvements were negotiable, that the purpose of our decrees was to make better Catholic schools. That and more. But it seemed, even then, that the cardinal was determined to reject all our words.

"You want an ultimatum?" he thundered. "Very well, I will accept your threat to withdraw from our schools. The date for your withdrawal is then June 1968." We were stunned to hear the finality of his announcement. Aside from the clearly disturbed reactions of Monsignor Montrose and Monsignor Clyne, the two superintendents who were most immediately concerned, the faces of the others on the cardinal's staff were expressionless. Monsignor Hawkes, who generally responded forcefully in meetings, sat attentively but quietly in a corner of the room as though he already knew what the cardinal would say.

At this point the cardinal launched into an attack on the decrees themselves. He accused us again of wishing to be a "high-grade community," which in itself did not entitle us to employment in the

---

and do not include these proposals and other specific measures. These excerpts contain the theological and philosophical principles on which we made our decisions. See also note 3 on page 121.

Catholic schools. Then he explicitly criticized the decrees as an indication that we no longer wanted to be a religious community! The sudden shift in the grounds of the argument as well as the outrageous slur on our lives took our breath away. Far from discussing our necessary educational and professional requirements, we were being accused, by virtue of the decrees, of no longer being religious women. How had this come about? We were in a state of shock. Had His Eminence read the decrees after all? Or had the small group of dissidents succeeded in gaining the ear of the cardinal over the last few months?

But rather than argue this latest inflammatory issue—indeed we felt at a loss to know how to do so—we tried to turn the conversation back to the misunderstood "ultimatum," to the lack of vocations because of our personnel crisis, to the grave consequences for staffing our schools, to the focus of the present meeting, which, we had hoped, was our educational policy.

His Eminence chose to return to the issue of religious life, perhaps feeling that this area was a safer one. For how could he, the cleric renowned for his creation of a vast archdiocesan school system, argue against quality education or better teacher preparedness? Or perhaps he knew that as the foremost Church leader in the Los Angeles hierarchy, his reproof of our religious lives would compromise our renewal efforts. So his argument was to be, then, not better teachers in his schools but approved religious persons in his educational system. Perhaps he felt he could threaten us into relinquishing our decrees.

After making the hurtful charge against the sisters' lives, he now softened his attack, for his next words were temporarily placating. The decrees, he stated, were "masterfully done," even "scholarly." However, he added, they epitomized a philosophy he would not permit in his archdiocese. He had, he assured us, "stupendous [sic] communities of religious in the archdiocese who would be scarred by the influence of the Immaculate Heart Sisters."[6]

This theme—the example set by our community in the archdiocese—was evidently another strong factor in the cardinal's decision to forego negotiation, for he repeated it several times in the course of the meeting. Soon His Eminence turned back to the numerous grievances he had against the Sisters of the Immaculate Heart of Mary.

---

[6] IHM General Council, Cardinal McIntyre, and advisors. Minutes of meeting, October 16, 1967, 2. A/IHMCOM.

Hollywood at night—a view of Western Avenue (1955) from Immaculate Heart College campus. The chapel was a beacon of serenity for many as they traveled the streets of Los Angeles, California.
(IHM archive photo)

Mother Eucharia Harney was a charismatic and dynamic influence in the community; she held office from 1939 to 1951. (IHM archive photo)

Although she mourned the loss of canonical status, Mother Eucharia remained deeply committed to the new community. (IHM archive photo)

Sisters of the Immaculate Heart of Mary, Los Angeles, 1960. Never again so still and silent. (IHM archive photo)

Marie Bruch Caspary and Jacob Caspary with daughter
Anita on the day of her entrance into the community,
September 24, 1937. (Photo courtesy of Caspary family)

Sister Mary Humiliata, I.H.M.
"Religious life agreed with me.
I found much peace and
happiness in the convent."
(IHM archive photo)

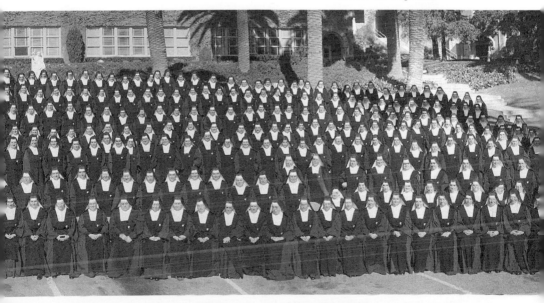

Mary's Day, 1966. Under the leadership of Sister Corita Kent, this became one of the community's major celebrations and a cause of controversy. (IHM archive photo)

In the later '50s and '60s Immaculate Heart College was marked by an unprecedented growth and vitality among the faculty. Leading off in a flood of national publicity was the art department with Sister Corita Kent, I.H.M.
(Photo courtesy of Corita Art Center, Los Angeles, California)

College president Sister Mary William (Helen Kelley), Mother Humiliata, Bob Hope, Martin Gang, chair of the college board of regents, and Cardinal McIntyre. Hope received the Pacem in Terris award from Immaculate Heart College. Many parents from the entertainment industry sent their children to schools staffed by Sisters of the Immaculate Heart. (Photo courtesy of *The Tidings,* June 24, 1966)

It was not uncommon for many sisters in elementary education to hold two full-time positions. Pictured is Sister M. Ethel Swain, I.H.M., who was principal and second grade teacher at Holy Spirit Catholic School, Los Angeles, California, 1961.
(Photo courtesy of Ethel Swain, I.H.M.)

The cover of *Time* magazine for February 23, 1970, featured Anita Caspary, I.H.M., and James Shannon, former auxiliary bishop of St. Paul, Minnesota, whose parallel struggles to implement the reforms of Vatican II high-lighted the turmoil within the Catholic Church after Vatican II.
(Photo courtesy of Time, Inc.)

In 1955 Cardinal James Francis McIntyre dedicated La Casa de Maria Chapel at the IHM novitiate in Montecito, California. Standing at his right is Msgr. Benjamin Hawkes.
(IHM archive photo)

Anita M. Caspary, Mother General
(1963–70), President (1970–73)

Agnes E. Flynn (Sister Elizabeth Ann),
Vicar General

Regina McPartlin (Mother Regina),
First Councilor, Mother General
(1951–63)

Although remarkably
diverse personalities,
the IHM Council
(1963–70) agreed that
the whole structure of
religious life urgently
needed redesign.
(IHM archive photos)

Charlene Mary Schaffer
(Sister Charles), Second Councilor

Dorothy Lester (Sister Gregory),
Secretary and Third Councilor

Eugenia Ward (Sister Eugenia),
Treasurer

In the early twentieth century, the Sisters of the Immaculate Heart purchased land in the beautiful Hollywood hills. This 1955 photo shows the motherhouse and high school (lower left), Immaculate Heart College (center) and library (center right). Currently, the administrative offices of Immaculate Heart Community, the Corita Art Center and the remodeled Immaculate Heart High School remain on part of this property. (IHM archive photo)

Mary Mark Zeyen, I.H.M. Elected the first vice-president of the new community and chair of the first board of directors, 1970–73. (IHM archive photo)

Immaculate Heart Community members renew their personal commitment "to build relations in society that foster access of all persons to truth, dignity and full human development." IHM goal statement, IHM archive photo)

Color, variety and unique individuals mark the new Immaculate Heart Community, 1987.
(IHM archive photo)

Present-day Immaculate Heart High School carries on the IHM tradition by providing an excellent education for young Catholic and non-Catholic women. Operated by the new Immaculate Heart Community, one hundred percent of IHHS graduates attend college.
(Photo courtesy of Immaculate Heart High School, Los Angeles, California)

After thirty-four years I can still hear the cardinal's irate accusation. Without a moment's acknowledgment of our reasoning, he rushed on to deliver his string of complaints. "For years now you have been disobedient to me and to my office. You've continued to have your speakers without my approval. Your sisters can be seen at all hours of the night attending, or even speaking at public meetings in public auditoriums, and on topics with non-Catholic speakers. I get calls night and day about what the Immaculate Heart Sisters are doing now. . . . And only last month, you, Reverend Mother, went scurrying off to Rome for another one of your consultations with more experts, I presume!"[7]

His insistence on our defiance and his allusion to Rome finally gave us the opportunity to defend ourselves. I hastened to assure him of our good intentions. I remember stating:

> Your Eminence, we have great respect for the office of the Ordinary. We have made every effort to conform to your wishes. But with respect to our rules, our spiritual lives, and our General Chapter, we are subject to the Vatican. The Church has given religious women a mandate, as you know, to test if we are in touch with the modern world. We've been told to renew our lives and to do this, the Vatican approved experimentation. That is what we're trying to do.

I took a deep breath. Then I resumed:

> The documents that you have are from our recent chapter. They were issued from the Chapter of Renewal. It has the force of law for us, Your Eminence. Even if we wanted to, we cannot change a word of it. Not I, nor even the IHM General Council here. This is what we will be governed by—until the next session of chapter.

My last statement elicited shocked disapproval from the cardinal, and he dismissed out of hand my assurance that we could, if he wished, call another meeting of the sisters' chapter to verify the convictions of the sister delegates. It was difficult—no, impossible—for him to believe that a General Chapter of religious women could have the authority we gave it, above that of the officers of the community, a distribution of "power" utterly foreign to his office.[8]

---

[7] For the specific charges, see "Actions on the part of the Ordinary which have created difficulties for the Sisters of the Immaculate Heart." Unpublished photocopy not dated. See Appendix B, p. 231.

[8] It was, most likely, this same inability to understand the necessity for a priests' senate mandated by the Second Vatican Council in 1965, a directive the cardinal was

The cardinal was clearly frustrated. He did not like what he was hearing. He did not like it that a woman was long in her explanations to him; that she talked of experimenting with the lives of religious; that he, who had attended the Second Vatican Council as a cardinal, was being reminded of some of its provisions. He was the guardian of canon law, not a group of sisters in a convent in Hollywood who wanted to wear contemporary clothes and whose lives sounded more and more like those of lay women. As he thought about all this, his voice, barely controlled now, rose even higher and louder. Again, I can see the dramatic scene and hear his pronouncement: "Very well, you can keep all your experiments and your fine decrees. But I tell you this, you won't be staying in my schools." And with that he turned to Bishop Manning next to him and waved his arm in our direction.

"See that a committee is appointed right away, all those with educational responsibilities—school superintendents, pastor representatives, along with the sisters' council here—so we can see to their orderly withdrawal from our diocese next year." The room was suddenly terribly quiet. The cardinal's face was flushed. I was sure my own was burning. Quickly we searched the other faces around the table—the bishop, the vicar, the priest-superintendents. No one said a word. Not one of his staff dared, for the cardinal had crossed that line where the give-and-take of discussion ended. No more explanations were possible now.

My thoughts raced rapidly. Perhaps if we held on, some negotiations might be worked out at a later date. Or would this end with the IHMs being fired and other religious women in the process of renewal paralyzed with fear? Was I simply seeing a powerful man facing his moment of incomprehension—the collective power of women relying on an authority greater than his own, the principles of renewal generated by his own hierarchical brotherhood?

Suddenly, as if by a signal, all those present began speaking simultaneously, whether out of embarrassment or relief that the worst course imaginable was concluded. The verbal skirmish ensuing was a jumble

---

unwilling to implement. His rationale was simply that he already had in place a consultative structure composed of his administrative appointees. "There is no record that McIntyre ever explained his position either to the priests themselves or to the press and that was a serious tactical mistake. Once again, his lack of communicational skills worked against him because many interpreted his failure to even discuss the issue as an unwillingness to implement a conciliar directive." Weber, *His Eminence*, 2:523–525.

of the meanings of words like "real religious life," "negotiable," and "experimentation" from priests, school officials, and sisters alike.

Although the meeting seemed long and frustrating, it had lasted only about thirty minutes. Thirty minutes in which such strong emotions, but so little substantive discussion prevailed. Thirty minutes in which our nearly eighty-two years of loving service in the Archdiocese of Los Angeles was put in jeopardy. Although most of the meeting seemed fruitless, I had at least made clear one point: that neither my council nor I had the authority to change the decrees. That had to be left to the Chapter of Renewal, which was not yet officially concluded.

With the sounds of chairs being pushed back and some lingering, scattered words as the cardinal dismissed us and left the room, we then heard the gentle voice of Bishop Manning, quietly urging further study of our decrees on both sides. Mother Regina and I took a few moments to talk with him. He ended the meeting by saying, "If this is from God, it will succeed; if it isn't, you wouldn't want it to succeed."[9]

A somewhat bedraggled delegation of sisters returned that afternoon to the motherhouse in Hollywood. At once the General Council called a meeting of the delegates to the Chapter of Renewal in order to ascertain their willingness to uphold the decrees promulgated the preceding Saturday. To their horror, they now had to face almost certain expulsion as teachers from Los Angeles's parochial schools and convents, and quite possibly from other diocesan schools as well. How ironic that the tactic suggested by Cardinal Hildebrand Antoniutti, but not employed by us, had now become a reality that we had to face.[10]

In the days before the next chapter meeting, the council and the delegates felt that it would be important to gain the opinions of prelates of dioceses outside Los Angeles in which our sisters taught. We had already learned that the cardinal had written to every diocese in the state of California. Although some of those bishops voiced objection to one or another decree, no discussion of expulsion from their schools was touched upon or even hinted at, nor did any of those bishops construe the proposed modifications of our Rule as a "threat" or an "ultimatum."

Sisters Elizabeth Ann Flynn and Mary Louise Krug met with Bishop Francis J. Furey of the San Diego Diocese on October 18, 1967. They

---

[9] See also Sister M. Charles Schaffer, I.H.M. Letter to the sisters in IHM convents, October 26, 1967. A/IHMCOM.

[10] For details of Cardinal Antoniutti's suggestion, see Chapter 8, pp. 76–77.

found him to be friendly, yet businesslike, asking only that the facts relating to his schools staffed by the IHMs be provided soon. Later, Father John Dickie, San Diego diocesan superintendent of schools, mentioned that Bishop Furey had been personally contacted by Cardinal McIntyre to gain his support. Furthermore, the bishop noted, the habit was a big issue with the cardinal.[11] Bishop Furey, however, was of the opinion that the sisters should wear a habit or secular clothes, one or the other. For him, as for many other members of the hierarchy at that time, clothes evidently did not define the religious.

Other sisters visited Bishop Alden Bell of the Sacramento Diocese and Bishop Aloysius Willinger of the Monterey-Fresno Diocese both on the same day, October 18, and reported that the bishops were friendly and understanding. And Bishop-elect Harry Anselm Clinch was very encouraging and added that we had to try to continue our struggle.[12] Bishop Floyd S. Begin of Oakland was even more forthright, saying that we "must be 'ruthless' in our decision to educate our Sisters."[13]

The most forthright and positive support for our renewal decrees from a Church authority came from Bishop Remi De Roo of Victoria, British Columbia, where thirteen IHM sisters staffed several schools, two of them serving the native peoples of that region. Bishop De Roo was one of the youngest bishops to be ordained during the Second Vatican Council. Early on he gave his permission for the sisters to experiment in their apostolate. After receiving a synthesis of the decrees, he expressed agreement and encouragement for our renewal efforts in his supportive letter to the then vice president of the Immaculate Heart Sisters, Sister Mary Mark Zeyen.[14]

---

[11] This preoccupation with the clothing of women religious by clergy still seems to persist. In an undocumented and erroneous historical account, Monsignor Weber wrote, "Immediately after the conclusion of the [IHM] Chapter, in early August, Sister Anita Caspary left for Rome, where she met with Cardinal Suenens who discreetly advised her not to be seen in the Eternal City without her habit." Weber, *His Eminence*, 2:422. Cardinal Suenens never discussed my personal attire with me.

[12] Minutes of the Ninth General Chapter of Affairs. Meeting Eight, October 22, 1967:1, and Meeting Ten, November 22, 1967:2, in *Sisters of the Immaculate Heart of Mary, Los Angeles: Community History Part II. October 13, 1967–March 25, 1968.* Unpublished photocopy. A/IHMCOM.

[13] Sister M. Charles Schaffer, I.H.M. Letter to Sister Anita Caspary, I.H.M., October 26, 1967. A/IHMCOM.

[14] Bishop Remi De Roo. Letter to Sister Mary Mark Zeyen, I.H.M., September 25, 1969. A/IHMCOM.

The response of Archbishop Joseph T. McGucken of San Francisco was, like that of a few other churchmen, more complex. He told Sister M. Charles Schaffer, the delegate visiting him in November 1967, that he considered the Sisters of the Immaculate Heart of Mary "very fine teachers" and wished to keep them in his archdiocesan schools. However, he also had some concerns about what he regarded as an over-emphasis on psychology and sociology in our documents, adding in a refreshing bit of candor that he had some of the same sort of difficulties with his priests![15]

Archbishop McGucken wrote me a letter saying that he had

> studied these decrees many times and compared them with the decrees of the Second Vatican Council, the *Motu Proprio Ecclesiae Sanctae*, and the commentaries on these documents . . . [and] I can see in these [IHM] decrees many good things which should help to fulfill the Conciliar mandate toward renewal and adaptation of the religious life to the conditions of our times. . . . there would be no quarrel with the effort involving the quality of education, the teaching conditions, or to provide for the education of the Sisters. I believe all of the Bishops would try in every reasonable way to be cooperative with these efforts.[16]

As a caveat, the archbishop wrote that he thought he detected in our decrees a kind of "secular humanism, or exaggerated personalism, in conflict with the well-established theology of the spiritual life." In some aspects of our external apostolate, "the authority and the responsibility of the bishops and the pastors" were not sufficiently considered by the IHM sisters.[17]

Thus the archbishop confronted the basic contradiction of the two antithetical positions of the Church-in-renewal. On the one hand, the enabling guide, or norms for renewal, empowered special chapters of religious groups to experiment through proposals from their chapters. On the other hand, trouble begins when "the experimentation is extended to matters contrary to the common law of the Church without the required permission of the Holy See." Even here, the archbishop wrote:

[15] IHM Ninth General Chapter. Minutes of Meeting Ten, November 22, 1967:2. A/IHMCOM.
[16] Joseph T. McGucken, Archbishop of San Francisco. Letter to Mother M. Humiliata, I.H.M., February 27, 1968. A/IHMCOM.
[17] Ibid.

> the Holy See *will grant* [underlining his] permission for prudent
> experimentation, but most probably not for wholesale and head-
> long changes which are contrary to the Second Vatican Council
> and the "Motu Proprio" itself—changes which alter the very na-
> ture of the Institute."[18]

"Prudent"? "Wholesale"? "Headlong"? "The very nature of the Institute"? To what extent was the contradiction itself a semantic problem?
We puzzled over these questions. At the IHM chapter session called
after that momentous meeting of October 16, 1967, the delegates heard
a full report of the visit with Cardinal McIntyre and the other bishops.
The delegates' response was one of sorrow at the misunderstanding,
mingled with suggestions for various types of replies to Cardinal
McIntyre. There followed a strong protest by the delegates over the
cardinal's condemnation of our identity as a religious community, the
alleged threats of His Eminence, and the ultimatum attributed to us.
Then a vote of the delegates as to their remaining steadfast to the decrees was taken. On October 22, 1967, the result was unanimous assent
to the decrees.

The delegates, understanding the importance of collective action
rather than a letter from the mother general, moved that a joint statement be sent to the cardinal. The essence of the letter made clear that
we did not wish to withdraw all our sisters simultaneously from our
schools; rather the chapter wished to see a certain small percentage,
which was negotiable, have the chance to finish their degrees, etc., but
the majority of sisters wished to continue teaching in the schools. Some
few who wished to serve in other ministries other than teaching were
to have the opportunity to serve God and the Church in other ways.
Further, members welcomed the opportunity to meet with His
Eminence to clarify certain points in the decrees that might have been
misinterpreted as intransigence.

This letter was sent to the cardinal. As requested by the chapter
members, another letter reporting the results of the special meeting of
delegates on October 22, 1967, and describing the general tenor of the
near disastrous meeting with the cardinal on October 16 was sent to all
community members. Part of the letter to the community reads:

> The reaction of His Eminence was generally negative not only on
> the issue of the schools but also on the documents on prayer and

---

[18] Ibid.

local government and a proper way of life for religious. Sister Anita Caspary told His Eminence that she was not authorized to speak for the Chapter in reference to his objections. Hence, it was felt necessary to call a meeting of the Chapter delegates on Sunday, October 22. At this meeting the Chapter delegates unanimously reaffirmed by secret ballot their support of the Chapter Decrees.[19]

In the cardinal's response to the decision of the chapter delegates and the proposal for further conciliatory meetings, he chose to ignore the sisters' offer and returned instead to the idea that the "ultimatum" was ours. His letter included the following:

> It would appear that the action of the Chapter presents to the Archdiocese of Los Angeles an ultimatum that does not even admit of discussion or negotiation. This ultimatum, with its elements, is not acceptable to the Archdiocese of Los Angeles and its Ordinary. Consequently, there is no other alternative than to accept the threat of the community that they withdraw from the teaching staffs of our parochial schools in the Archdiocese.[20]

In addition, the cardinal emphasized what he called "ecclesiastical jurisdiction," the consequence of which was our non-acceptability as teachers in Los Angeles archdiocesan schools because of our experiments with the habit, prayer at flexible times and locations, a more realistic retiring time, and alternatives to a single superior in each convent, etc. In this letter, for the first time, the cardinal connects the renewal steps to the sisters' vows, implying that our changes were antithetical to the three vows. Looking back, we realized that here was indeed a veiled threat: go back to the old ways if you want to keep your vows. His words were clear, his cutting remarks on our continuing dedicated religious service freely proffered:

> . . . we are unwilling to have a supposed religious community of women teaching in our parochial school system and having residence in our convents when in reality, these schools and convents will no longer enjoy the traditional and well founded practices of being directed by women dedicated by vow and by practice to a

---

[19] Sister Anita Caspary, I.H.M. Letter to the IHM Community, October 22, 1967. A/IHMCOM.

[20] Cardinal McIntyre. Letter to Mother M. Humiliata, I.H.M., October 24, 1967, 1–2. A/IHMCOM.

> life of religious rule and conformity to a practice long established
> and highly regarded. . . . The necessity of this comment is occa-
> sioned by the statements in the decrees of your recent Chapter and
> as has been evidenced in the conduct of your community for the
> past year or two.[21]

And our "failure" to recognize his "ecclesiastical jurisdiction" merited
a further admonition. The sisters who lived in parochial convents
(prior to being dismissed from teaching at the close of the school year
in June 1968) had to conform to preconciliar regulations, that is, to
practices "not offensive to ourselves or to our people."[22]

But the die was cast. Whether the original statement (in his letter of
October 24, 1967) was meant as a threat to make us change our minds,
whether we really were not wanted because of our generally progressive ideas, or whether it was merely a question of control by authority,
there was no sure way of knowing. It seemed obvious that he was answering alleged threat with threat. Later I was informed that a member
of the chancery office was at lunch on October 26, 1967,[23] with several
other priests. The cardinal was reported to have said, "They want a
fight and so I will fight to the finish." Another prelate joined the discussion, saying he supposed the problem would be solved "the Italian
way," that is, the cardinal would ask the Vatican for an apostolic visitator who most probably could secure a compromise.

The month of October 1967 brought many speculations. According
to one report, the cardinal was of the opinion that the threat of financial
need on our part would force us to capitulate. With the loss of teaching
positions, our need for financial support was a great responsibility that
he knew we did not take lightly. Many, along with the cardinal, surmised
that these grave circumstances would force us to modify or repeal our
decrees and abandon our quest for renewal. Most probably what supported his assumption was the exodus of many sisters from other
communities across the nation. During this period many communities
experienced the loss of some of their most highly educated women,
thus depleting anticipated resources and financial support.[24]

[21] Ibid., 2.

[22] Ibid.

[23] This conversation as retold to me occurred two days after I received McIntyre's
very strongly worded letter of October 24, 1967.

[24] Joseph T. McGucken, archbishop of San Francisco. Letter to Mother M. Humiliata,
I.H.M., February 27, 1968. A/IHMCOM.

What the cardinal failed to realize was that the collective IHM reputation, the strength of character of each sister, and a deep faith that we
were following the Spirit of God through renewal would provide the
solid foundation to meet this challenge. In the years since that time
many of our sisters not only found decent jobs but were aggressively
sought out by employers. We gathered our resources not only to sustain
ourselves but also to assist those in need. In this respect the cardinal
surely underestimated the IHM women.[25]

But at this time we could not know whether the cardinal's use of the
word "ultimatum" was just a strategy designed to force us to reject our
renewal plan or whether he meant literally every word in his letter of
October 24, 1967. We therefore had to assume that he meant it when he
stated that our decree on apostolic works was not acceptable to the
archdiocese, did not admit of discussion or negotiation, and left no
alternative but to accept the "threat" of our sisters not being allowed to
staff his schools.

The verbal skirmishes throughout the month of October over "threat"
and "ultimatum" as interpreted by the cardinal on the one hand and
our use of "educational decrees as negotiable" on the other showed the
futility of our reasoned arguments on education to convince the cardinal. He never approved of nor believed in the clear directive promulgated by Pope Paul VI: "It is the institutes themselves which have the
main responsibility for renewal and adaptation."[26]

With these issues before us, no easy resolution of our problem was
possible. While our choice of education for the sisters, and therefore
excellence for our students, was called a "threat," we remembered with
great vividness the very real threat of May 1965, when the cardinal
warned us,"You will suffer for this."

In his reply to my letter of October 23, 1967, His Eminence stated
that meetings with his appointed committee would be welcome. But just
as this more sanguine note in our ongoing dialogue gave us a glimmer
of hope, a new and disturbing event occurred in the form of a letter

[25] Over the years many people have stated that Cardinal McIntyre and members
of the Catholic hierarchy underestimated the power of women religious to take care
of themselves financially as well as spiritually. Obviously our experience proves
that they were wrong.

[26] Norms for Implementing the Decree: On the Up-to-Date Renewal of Religious
Life (*Ecclesiae Sanctae*), in *Vatican Council II: The Conciliar and Post Conciliar Documents*, ed. Austin Flannery, O.P. (Northport, N.Y.: Costello Publishing Co., 1981) 624,
no. 1.

dated November 6, 1967, from Archbishop Luigi Raimondi, the apostolic delegate in Washington, stating that the Sacred Congregation in Rome had appointed the Very Reverend Thomas R. Gallagher, O.P., as apostolic visitator to our community. Here, then, was "the Italian way" our source had predicted. The letter expanded on the valued experience of Father Gallagher. He had been with the apostolic delegation in Washington for two decades. He was also a consultor both for the Pontifical Commission for the Revision of the Code of Canon Law and for the Sacred Congregation for Religious. Clearly his visitation would be of great import.[27]

Meanwhile the cardinal called a special meeting of all pastors in the Los Angeles Archdiocese whose schools we staffed, to inform them of his strong opposition to our new decrees. This meeting occurred without providing us any opportunity to explain our position. It became increasingly evident that His Eminence was planning our exodus from Los Angeles schools or was at least getting ready for that eventuality if his threats were to fail. By October 30, 1967, he had arranged for the special meeting, which included the archdiocesan staff responsible for education, the IHM General Council, and education specialists. Only fourteen days after our momentous meeting of October 16, 1967, he was preparing for the departure of the IHM Community from the archdiocesan parochial schools. Events were moving swiftly.[28]

This threat of removing us is verified by a letter from Cardinal McIntyre to Archbishop McGucken of San Francisco. He wrote:

> May I expatiate on my present frame of mind with regard to this subject. We have, in our letters to Mother Humiliata, reiterated our unwillingness to accept the new decrees both from the standpoint of pedagogy and the spiritual life. It is my purpose to insist that unless they maintain a reasonable adherence to the rule of the community as it existed at the time when the vows were taken by most of the existing members, we shall be unwilling to employ them in our schools. This will be our ultimatum to the ultimatum expressed in their decrees. You will remember that this ultimatum was quite positive.

[27] Archbishop Luigi Raimondi, Vatican apostolic delegate to the United States. Letter to Mother Mary Humiliata, I.H.M., November 6, 1967. A/IHMCOM.

[28] Cardinal McIntyre. Letter to Mother M. Humiliata, I.H.M., October 30, 1967. A/IHMCOM.

Be that as it may, our decision will be that we shall not have (them) teaching in our schools and living in our convents under the guise of religious women (with) a quasi secular rule. Candidly, I feel that the community will compromise and they will not wish to move out of twenty-five of our schools.[29]

The threat, then, was to arrange for this departure. There was apparently a delay of several months before the special meeting occurred. Perhaps this was to allow all parties to come together for further behind-the-scenes discussions. The meeting of educational personnel held on December 7, 1967, was presided over by Bishop Ward,[30] who opened it with a prayer and proceeded to state that the intent was "to have a meeting of minds," by which he apparently meant the method and timing of the sisters' withdrawal. When I noted that His Eminence had sent a letter earlier, stating that both June 1968 and June 1969 were possible dates for our departure, Bishop Ward agreed that even though the cardinal had been "unable to accept the religious and educational proposals," the departure date could be extended to June 1969. Striving to focus on the reasoning behind the cardinal's ostensible willingness to wait a year, I felt it important to assert our own requirements for continued service in the period from July 1968 through June 1969: "For this period, our schools could be staffed under two conditions: that we may be permitted to live the proposed way of religious life and according to the conditions of our educational decrees."[31]

This reassertion of the central issues of our community's 1967 decrees immediately produced from Bishop Ward a negative reaction: "As I see it, 1968 is the deadline because you are reaffirming your Chapter Decrees."[32] The meeting, preserved verbatim by a sister present at the meeting, proceeded in the same vein.

---

[29] Cardinal McIntyre. Letter to Joseph T. McGucken, archbishop of San Francisco, November 2, 1967. Archives of the Archdiocese of San Francisco. According to the 1967 statistics in the IHM archives, we staffed over thirty-five schools in the Los Angeles Archdiocese.

[30] IHM General Council. Minutes of meeting with officials of the Archdiocese of Los Angeles, December 7, 1967, 1–20. Because of the grave issues discussed at this special meeting, the minutes include a verbatim dialogue. A/IHMCOM. See also Ward, interview, 1–40.

[31] IHM General Council. Minutes of meeting, December 7, 1967, 2. A/IHMCOM.

[32] Ibid.

Mother Humiliata: "Yes, we are affirming our Decrees. We really cannot retreat from what we believe to be our way of life."

Bishop Ward: "You're still holding to the same conditions?"

"Yes, your Excellency," I replied.

Bishop Ward: "Then the terminal date is June, 1968."

"The extra year is not, then, the terminal date?"

Bishop Ward: "That's it, then. The meeting is over. In general fashion, what things must be put in order?"

Mother Humiliata: "Well, we should notify the staff, particularly the lay teachers; and we should explain to the parents why we are being asked to withdraw."

Msgr. Hawkes: "We will notify these people."[33]

The monsignor's emphasis on "We" was unmistakable. Several more attempts to take the initiative in informing the lay teachers and parents were met with the flat assurance by the hierarchy that they would do the notifying. Meanwhile Monsignor Hawkes returned to the charges against us. We were mindful that he was the cardinal's right-hand man and that he spoke for the cardinal. His voice seemed harsh and peremptory.

Msgr. Hawkes: "Let's clear up your decisions to make no changes and your departure date. It is all based on your attitude toward **religious** life. The diocese was never opposed to your withdrawal from schools. We never opposed this—you were slow in doing this.[34] Other communities did this a long time ago. The prime reason for His Eminence's objection is that you have no fixed religious life. The whole issue is that he will not have you without a fixed religious life."

Mother Humiliata: "We have never decided to withdraw from schools. We have decided to uphold our Chapter Decrees."

Msgr. Hawkes: "Then you reaffirm your decision. When do you plan to leave our convents?"[35]

[33] Ibid.
[34] Ibid. The word "this" refers to the topic of contracts. Monsignor Hawkes mentioned that the newer communities in the diocese had contracts but that those present for a long time (e.g., Immaculate Heart Sisters and Sisters of St. Joseph of Carondelet) did not. See also minutes of meeting of October 16, 1967. A/IHMCOM.
[35] IHM General Council. Minutes of meeting, December 7, 1967, 4. A/IHMCOM.

Faced with such an immediate request, I temporized. I thought once again of the enormous struggles ahead for the sisters as they tried to prepare for a total change of lifestyle, leaving a secure professional situation, a communal structure, and a familiar habitat, some having "left" the world twenty, thirty, forty, even fifty years earlier. And if they were not to be in the employ of the archdiocese, where then? How then? Particularly painful was the thought of the financial hardships facing all the sisters, but especially those who were older or ill:

> Mother Humiliata: "If our sisters could remain through this coming summer, it would help."
>
> Msgr. Hawkes: "If you have made the decision to abide by your Decrees, then you should write to His Eminence and say what you wish to do with regard to time. If you should have undue hardships, ask a favor of His Eminence—know the facts—consult with him—ask his advice. His Eminence has always been charitable to the religious in this Diocese—he will listen!"[36]

But our experience in the last few years did not augur well for such largess on the cardinal's part, so this invitation by Monsignor Hawkes only served to remind us of the cardinal's insistence on ecclesiastical jurisdiction, even in matters outside his purview.

Throughout the discussion no one present seemed to know how far the cardinal would bend in allowing our sisters living under the decrees to teach in parochial schools or even to live in the Los Angeles convents where they now resided. The final decision would be handed down by the Vatican, an authority we thought would favorably review our sincere efforts at renewal, especially since our reforms originated with the Second Vatican Council. This extremely tense meeting, with its several dramatic high points, emphasized in tones and gestures, was, after all, very bland in its outcome.

It was our understanding from the exchange of two letters in October, 1967, that the December 7, 1967, special meeting with archdiocesan authorities and education specialists was to arrange how and when the schools would be vacated. And although the focus of the priests was for the most part on the schools, the cardinal's chancellor, Monsignor Hawkes, brought the discussion around to our lifestyle, which included our experiment with secular clothes. Surely this was the sticking point

---

[36] Ibid.

with His Eminence, as Bishop Ward attested in his interview years later.[37]

Once back in the motherhouse, the General Council, lacking any other option, agreed to send another conciliatory letter to the cardinal, attempting to encourage his staff to adopt a more positive approach to the problem of staffing vacancies in his schools. We also wished to convey our desire to cooperate wherever possible. Thus my letter of December 18 to him reads as follows:

> The Chapter Decrees on Education are negotiable. We wish to come to an agreement concerning the practical problems encountered in the implementation of these decrees. For example, the mutual selection of schools for staffing by our Sisters could include a number of schools which already substantially meet the desired educational standards expressed in the Decrees. We sincerely believe that transition periods and special contractual provisions could be worked out for other schools.
>
> We have never desired the withdrawal from archdiocesan schools and we seek to avoid this eventuality. We respectfully request that the possibility of necessary withdrawal from some schools not be considered to be any form of ultimatum. Our representatives are prepared to meet with Your Eminence or any representatives whom you may wish to designate for the purpose of negotiations with respect to our Decrees on Education. As an indication of our readiness to pursue this matter amicably we have prepared a discussion outline which we would like to propose as material for a future meeting, along with the items you might suggest. We are progressing in good faith to implement those Chapter decrees which deal with the issues Your Eminence described as involving "ecclesiastical jurisdiction" (letters of October 24 and 30). This entire matter has been referred, as you know, to the Sacred Congregation, whose decision we await. We wish to state again the experimental nature of these Chapter enactments and the consequent necessity of continually weighing their value.
>
> We are having a meeting with the entire community on December 29 as is customary. We would very much appreciate a reply by that date, if such is at all possible.

---

[37] In another passage in this 1992 interview, Bishop Ward stated, "According to one [unnamed] cleric, the IHMs discarding of the habit 'was the ignition point . . .' that brought the Cardinal's anger with the unconventional IHMs to a peak." Ward, interview, 20.

> We realize that this may be an imposition because of Christmas
> holidays; yet a resolution of the difficulties would assist in bring-
> ing peace of mind to our Sisters. . . .[38]

The answer of His Eminence, written the following day, indicated
strongly that educational problems could not be discussed until the
question of "ecclesiastical jurisdiction" (the whole question of the Immaculate Heart changes pertaining to religious life) was settled. His
Eminence felt that in my correspondence I had ignored the question
pertaining to religious life, over which he had responsibility. What
seemed obvious, however, was that once again it was the question of
our identity as religious that was for him the real problem. He summarized it as follows:

> Our policy as stated was and is that we wish sisters teaching in our
> parochial schools and residing in our convents to live a life of reli-
> gious rule and practice, inside and outside the convents and schools,
> and to wear a uniform habit that is immediately recognizable as
> the garb of a woman dedicated to the service of God in religion.
> Such a rule and garb, of course, must have the approval of the
> Sacred Congregation for Religious and be in accordance with vows
> taken and to be taken.[39]

Once again, as he had done in a letter dated October 24, 1967, he
linked the wearing of the habit to the three vows sisters profess, suggesting that both were equally the preeminent mark of religious women.
He seemed unbending on this issue, even though it had long since been
pointed out to him that we had received official limited permission to
experiment with alternatives to the habit from Father Bernard Ransing,
C.S.C., of the Sacred Congregation for Religious, almost two years earlier, on March 25, 1965.[40]

Because of the cardinal's insistence through messages sent by way
of his staff that we had no fixed rule, were given wholly over to experimentation, and were living, in his opinion, like seculars and not religious

---

[38] Mother M. Humiliata, I.H.M. Letter to Cardinal McIntyre, December 18, 1967.
A/IHMCOM.

[39] Cardinal McIntyre. Letter to Mother M. Humiliata, I.H.M., December 19, 1967.
A/IHMCOM.

[40] Bernard E. Ransing, C.S.C. Letter to Mother M. Humiliata, I.H.M., March 25, 1965.
A/IHMCOM. At this time Father Ransing was secretary to Cardinal Hildebrand
Antoniutti, prefect of the Sacred Congregation for Religious at the Vatican.

women, the IHM chapter, at its meeting on December 26, 1967, commissioned that a documented history of our educational apostolate and an apologia for our way of life be written and sent to His Eminence immediately.[41] Because of the misunderstandings, confusion, and disappointments of the parents of children in our parochial schools, we sent out small committees to the parishes in whose schools we taught. We also sent a packet of letters, clippings, and editorials with the following cover letter to the parents of each child. Reactions were varied, but on the whole we felt that parents understood our reasoning and knew that we did not wish to leave the schools. The cover letter to them read as follows:

Dear Friends,

You will hear that after 82 years in the Archdiocese of Los Angeles, the Sisters of the Immaculate Heart are being asked to stop teaching your children in the parochial schools of the Archdiocese. We would like to make clear that we have tried, by every means possible, to avoid such an eventuality.

We think it important for you to know that our recent changes, which have in turn prompted this action, have been in response to a directive which Pope Paul VI issued after the close of the Second Vatican Council. The Holy Father urged all religious communities to examine and renew their way of life and to engage in wide-ranging experimentation to achieve this renewal. . . .

From our conferences and correspondence with the Chancery Office, we are convinced that our remaining in the schools is a return to our former way of life. The question of uniform dress is an obvious but minor part of the discussion. More central to the discussion are regulations for a fixed time for rising and retiring, fixed hours for prescribed prayers, a highly centralized mode of local house government and other points of like nature. This mode of living may have suited former times, but it is a hindrance to present demands of apostolic life in schools and hospitals. In trying to understand the situation in which we find ourselves neither you nor we can look merely to the superficial aspects of the problems involved. Rather, we must go far more deeply into some of the most serious questions confronting Catholics today. As we view the whole panorama of religion in our day, three critical issues affecting your children stand out:

[41] Sister Elizabeth Ann Flynn, "Background on the Ninth General Chapter's Decree on Education" (Los Angeles: Unpublished work, December 1, 1967). See Appendix A, p. 225.

FIRST: The role of the Church in the lives of young people has weakened.

SECOND: Catholic schools need a challenging new level of quality.

THIRD: The attractiveness of religious life in the entire United States in its traditional form is increasingly questioned, as national statistics show. . . .[42]

Of course, these explanations were displeasing to His Eminence, who had sent his own form letter to the pastors of his archdiocese. The letter was also distributed to parents, presenting his argument for asking the Sisters of the Immaculate Heart not to teach in his schools. The words "withdraw" and "ultimatum" were again attributed to the sisters as being the first to use them.

The concern many felt in the Los Angeles Archdiocese and in the nation over the loss of so many sisters to the schools was expressed by numerous letters to the community and to bishops near and far. Some of these communications contained requests to be allowed to intervene, to be the mediators in a matter deemed so important to the whole country. Especially anxious were the pastors whose parish schools had been staffed by the Immaculate Heart sisters. One such parish, St. Anthony's Parish in Long Beach, California, where Monsignor Bernard Dolan was pastor, was staffed by IHM sisters from its beginnings.

For Monsignor Dolan, a gregarious and good-natured man, the situation demanded action. Therefore he called me to learn my feelings about having a meeting with the cardinal to talk about saving the situation at least for the twelve grades at St. Anthony's. I was pleased by this well-meaning invitation but somewhat dubious about how the cardinal would react. I agreed to the meeting, thinking that with the added impetus of such a forceful and loyal prelate as Monsignor Dolan it might be of some help. After all, I knew that Monsignor Dolan was a good friend of Cardinal McIntyre's and a "valued and treasured member of McIntyre's inner circle."[43] Furthermore, as former chancellor of the Los Angeles Archdiocese under Archbishop John J. Cantwell and one who had been accorded several prestigious titles such as papal chamberlain and protonotary apostolic, he commanded a great deal of respect in the archdiocese.[44] The meeting was set for January 15, 1968.

---

[42] Sister Anita Caspary, I.H.M. Letter to all persons served by the Immaculate Heart Sisters, January 8, 1968. A/IHMCOM.

[43] Weber, *His Eminence*, 2:497.

[44] Ibid., 497–498.

On the appointed morning I found myself rather anxiously awaiting His Eminence in the anteroom of his office, while Monsignor Dolan
paced back and forth. Both of us were dressed in black, looking as
formal as possible. Monsignor wore his clerical garb, and like most of
our sisters at this time, I was in secular clothes. I had chosen a black,
tailored suit, very modest and formal, which I thought could hardly
offend the most conservative of priests.

I do not remember any exchange of greetings as we were ushered
by an aide into Cardinal McIntyre's office. The first thing I do remember was the cardinal's very loud and angry voice, shouting "You can no
longer call yourself a religious in that clothing! How dare you come to
my office this way!"[45] I was shocked into silence. So was the normally
genial and talkative pastor of St. Anthony's. When I turned to him for
support, I was stunned to find that he had fled the room. I had no
choice but to listen to a long, condemnatory speech, after which I left
with as much dignity as I could muster. St. Anthony's was never mentioned.

I had scarcely reached the refuge of my office when the phone rang.
It was Monsignor Dolan, apologizing for his hasty retreat. He gave
only one excuse: "I could not stand to see a woman insulted like that."
The fate of St. Anthony's and the IHMs was now sealed. Monsignor
Dolan died the following summer on the feast of the Immaculate
Heart. Those who knew him well said that he died of a broken heart.

Another such attempt at mediation occurred later on the part of a
well-known businessman, Mr. Walter Laband, who was also a bene-
factor of one of our hospitals, Queen of the Valley Hospital, in West
Covina, California. Mr. Laband seemed to be the perfect choice to intercede with the chancery office on our behalf. He was a man of distinction who knew his way around the world of high finance, as did the

---

[45] Cardinal McIntyre's preoccupation with the habit of women religious bordered
on a fixation, in my opinion. In a letter written to me, Bishop Ward wrote, "His
Eminence has commented to me that yesterday in the parking place of the Cathedral of St. Vibiana, he was attracted to the costume of a young lady described to him
as a member of your community. Her costume was entirely comparable to the dress
currently in vogue amongst lay women. Her skirt was knee length, and she wore an
Eton jacket. Her headdress comprised a modified veil. Without this contracted veil,
there would have been no indication given in her appearance that she was a religious." Bishop John J. Ward. Letter to Mother M. Humiliata, I.H.M., May 5, 1967.
A/IHMCOM. After thirty-five years I still have not been able to find out which
sister possessed an Eton jacket in 1967.

cardinal himself. He too was a "builder," having contributed generously to the hospital's building program. When he suggested that I should invite Monsignor Hawkes to a dinner at the motherhouse to talk with him and me, I felt it only right to agree to his plan. I did not think that it would be easy, but I remained hopeful because of the charm and diplomatic skills of Mr. Laband.

So the silver and china were our best and the menu was carefully planned for that evening in March, 1968. The early part of the evening proceeded smoothly enough, both Mr. Laband and Monsignor Hawkes exchanging anecdotes and information about financial problems in and around the archdiocese as well as stories about persons they both knew. The sisters moved quietly in and out of the dining room as they brought in the various servings of the dinner, returning with plates of delicacies that we hoped would please the monsignor.

Then the conversation grew more serious as Monsignor Hawkes focused abruptly on our reluctance to change our views regarding the religious habit. As a man of the world who had already seen the hospital sisters in secular clothes, Mr. Laband had no problem with a change of habit, but he deferred to the monsignor on the subject and gradually attempted to turn the topic away. I began to grow anxious. I knew of the monsignor's forceful persistence. I also recalled vividly the cardinal's meeting in January with Monsignor Dolan and myself, and the cardinal's strong reaction to my simple black dress. Whereas Mr. Laband wanted to discuss the larger picture of staffing needs and the Catholic apostolate, Monsignor Hawkes insisted on the importance of the issue of our dress in the mind of the cardinal. No explanation or talk of experimentation was of interest to him. His Eminence had no patience, he said, with the IHMs and their proposals. The habit was the thing that divided the sisters and the cardinal.

Mr. Laband grew silent, unable to cope with the whole problem of proper clothing for religious women; he had come to discuss larger questions. But Monsignor Hawkes, who by this time had lost his temper, had had enough. He shouted, "Why can't you sisters have a habit, put it in the closet, and just wear it on feast days?" His face had reddened; his hands were shaking. The scene was so contrary to his usual cold imperturbability that I was a little frightened. Could he be on the verge of a heart attack or stroke? He crushed his napkin into a ball and threw it on the table beside his dessert plate. It was all over. The sisters who were serving vanished without serving coffee. They were unprepared for what they had witnessed—such feeling, such anger about the habit?

I had nothing left to say. To talk about our belief in integrity, about keeping faith with our 1967 Chapter of Renewal, our experimentation process, or even the documents of the Church from the Second Vatican Council all seemed like a foreign language. Monsignor Hawkes left hastily. Mr. Laband, uttering some brief, polite words, left crestfallen. He was no doubt more than a little unsettled by the encounter, in which his diplomatic skills were of no avail. It was, no doubt, difficult for him to comprehend the rejection of a proposal on the basis of dress which was used by a number of communities but which for us was a compromise on more than the habit. Once again the kind intentions of friends had come to naught.

Meanwhile His Eminence, concerned about the staffing of his archdiocesan schools, inquired about the exact number of sisters who would be leaving the schools because of their decision to follow the IHM decrees. He added that provision would be made for those sisters who wished to remain and teach in the schools if they adhered to the regulations that had prevailed over the years.

When this communication was read to the delegates of the next session of the Chapter of Renewal, the group decided to answer as a body rather than from my office alone. They felt the need for a response that would represent the entire community. We wanted to summarize the beliefs that had given rise to the incredible happenings of the previous months.

The letter we sent, which follows here, was respectful, comprehensive, with lingering hopefulness, but ultimately resigned:[46]

Jan. 25, 1968

Your Eminence,

On January 20th Sister Anita Caspary gave a report to the Chapter delegates of her meeting with you on January 15. We have reviewed the entire situation in the light of our correspondence and conferences with you since October when we presented our document to you.

---

[46] In this letter I am referred to by my baptismal name. Our beloved Mother Eucharia Harney, I.H.M., in her penchant for symbolic and Latinized names, had strongly suggested that the name "Humiliata" be given to me at reception, signifying a virtue she wished me to cultivate. Through the years this was both a source of confusion and humor for me. Horrified at the incorrect Latin form, Sister St. Paul, my Latin teacher, persistently reminded the community that *humiliata* in Latin accurately translated means the "humiliated one," not "humility." During my first years

At this time we respectfully wish to restate our understanding of the situation and to conclude reluctantly that we are, indeed, at an impasse.

As a pontifical institute, subject directly in matters of our internal life only to the Sacred Congregation for Religious, we were obedient in the spirit and procedure of our Ninth General Chapter to the relevant documents of Vatican II and to Pope Paul's "Motu Proprio." The conclusions of the Chapter, therefore, we can only consider to be valid and binding on all members of the institute, as, indeed, have been the decrees of our past general chapters. We sincerely believe that these Decrees constitute acceptable guidelines for a religious life.

We did not close our ears to your request for reconsideration of some aspects of our renewal. We struggled to find some way in which your authority, our autonomy, and the sensitivities of the people with whom we work might be reconciled. We do not dispute your right to terminate our employment in schools under your jurisdiction. What we question is the fairness of your suggesting that some members of our community might gain acceptability in the archdiocesan schools by the sole means of repudiating the spirit and intent of our lawfully-arrived-at Decrees which have traditionally had the force of law and which bind all members. It is difficult to interpret this as being anything less than disruptive of community harmony and integrity.

There seems to be little doubt that great and vital changes are needed in the Church. That is why the Second Vatican Council was convened. *It was in obedient response to Mother Church and her directives to religious following Vatican II that our Chapter desired to act.* [Italics ours] We feel that if any unit in the Church which is authorized to initiate changes for itself is hindered from doing so by another, the integrity of the whole is threatened. This is not to argue that all of the changes we have proposed for ourselves are unquestionably correct or essential. We are convinced, however, that it was our unquestionable right to have arrived at them in the manner directed by Rome.

In view of all that has transpired, culminating in your decision regarding the conditions for our remaining in the schools of this Archdiocese, we, the Sisters of the Immaculate Heart, will proceed to withdraw from the schools we staff in June, 1968. We feel in justice that the decisions involved, however painful both for your Eminence and for the members of our community, must be acted upon at this time. Those responsible for and concerned about future plans for students and schools

---

of teaching the younger students struggled not only to understand my name but also to pronounce it. On one occasion I received a Christmas gift with a card addressed to Sister Mally Olive. Needless to say, I readily embraced my baptismal name when such changes were permitted.

must make suitable arrangements immediately. Our deep concern for parents, pastors, and students will insure the greatest care on our part that this difficult transition be made as cooperatively as possible.

Sincerely yours in Christ,

[Signed: "The Sisters of the Immaculate Heart"][47]

But there was something more. His Eminence had read penetratingly into the further thinking of the decrees, further, no doubt, than even some of the Immaculate Heart Community. He had perceived the suggestion, not yet decreed but only stated obliquely, that other apostolates in the areas of peace, poverty, race, and alienation of every kind were about to draw sisters into broader fields of endeavor than the parochial schools. Perhaps he sensed, and quite correctly, that the future of a large number of women in the American Church were about to leave the confinement and conformity of the Catholic classroom for new apostolates. He had read, no doubt, the statement in the chapter document, "We want to be 'closely involved in temporal affairs of every sort': education, political institutions, international relations, the arts and professions, culture, and economic affairs."[48]

Actually this statement was prophetic rather than immediate in its impact, but ironically the expulsion of the Immaculate Heart Sisters from the schools of the Los Angeles Archdiocese hastened the fulfillment of the prophecy. Had the decree on education been blessed with the approval of His Eminence, most of the sisters would no doubt have returned to their classrooms. When those classrooms were shut, new doors began to open; new opportunities for untried apostolates were, in a sense, forced upon them.

Meanwhile the announcement that over two hundred sisters were to leave their teaching posts in over thirty-five Los Angeles Archdiocesan schools alone shook the Catholic world. Newspapers across the country revealed their attitude toward change by their sensational headlines: "Nuns' Stand Seen as an Ultimatum" and "McIntyre to oust 200 updating Nuns." Had the cardinal issued an ultimatum, or had the sisters held out for miniskirts? Misinterpretations and dramatic re-

---

[47] Sisters of the Immaculate Heart of Mary, Los Angeles, California. Letter to Cardinal McIntyre, January 25, 1968. A/IHMCOM.

[48] This sentence appears in the complete edition of the 1967 chapter decrees. A/IHMCOM.

tellings of the meeting took up columns of both secular and Catholic publications. But the full story was to include many more than those who taught in Los Angeles. The community's 525 sisters who desired to support their chapter's proposals for change (excepting the forty to fifty sisters who did not wish for change) were to be affected by the cardinal's stance.

Now the sisters had much to do besides hearing from friends who meant well or read the latest account of their supposed intransigence in the media. The deadline of the end of the school year, June, 1968, would soon be upon them. There were records and files to be put in order, convents to be inventoried, work for the coming year to be found, apartments and rental houses to be located. There were pastors to deal with and parents to be given endless explanations.

Since the Sisters of the Immaculate Heart were a pontifical institute rather than a diocesan order, Cardinal McIntyre did not have jurisdiction over their *internal* affairs. As the conflict moved up the hierarchical levels of authority, he continued to exercise his strong opposition to the chapter decrees in the only clearly appropriate area for the Ordinary, that of the archdiocesan schools. According to Monsignor Weber, in the cardinal's mind, the sisters' apostolic work, for example teaching, was inextricably bound up with the sisters' proposals for internal spiritual renewal. For him, "the whole notion of education was intertwined in the religious status, training and living of the community . . . and 'the convent they lived in should be subject to a determined and definite rule of life and a spirit of religion, not a secular spirit.'"[49] Thus, by opposing our decrees concerning teaching and the education of the IHM sisters, including the wearing of secular clothes in the schools, he was opposing our internal experimental changes. Furthermore, the many written and oral complaints from the cardinal through the sixties demonstrated clearly that he had characteristically been more than a little willing to be involved in issues other than education.[50]

Those sisters who supported the IHM decrees but felt that their vocation to the religious life and teaching in a Catholic school were synonymous were forced to find employment outside the Los Angeles Archdiocese. Some of these suffered a vocational crisis that led to

---

[49] Weber, *His Eminence,* 2:424.

[50] "Actions on the part of the Ordinary which have created difficulties for the Sisters of the Immaculate Heart." Unpublished photocopy, 1965–67. See Appendix B, p. 231.

eventual departure from our community. But for the larger number, who could accept the thesis that "every humanizing work is a Christian work,"[51] a new idea of religious life began to develop. Cardinal McIntyre, by his very opposition to our stance, provided the grounding for a deep solidarity among the Immaculate Heart sisters. His intransigence sharpened our commitment to develop new horizons of Christian ministry still in their early stages.

Meanwhile, as the news of the local conflict with His Eminence escalated in volume and media coverage, letters flew to and from the apostolic delegate in Washington, D.C., to Church officials at the Vatican. The male hierarchy did not know what to do with us except to repeat the pattern of the past. And so another visitation to the Immaculate Heart Community was scheduled, but this time the Vatican was to be directly involved.

[51] This sentence appears in the complete edition of the 1967 chapter decrees. A/IHMCOM.

Chapter 12

The Vatican Visitations

After that fateful meeting in October 1967, one dramatic confrontation after another, with unbelievable haste, filled our days. In early November Archbishop Luigi Raimondi, the Vatican's apostolic delegate to the United States, wrote a letter to me announcing that the Sacred Congregation for Religious had mandated another visitation.[1] The message conveyed a tone of a summons from a high ecclesiastical court of the Church. Very Reverend Thomas R. Gallagher, O.P., a Dominican priest from Washington, was to be the apostolic visitator. His reputation for high-level Church negotiations was by this time not unknown to us.

Years of submission to the Holy See and reverence for the Catholic Church inspired more than a little awe and anxiety in many IHM members at this announcement. After all, we had been through several visitations before the 1967 Chapter of Renewal. We had exchanged with the local hierarchy numerous explanatory letters about our life and ministries, covering every possible point of dispute, it seemed to us. What more did they want? Did someone request another visitation? Further, what was Father Gallagher's real purpose in coming?

Over the years there has been much speculation and discussion as to who initiated this visitation. There were several indications that Cardinal McIntyre requested help from the Vatican and its agencies in order to bring us to his point of view. In an interview given in 1992, Bishop John J. Ward related that after the cardinal was unsuccessful in persuading us to relinquish the renewal process, he turned to Pope Paul VI. Ward stated:

[1] Archbishop Luigi Raimondi, apostolic delegate. Letter to Mother M. Humiliata, I.H.M., November 6, 1967. Archives of the Immaculate Heart Community (hereafter referred to as A/IHMCOM).

As a result, all Cardinal McIntyre could do was go to the Holy Father and say, "Look, we would like a review of this. I've asked the sisters to do this and they have not done it, so I am relating it to you. Would you set up a Board of Inquiry?" The first Board of Inquiry was Father [Thomas R.] Gallagher, [O.P.].[2]

In his biography of Cardinal McIntyre, Monsignor Weber's account differs radically from that of Bishop Ward, who was an auxiliary bishop and a close advisor to McIntyre during this period. "Though he personally disagreed with and opposed many of the experimental changes proposed by the sisters in their religious life, McIntyre was content to leave that aspect to the Sacred Congregation for Religious 'which had jurisdiction in such matters.'"[3]

Again in contrast to Weber, Bishop Ward's statements continue to demonstrate the collaboration between the cardinal and the officials from the Vatican.

He [Gallagher] was appointed by Rome. Cardinal McIntyre goes to Rome and says, "Look, I'm having difficulty with this pontifical-right religious community." So, Rome appoints Father Gallagher, who comes out, to make an inquiry. He interviews the Mother Superior, the staff, he interviews all of them, he came back and he got no place. . . . Then the episode of the habits came out. Then Cardinal McIntyre made his decision because it was his diocese; he could say who was going to teach in his schools.[4]

The Apostolic Visitor's Inquiry

With less than two weeks from the time I received notice of his appointment as apostolic visitor, Father Gallagher arrived at the motherhouse during the week of November 19, 1967, to conduct his inquiry. He was reserved, distinctly aloof, and dignified in his white Dominican habit, incongruously conspicuous among the colorfully dressed sisters, almost all of whom had now adopted lay attire. Using a set form of questions to interview each sister, he remained a few days.

---

[2] Bishop John J. Ward. Interview by Marshal H. Mercer, December 10, 1992. Audio-cassette transcript, 40.

[3] Msgr. Francis J. Weber, *His Eminence of Los Angeles: James Francis Cardinal McIntyre* (Mission Hills, Calif.: St. Francis Historical Society, 1997) 2:425.

[4] Bishop Ward, interview, 40 (see note 2 above).

Then he announced that the visitation would continue again beginning in early 1968. He regarded the issues as too numerous to be brought to a hasty conclusion; thus he needed more time. However, prior to his departure he requested from the IHM General Council a copy of our Rule and the background out of which it developed. This was posted to him in early January 1968.

In this same month Cardinal McIntyre requested from us the number of our sisters he might expect to see teaching in the archdiocesan schools. His request did not specify the school year, though we suspected it to be after June 1968, in view of the impasse at the meeting with the chancery office and educational personnel on December 7. During this period the IHM education commission sought from each sister a statement of her availability to teach.

Almost immediately after the requested material had been sent to Cardinal McIntyre, Father Gallagher issued a short communique to me on January 12, 1968:

> In view of the authority vested in me as the Apostolic Visitator of the California Institute of the Sisters of the Immaculate Heart of Mary, I herewith enjoin you to desist from any and all efforts to ascertain from members of the community their intentions with regard to their future teaching in the schools of the Archdiocese of Los Angeles. Such replies as have been elicited in this manner are to be disregarded without prejudice to the individuals who submitted them.[5]

Apparently Father Gallagher, learning about the canvassing of teachers by our education commission, interpreted this "census" as an attempt by the officers of the community to unduly influence, and thereby determine, the opinion of the sisters regarding the 1967 chapter decrees. To agree to teach in Los Angeles's parochial schools on the part of any sister meant to Gallagher a rejection of the IHM decrees.

With two hierarchical agencies demanding answers and attention, my central task was to keep the vision of the IHM decrees before the community. In retrospect, it is evident that at this stage of the tension with the cardinal and his supporters, the IHM decrees kept getting reduced to one of two issues: the sisters should wear some type of habit and continue to teach in the Los Angeles Catholic schools, or the

[5] Thomas R. Gallagher, O.P. Letter to Sister Anita Caspary, I.H.M., January 12, 1968. A/IHMCOM.

decrees were a collective challenge and an ultimatum to the cardinal's authority. Both of these reductions were a far cry from the central meaning of the decrees; both represented a terrible injustice and a skewed interpretation of our vision of service and ministry. Thus the tangled web of opinions—willingness to teach, necessity for educational preparation, dedication to the teaching professions, loyalty to the 1967 chapter decrees, and the habit—was now so intricately interwoven that the IHM sisters and certainly the IHM General Council felt a kind of hopeless frustration with the whole situation.

The dissemination of Gallagher's letter to the community and his implication that the IHM General Council was attempting to ascertain the loyalties of the sisters aroused anew the sisters' indignation and tension, so much so that the tenor of community life was completely changed. Feast days such as Easter, Pentecost, and even the Feast of the Immaculate Heart were no longer carefree days of freely talking at any time, of singing all our customary songs, of enjoying the cooks' most delicious dishes. Sisterly exchange of small gifts on such days still took place, but suspicion and watchfulness of each person's choice of friends and associates made community life as we had known it a thing of the past.

Father Gallagher's letter contained further admonitions. He had given each sister a questionnaire to complete. His letter mandated strict confidentiality. "All members of the community are to be notified by the Mother General that their interviews with the Apostolic Visitator, the replies to his questionary and correlated materials are strictly confidential and that no one in the community has a right to know of these communications."[6] This statement appeared unduly cautionary to us, especially since no official pressure had ever been brought to bear on any member of the community to disclose such documents or their contents. The motivation from which most of us, I am sure, wrote our answers to the questionnaires was the hope that this statement might convince the reader (whoever that might be) that the beliefs we held were deeply personal and sincere.

The questionnaire called for the identity of each sister, her date of profession of vows, and her date of birth. The first of the four questions asked concerned religious life, that is, the concept as expressed in the decrees: Are you in accord with these decrees?

---

[6] Ibid.

For my part, answering this request was a chance to explain how I felt about a matter close to my heart. My answer to this first question was as follows:

> I think the form of religious life we are striving to describe in our Decrees is one we have, in many ways, been living for some time. We have come to see that certain customs and conventions of convent life as they were previously set down really became a means for casting off personal responsibilities, for masking immaturity, for evading the making of decisions and thus, for not sharing the onus of decisions made. Further, during the past few years, we have seen numerous examples of personal tragedy, failure and the desire to abandon religious life, produced by over-institutionalization and overextension of our sisters. We have also seen the danger of demanding from a sister both a generous response to the valid needs of those she serves and at the same time asking her for rigid adherence to an inflexible horarium and a series of obligations within the convent.
>
> We thus have come, over a period of time, to live in a more human fashion, to allow human relationships to deepen and broaden, to seek to worship and pray in a way that makes community meaningful, to develop a personal loyalty to Christ that binds us together, making solitude rich and loneliness rare. We are developing a new respect for each other, a new allowance for each other. We are seeking to make each person aware of what she contributes to the community, not by what she does, but by what she is.
>
> What our chapter set down in words is a way of life which theoretically and practically is a description of what we are as well as what we hope to be. To live according to the Chapter Decrees is more demanding than the ascetic practices of silence, penance or prolonged prayer. This way of life does not attempt to measure the individual by fixed external criteria. Instead, the person's fitness for the life is evaluated by her honest attempt to create Christian community, which demands self-sacrifice. To grow in the concept of Christian community, our Decrees enjoin us then to expand the vision of the religious beyond the petty world of self. The life described by the Decrees cannot be lived without faith in and dependence on God. It can be sustained only by one who seeks daily to follow Christ more closely in knowledge and love.[7]

[7] Anita Caspary, I.H.M. Personal papers.

Other questions from Father Gallagher were concerned with relations of the community with bishops, priests, laity, and with the wearing of the habit. As an apostolic delegate, Father Gallagher would most likely have already known of the permission granted to religious all over the world: the opportunity to experiment, adapting their clothing to the needs of a modern ministry and apostolic work. Hence it is highly likely that the presence of the issue in the questionnaire was due in large part to Cardinal McIntyre's own views.

In my comment on the wearing of the habit, I included not only my own perspective but that of other religious women as well.

> I think the habit in its traditional form marks us as persons of another era. It tends to speak more of the power of the Church than of the love of Christ to men. Sisters also tend to let the habit speak for them while they have very little idea of the message it brings, at least to some. Experimentation may determine that an easily recognizable sign is good or that uniform styles or colors are necessary. Meanwhile, the Sisters of St. Joseph of Carondelet have expressed in their Chapter reports of last month some of the thinking of our own Chapter Decrees: "Since in the minds of many, the traditional habit is medieval and more of a costume than a dress, it seems logical to move from the seventeenth to twentieth century dress in one step rather than to adopt an individual garb that will require further change."[8]

While these questionnaires were being gathered and sent to Father Gallagher, another important document was being mailed by a small group of IHMs to Cardinal Hildebrand Antoniutti, prefect of the Sacred Congregation for Religious. The sisters who disapproved of the changes were holding their own meetings (of which, through rumor, I had been made aware). At one of those meetings, Sister Eileen MacDonald was elected to represent this group. Soon after, Sister Eileen announced this election to me and gave me a copy of the plea she had addressed to Cardinal Antoniutti. The letter read:

> As the temporary chairman of approximately a tenth part of the members of the California Institute of the Sisters of the Immaculate Heart of Mary, presently under investigation by the Sacred Congregation for Religious, I have been authorized by this group to request your kind indulgence in the consideration of our problem.

[8] Ibid.

Since the governing body of the Institute has committed itself to the withdrawal in June of 1968 of all Sisters engaged in the teaching apostolate in the schools of the Archdiocese of Los Angeles, we who wish to continue in this principal work of our Institute since its foundation in 1848 are faced with a dilemma.

Although our Mother General had asked for the names of those Sisters who wish to continue to teach in the parochial schools of this Archdiocese, the General Chapter resolved that such Sisters would be acting contrary to the will of the Chapter. Such a decision makes our status ambiguous. Consequently, we need the opinion of a higher superior to clarify our rights. . . .[9]

There appeared to be something of a contradiction between Sister Eileen's desire to see the action of the mother general upheld (actually the request came directly from our sisters' education commission) while at the same time approving of Father Gallagher's prohibition of any such request. Later in the letter Sister Eileen conveyed her opinion of the chapter decrees:

The strongly opposing views between our group and the rest of the members of the Institute represent two irreconcilable points of view regarding religious life. We are eager to implement the renewal ordered by Vatican II; however, we are opposed to what appears to us a complete secularization of our Institute by the present Chapter.

We wish to emphasize the fact that we desire to remain members of the California Institute of the Sisters of the Immaculate Heart of Mary. We do not wish to form a new congregation. Pending the decision of the Sacred Congregation for Religious on the decrees of our General Chapter, we request from you a clarification of our status as a dissenting group and authorization to continue to teach in the schools of the Archdiocese of Los Angeles.

We regret adding to the burden of your office, but our distress at having to abandon the souls of children enrolled in our schools urges us to seek your approval. In the spirit of submission, we await your decision.[10]

I read the letter and concluded the interview with Sister Eileen, relieved that the truth of her group's position was now out in the open.

---

[9] Sister Eileen MacDonald. Letter to Cardinal Hildebrand Antoniutti, February 26, 1968. A/IHMCOM.

[10] Ibid.

Now the rumors and counter-rumors that had riddled the contentment of the sisters in the motherhouse were no longer mere conjecture. The leadership of those opposing the chapter decrees had now come to light; I could now fully comprehend the past course of events, only guessed at earlier. But what would happen next I could not even imagine.

The Famous Four Points Letter

As Father Gallagher had promised, he returned to the motherhouse in late January 1968 to finish his visitation. I am sure that he detected a cooler reception during this visit; his memo had prepared us for the fact that our renewal program, even our community spirit, was incomprehensible to him. After his second leave-taking, on February 29, 1968, I received another communication from him. The letter, which was to become famous (or infamous) in the literature on the renewal of Catholic religious life, was to affect not only the IHM sisters but hundreds of other orders around the world. The body of the missive was not actually from Father Gallagher; rather it was a directive to him from the prefect of the Sacred Congregation for Religious, Cardinal Antoniutti. We received this letter in early March, less than five months after our momentous meeting with Cardinal McIntyre on October 16. Due to its great importance, it is presented in full.[11]

February 21, 1968

SACRA CONGREGATIO
DE RELIGIOSIS
Prot.: No 493/65

Dear Very Reverend Father,

This Sacred Congregation has received your preliminary report on the Visitation that you have made to the Sisters of the Immaculate Heart of Mary of Los Angeles; we are most grateful to you for it, and for all that you have done in the accomplishment of the delicate task that we have asked you to undertake.

---

[11] Cardinal Hildebrand Antoniutti, prefect of the Sacred Congregation for Religious. Letter to Very Reverend Thomas R. Gallagher, O.P., February 21, 1968. Document no. 493/65. Photocopy. A copy of this document was accompanied by a cover letter from Father Gallagher to me. A/IHMCOM.

We appreciate the urgency of the matters which you indicate as requiring the immediate attention of the Holy See, and we have therefore taken the following decisions, which we ask you, in your capacity as Apostolic Visitator, to make known to the Sisters:

First: The members of the Institute have to adopt a uniform habit, which will be in conformity with the prescriptions of paragraph 17 of the Decree "Perfectae Caritatis." The use of lay clothes is not against the above-mentioned Decree, but violates Common Law and the prescriptions of the "Motu Proprio" Ecclesiae Sanctae II, par. 6, which states that: "The General Chapter is empowered to modify on an experimental basis certain prescriptions of the Constitutions . . . provided that the purpose, *nature and characteristics of the Institute are preserved intact.*"[12] The habit pertains to the nature and characteristics of any Institute for which it has been approved, and the interpretations given to the Sisters in this regard by certain so-called "competent theologians" have absolutely no foundation, either doctrinal or juridical.

Second: Every community of the Sisters of the Immaculate Heart should meet daily for some religious exercises in common. They should at least attend the Holy Sacrifice of the Mass together every day.

Third: The Sisters should keep in mind their commitment to education as specified in their Constitution: The specific end is to labor for the salvation of souls through the work of Catholic education in schools and colleges . . . (Art. 5). Here, too, the above quotation from the "Motu Proprio" Ecclesiae Sanctae II is applicable, namely that the purpose (specific end) of the Institute must be kept intact.

Fourth: The Sisters must observe the prescriptions of the Conciliar Decree "Christus Dominus" (NN. 33-35) and of the "Motu Proprio" Ecclesiae Sanctae I (NN. 22-40) in regard to collaboration with the Local Ordinaries in the works of the Apostolate in the various dioceses. These prescriptions hold for all Religious, *especially for those of Pontifical Right.*[13]

The above decisions are taken with particular concern for the common good of the Church and for the religious education of the children who are so precious to Her. We ask you to strive by every means possible to obtain the generous collaboration of all the Sisters in carrying out the above directives in a spirit of humility, obedience and love of Holy

---

[12] Emphasis of these words is Cardinal Antoniutti's.

[13] Emphasis added. Pontifical right, which we held, is a canonical status for a religious congregation within the Catholic Church. See the work of Margaret Susan Thompson, "The Validation of Sisterhood: Canonical Status and Liberation in the History of American Nuns," in *A Leaf from the Great Tree of God: Essays in Honor of Ritamary Bradley, SFCC,* ed. Margot H. King (Toronto: Peregrina Publishing Co., 1994) 38–78.

Mother the Church. Insist, too, on the need for unity and harmony among the members, since we have been receiving urgent requests for the protection and preservation of the Institute, from some of the Sisters who are firm in their intention not to accept the drastic changes that have been introduced.

With renewed sentiments of gratitude, I remain,

Faithfully yours in Our Lord
(Signed) H. Card. Antoniutti[14]

Responses to the Four Points

This document was first given to the chapter delegates and then to the entire community. The shock of these "Four Points"[15] (except for the attendance at daily Mass, which was already in effect throughout our institute) as being necessary to the *nature* of religious life created tumult in the minds of our sisters. Questions and challenges pervaded our conversations. Why should adherence to these particular "Four Points" be the essentials of religious life? As a community we had entered the hospital apostolate years ago with Cardinal McIntyre's blessing. We never doubted that our goal to excel in teaching and hospital work ever weakened our religious commitment. Soon the news of this recent development in "The Immaculate Heart Story" reached other communities whose sisters had been experimenting with habits and forms of new apostolates, and so on, to an extent far beyond our first timid attempts. Needless to say, those religious were as taken aback as we were.

Of course, the first question from the Immaculate Heart Sisters and from other progressive groups was "Why the IHMs?" None of the other orders had received any such statement concerning the "essentials" of religious life. Still others—the conservative religious groups—felt that there must be some hidden scandal in our community that had angered Cardinal McIntyre. But the most obvious answer for many of us was the fact that none of the other communities had their motherhouse in the Archdiocese of Los Angeles and thus were not within his immediate religious jurisdiction.

---

[14] Signature of Cardinal Hildebrand Antoniutti, prefect of the Sacred Congregation for Religious. A/IHMCOM.

[15] I use the term "Four Points" to refer to this letter and the central issues about the nature of religious life that arose from our struggle.

Other questions troubled the sisters. Much concern, for example, centered on the use of the term "religious." The "Four Points" letter stated that the habit "pertains to the nature and characteristic of any Institute for which it has been approved. . . ." How could it be, the sisters argued, that the use of lay clothing should be in violation of the nature and characteristics of the institute, especially since most Catholic orders wore habits that were the secular clothes of their foundress's own day?

Undeniably, as we now knew, the word "religious" had been used somewhat ambiguously in *Perfectae Caritatis,* the Second Vatican Council's decree on religious life. The document refers to lay religious life as pertaining to persons, such as sisters, and those dedicated to vows, but not clerics. The term was accented strongly in our discussions because of the uncertainty of our future status. Was "religious," then, a noun or an adjective? Was the term so limited that it was confined by dress, hours of rising and retiring, or certain set types of work? Or did it refer, as we had supposed, to one's association in a group striving, in union with the Church's mission but not bound by legal minutiae, to do the work of God?

In a letter dated March 4, 1968, informing the sisters of the "Four Points," I expressed the troubling contradiction I found in the document from the Sacred Congregation of Religious.

> A response to these directives [from Cardinal Antoniutti through Father Gallagher] clearly cannot be made without consultation with the membership of the community. They [the directives] reflect deep confusion and contradiction in official ecclesiastical directives relating to the implementation of the Decree on the Renewal of Religious Life. On the one hand, Vatican II Decrees ordered religious to renew their own way of life in a daring and courageous way; on the other hand, the Bishops have been given expanding authority over the personal and institutional life of religious. (The enclosed documents illustrate that the Church is of two minds on the matter). . . . The dilemma is acute; juridical power still rests with those who are reluctant to approve the broad experimentation authorized by the "Motu Proprio" for Religious. This creates great suffering and anxiety for the community as a whole and for each member. Since there seems little hope for an easy or early resolution of the dilemma, we ask for your prayers that all of us remain open and docile to the Holy Spirit, and that we persevere in our concern for the common good of the Church.[16]

[16] Anita Caspary, I.H.M. Letter to IHM Community, March 4, 1968. A/IHMCOM.

In addition to summarizing this dilemma for our sisters' consideration, I also provided them with copies of the pertinent passages from
those conciliar documents that referred to the expanded role of the
bishops. A passage from *Christus Dominus* described the expanded role
of the bishops and demonstrated the seriousness of the dilemma:

> Religious should at all times treat the bishops, as the successors of
> the apostles, with loyal respect and reverence. Moreover, when-
> ever legitimately called upon to do apostolic work, they must carry
> out these duties in such a way as to be the auxiliaries of the bishop
> and subject to him. Furthermore, religious should comply promptly
> and faithfully with the requests or desires of the bishops when
> they are asked to undertake a greater share in the ministry of sal-
> vation. Due consideration should be given to the character of the
> particular institute and to its constitutions, which may, if necessary,
> be adapted for this purpose in accord with the principles of this de-
> cree of the Council.[17]

In a further reference to the role of bishops, Pope Paul VI wrote,
". . . all religious, even exempt, [i.e., pontifical institutes] are bound by
the laws, decrees and ordinances laid down by the local Ordinary affecting various works."[18] In another section that referred to clerics
rather than to nuns, Pope Paul, writing on the bishop's authority to leg-
islate in matters of secular clothing, stated: "The local Ordinary . . . to
prevent scandal to the faithful can prohibit clerics, both secular and
religious, even exempt religious, from wearing lay dress in public."[19]

Thus it would seem that the much vaunted "experimentation"
being urged for religious orders was circumscribed by a formidable
array of episcopal privileges and laws that might be invoked at any
time. Our sisters had recently become aware of the apparent contradiction of these two mandates. But we had thought that the authorization
to experiment was a kind of time-out-of-time, a period of suspension of
the usual regulations. Moreover, we thought that our special status as a

---

[17] *Christus Dominus*, in *Vatican Council II: The Conciliar and Post Conciliar Documents*, ed. Austin Flannery, O.P. (Northport, N.Y.: Costello Publishing Co., 1981)
1:584, no. 35, par. 1.

[18] Apostolic Letter, Written Motu Proprio, on the Implementation of the Decrees
Christus Dominus, Presbyterorum Ordinis and *Perfectae Caritatis*, in *Vatican Council II:
The Conciliar and Post Conciliar Documents*, ed. Austin Flannery, O.P. (Northport,
N.Y.: Costello Publishing Co., 1981) 1:605, no. 25, par. 1.

[19] Ibid., par. 2d.

pontifical institute gave us additional freedom to experiment within the archdiocese. Now we learned from these documents that even those institutes formerly exempt were to be included in all the newer rules with respect to the jurisdiction of local bishops. With the emergence of the "Four Points" directives, it seemed right and necessary to lay the bases of the contradiction before all the sisters for their consideration. And so I closed my letter to them with the announcement of a meeting the following Sunday afternoon, March 10, 1968, "to discuss all these matters as they affect . . . [each one] personally."[20]

Unexpected but Welcomed Support

Perhaps aroused by the arbitrary nature of the "Four Points" issued in February 1968 and publicized widely, although not by us, a number of canon lawyers, officers and past officers of the prestigious Canon Law Society of America, sent us unexpected but welcome support. As a group they did not pass on our decrees from the perspective of theology or practical wisdom but instead confined their judgment to the legal system of the Catholic Church. This letter was dated March 11, 1968:

> We have examined the contents of your decrees and have tried to evaluate them in the light of present legislation, in particular, the Code of Canon Law, the Decree on the Adaptation and Renewal of Religious Life from the Second Vatican Council, and the Motu Proprio Ecclesiae Sanctae which contains the norms for the implementation of the Council Decree.
>
> In our opinion, both the spirit and the explicit expression of your decrees are entirely within the law. We find nothing contrary to the norms of the Ecumenical Council in your chapter's recommendations. Quite the contrary, as canonists, we find in your deliberations and legislation a prompt, respectful compliance with the directions given by Pope Paul VI for the implementation of the Council Decree regarding the renewal of religious life. . . .
>
> Cordially yours in Christ,

Reverend Thomas L. Lynch, J.C.D.
   Vice-Chancellor, Archdiocese of Hartford
   President, Canon Law Society of America

---

[20] Sister Anita Caspary, I.H.M. Letter to IHM sisters, March 4, 1968. A/IHMCOM.

Reverend James C. McDonald, J.C.L.
   Vice-Chancellor, Diocese of LaCrosse
   Former Vice-President, C.L.S.A.
Rt. Rev. Msgr. John S. Quinn, J.C.D.
   Former President, C.L.S.A.
   Consultor to the Pontifical Commission for Revision of the Code
Reverend William W. Bassett, J.C.D.
   Faculty of Canon Law
   The Catholic University of America
Reverend James A. Coriden, J.C.D.
   Co-Chancellor, Diocese of Gary
   Former General Secretary-Treasurer, C.L.S.A.
Reverend Frederick R. McManus, J.C.D.
   Dean, School of Canon Law
   The Catholic University of America[21]

Some of the letters of support we received were less formal but equally encouraging, as, for example, the charming note that came much earlier from canon lawyer Father J. Elliott MacGuigan, S.J., of Regis College, Ontario, Canada, sent on November 21, 1967:

> Dear Sister Anita,
>
> . . . I have twice read the Decrees of the Ninth General Chapter . . . and I know them to be the best I have ever seen. And I shall use them as a model in my future apostolate with religious men and women. As I read them I was proud to know we had such intelligent and articulate church-women. May their tribe increase. I can hardly wait for Vat. III.
>
> In Christo,
>
> J. Elliott MacGuigan, S.J.[22]

Other groups of religious men related their own plans for renewal to ours and supported us as a community well before the publication of the "Four Points." Among them were the Jesuits of Loyola University, Los Angeles; the Jesuits of Alma College, Los Gatos; the Franciscans of Franciscan Theological Seminary, Santa Barbara; the Dominicans of the

[21] Father Thomas L. Lynch and others. Letter to Sister Anita Caspary, I.H.M., March 11, 1968. A/IHMCOM.
[22] J. Elliott MacGuigan, S.J. Letter to Sister Anita Caspary, I.H.M., November 21, 1967. A/IHMCOM.

Berkeley Priory; and the Christian Brothers of Mont La Salle. A three-page open letter sent by Father Robert Arrowsmith, S.J., of Loyola University in Los Angeles, was addressed to His Eminence Cardinal McIntyre and was signed by thirty Jesuit university faculty members, who said that the IHM decrees proposed "nothing contrary to sound doctrine and religious spirit" but contained "a genuine religious vitality which commands our respect as fellow religious."[23]

No sooner had the Jesuits' letter been received by His Eminence than he requested a meeting with them to be held the following day. The Jesuits went to the chancery office with the understanding that Cardinal McIntyre, while not approving of their position, would couch his disapproval in the language of diplomacy, perhaps even engaging in some civil theological discussion. What they found instead was a churchman who, after a perfunctory greeting, soon lost all control, quickly growing red in the face and shouting at them, "Why do you defend these women—they are bad women!" After what seemed an interminable period of ranting, the Jesuits left, shocked at what they had just witnessed.[24] When asked years later why the cardinal treated the Immaculate Heart Sisters so severely, one Jesuit who lived through those troubled times remarked that the IHMs had the misfortune of having their motherhouse in the cardinal's diocese. The Jesuits' headquarters were far removed.

The Franciscans from the Theological Seminary in Santa Barbara addressed their remarks in support of the IHM sisters to Dan Thrapp, religion editor of the *Los Angeles Times*. They used this forum to call attention to the lamentable distortion of truth in the local Catholic diocesan newspaper, *The Tidings*, which was viewed as the mouthpiece of the chancery office. The Franciscans took issue with the canard that it was the IHM sisters who "issued an ultimatum," while the chancery office maintained that the sisters "have not been dismissed." This ploy, the letter maintains, has had as its effect, if not in fact its purpose, the defaming of the sisters and the turning away of "the wrath of the parents . . . from the Archdiocese and onto the sisters. . . ." The letter was

[23] Robert Arrowsmith, S.J. Letter to Cardinal McIntyre, January 30, 1968. A photocopy was sent to Sister Anita Caspary, I.H.M. A/IHMCOM.

[24] Clinton Albertson, S.J., Ph.D., Oxon. Notes of interview by Fidelia Fleming Dickinson, December 19, 1997, Loyola-Marymount University, Los Angeles. I am grateful to Dr. Dickinson for this first-person account of the Jesuits' meeting with Cardinal McIntyre.

signed by ten of the priests and brothers who were faculty members at the seminary, four of whom were theology professors.[25]

Of particular importance was the support of women religious. Many communities became confused about their own future. Debates raged within individual orders; many members remained silent out of fear for their own institutions and their process of renewal. However, some were outstandingly courageous, such as Sister Francis Borgia Rothluebber of the School Sisters of St. Francis, who with fifteen major superiors of women in Milwaukee organized women religious of that region.[26] The sisters in the Los Angeles Archdiocese were particularly vulnerable, yet thirty women religious sent an open letter to Cardinal McIntyre speaking their truth to power. In this message they expressed their support of our efforts at renewal.[27] Of special note was the personal encouragement and involvement of Mother Mary Luke Tobin, major superior of the Sisters of Loretto, and Sister Helen Sanders, her assistant. These women championed our cause at the Vatican and sought to use their personal influence and power to intercede for us. Mother Mary Luke had attended the Second Vatican Council and understood well the Vatican bureaucracy.[28]

A Vatican Attempt to Control Public Opinion

In spite of the heartening of spirit these unsolicited letters gave us, the discouragement of the sisters was growing daily, and now some members, especially the younger ones, decided to leave religious life, plainly disheartened by what appeared to be an endless legalistic battle sapping the energies and enthusiasm of the community. They became further disillusioned, as indeed did the entire renewal-minded community, when we discovered that the Vatican's apostolic delegate, Luigi Raimondi, had on April 9, 1968, forwarded Cardinal Antoniutti's critical analysis of the IHM case to the chair of the Conference of Major Superiors of Women (CMSW), Mother M. Omer Downing, S.C. Raimondi

---

[25] Robert B. Pfisterer, O.F.M., and others. Letter to Dan Thrapp, religion editor, *Los Angeles Times*, February 1, 1968. Photocopy. A/IHMCOM.

[26] "15 Milwaukee superiors back IHMs," *National Catholic Reporter* (March 6, 1968) 6. Photocopy. A/IHMCOM.

[27] "30 L.A. sisters support IHMs," *National Catholic Reporter* (March 6, 1968) 6. Photocopy. A/IHMCOM.

[28] Mother Mary Luke Tobin, S.L. Letters to Anita Caspary, I.H.M. Personal files.

wrote, "It is the desire of the Holy See that it be brought to the attention of the religious communities of this country."[29] Because of its great importance to us and to all sisters engaged in renewal programs, but also because of the indignation stirred up among many major superiors, the apostolic delegate's letter to Mother Omer is included below.

One: The fundamental complaint underlying the protests recently lodged on behalf of the Sisters of the Immaculate Heart of Mary is really groundless: "The Sacred Congregation is blocking aggiornamento and is therefore against Vatican II."

Two: The genuine renewal as it is stated in the Decree *Perfectae Caritatis* (n. 2) must always be carried out "under the influence of the Spirit and the guidance of the Church."

The Decree *Perfectae Caritatis* (n. 4) and the *"Motu Proprio" Ecclesiae Sanctae* (n. 6) entrust to the religious Institutes the responsibility of carrying on the desired adaptation, but do not exempt the Holy See from the obligation of supervising, so that everything is accomplished in accordance with the Conciliar prescriptions. The Sacred Congregation which is responsible for the renewal of the religious Institutes (Reg. Eccl. N. 73, 5) has not only not blocked but rather has encouraged in every way, the orderly up-dating of the religious life, as can be attested by the many Communities which have sought its guidance and thus have first hand acquaintance with what it has done. At the same time, however, the Sacred Congregation must insist that the norms laid down by the Second Vatican Council be duly respected. It is on this point that, notwithstanding excellent intentions, some of the Immaculate Heart Sisters, and members of other Institutes, have been found wanting. Nowhere does the Council grant Religious unrestricted authority to experiment. Even the Special General Chapter is limited by the provisions of *Perfectae Caritatis* and *Ecclesiae Sanctae*.

Three: Regarding many of the innovations introduced by the Sisters of the Immaculate Heart of Mary, the Sacred Congregation has absolutely no objections and will be happy to approve them when such approval is necessary. For others, however, the Congregation reserves the right to give an answer in due time. Nevertheless,

[29] Archbishop Luigi Raimondi, Vatican apostolic delegate to the United States. Letter to members of the Conference of Major Religious Superiors of Women, April 9, 1968. Document no. 1068/68, 2: no. 4. A/IHMCOM. This document was sent with a cover letter by Mother Mary Omer, S.C., then president of the Conference of Major Religious Superiors of Women.

even at the present time, as the result of an Apostolic Visitation provoked by numerous appeals, the Sacred Congregation has deemed it its duty to intervene on the following basic points. . . .[30]

Four: It is surprising that such a wave of disedifying publicity has been stirred up around points which are not open to question, and that radio, press and television have been enlisted to publicize arguments which are devoid of objective foundation and which can only cause trouble. The appeals, letters, and petitions circulated on behalf of the Sisters of the Immaculate Heart of Mary give the impression of having been requested and solicited. Many of these present identical texts, along the lines of form letters, suggesting a campaign organized by one central office.

Five: Anyone who feels that the necessary and ardently desired renewal of the Religious Life can be built on the use of secular and worldly dress, on the elimination of community life, on subordination of the Religious Life to external activities, and on independence from the local Ordinary in the Apostolate, is falling into serious error and evidences an attitude basically contrary to that genuine renewal as is stated in *Perfectae Caritatis* (n. 2). One would be tempted to conclude that many of those who have undertaken to send letters, etc. have not read the Council decrees attentively or even the norms issued by the Holy See. One can only deplore tactics, which, even with all allowances made for good intentions, are objectively a distortion of facts creating confusion instead of providing genuine enlightenment.

It should be stated that the Sacred Congregation for Religious has likewise received very many letters from Sisters of different Institutes in the United States, spontaneously disapproving the campaign organized around the Immaculate Heart Sisters of Los Angeles, and have reaffirmed their complete accord with the directives of the Holy See, begging that their religious life be protected against unseemly innovations.

Six: All who are genuinely interested in the renewal of the Religious Life should weigh carefully the replies provided by the Sacred Congregation for Religious, and should strive to work toward genuine renewal in collaboration with all generous-minded Religious, carefully avoiding any measures which might cause scandal to the good and at the same time the best interests of the Church.

---

[30] Ibid. There follow the "Four Points." In the interest of brevity they are excluded here. See notes 11 and 15 above.

> This is not juridicism, but merely an attitude of respectful
> deference to the norms laid down by the Council and to the pas-
> toral discipline of the Church.[31]

When this communication was received around the country, virtually every sister, whether engaged in renewal programs or not, was
made aware of our case, in some details accurately and in others in-
accurately. Many responses to this letter were sent to Mother Omer,
to other major superiors, to the apostolic delegate, Archbishop Luigi
Raimondi, and to me as well. Those that I received were of course
highly indignant that our case had been used as the proverbial scapegoat for all such renewal efforts. Anger was focused on the misrepre-
sentations of our decrees and their purpose, at the Vatican attempt to
renege on the inspired promise of the documents of the Second Vatican
Council, and the backhanded manner of the attack against us. However, much to the surprise of many within and without Church circles,
a great resistance arose.

Resistance to Vatican Pressure

There were many excellent counters to this letter from Archbishop
Raimondi.[32] One of the most thorough and eloquent was written by the
major superior of the Sisters of Notre Dame de Namur, Sister Mary
Daniel Turner, who was provincial of her community at the time of this
struggle.[33] Later she served seven years as executive director of the
Leadership Conference of Women Religious, as the Conference of Major
Superiors of Women came to be called. Her next ministry was as su-
perior general of her international community, an office that took her to
Rome and the order's motherhouse in Belgium for six years.

In her letter Sister Mary Daniel forcefully and with an unusual di-
rectness toward Vatican authorities addressed the complexity of the
situation and the treatment given to us. For me, her letter summarized
the underlying substantive issues of our struggle: the use of power,
experimentation, and authority, and the concept of subsidiarity. She
wrote:

[31] Ibid.

[32] Sister Mary Daniel Turner, S.N.D. de N. Letter to Sister Anita Marie Caspary,
I.H.M., April 26, 1968. A/IHMCOM.

[33] Sister Mary Daniel Turner, S.N.D. de N. Letter to Archbishop Luigi Raimondi,
apostolic delegate to the United States, April 26, 1968. Photocopy. A/IHMCOM.

Before I address myself to the major contents of the letter, I must say I am embarrassed and ashamed that an official body within the Church could make public the quality of statements found in sections four (4) and five (5). . . . We who serve the Church as religious are saddened that however difficult and painful the present moment, the response for this particular Congregation is one so lacking in the Christian qualities of compassion, trust and dignity.[34]

One of the most problematic areas for Archbishop Raimondi was the public support for our struggle and the unwanted (and disedifying for him) publicity and protest this brought to the Catholic Church. Sister Mary Daniel challenged this interpretation.

The protest is basically about the Sacred Congregation's use of power [author's emphasis]. Why the Sacred Congregation chooses to use its power as it does, is not within my competency to judge. . . . Rather those who are troubled, are deeply so, because they question the use of power. . . . Publicity, wholesome or otherwise can also serve to sharpen the conscience of each of us. To indicate only one effect is to over-simplify the end results of mass media.[35]

In a very strong passage Archbishop Raimondi chastised those who equated the renewal of religious life with the adoption of secular dress, the elimination of community life, and an independence from the Ordinary of the diocese. For him this was a serious error and an attitude problem. On the contrary, Sister Mary Daniel argued that

experimentation with new forms, new expressions are critically needed. New forms of expressing these values are not indicative of a desire to eliminate community life. . . . There is a tension here between the authority of a congregation and the authority of the Holy See and of local Ordinaries. Only if we question in Christian love and truth, *when* and *how* [author's emphasis] the authority is used at each level, can we as People of God grow. Not to question is not to renew.[36]

Finally, she addresses the basic value in question—that of subsidiarity. A theological principle long held in Catholic thought, the principle of subsidiarity holds that individual persons and intermediate group-

[34] Ibid.
[35] Ibid.
[36] Ibid.

ings should be allowed and encouraged to assume responsibility for the common good. If possible, decisions that affect a group should be made by the group, in that way a model of shared responsibility and shared authority would exist. In her letter Sister Mary Daniel reflected on this principle in light of the renewal of religious life:

> Unless the nature of experiment is understood, appreciated and endorsed, the basic problem of the subsidiarity in this regard cannot be adequately handled. Moreover, unless women religious in particular, are respected as adults, as persons whose dignity demands that they be permitted to act according to a knowing and free choice and allowed to create structures that make choice possible (G.S. 17 and 24), no experimental programs are possible. Unless this basic respect is operating the Sacred Congregation could not permit the initiation of any experimental programs. It could not give to non-adults this kind of responsibility.
>
> I cannot say strongly enough that today's women do not see the approval of the Sacred Congregation as the ultimate criteria for determining whether or not a given form expresses a Gospel value. It is a body that should counsel, direct, guide and sanction. But women religious would hope that the counsel, guidance and sanctions are results of evaluations *after* experiments have been tried and not prejudgments made before experiments are undertaken.[37]

Sister Mary Daniel was not alone in her strong resistance to the arguments and tactics of the Vatican. Now that the Sacred Congregation for Religious had addressed its complaints in two documents by two Vatican authorities (Cardinal Antoniutti and Archbishop Raimondi), supporters answered using various means and media. One such ardent supporter was Sister Marie Augusta Neal, S.N.D. de N.[38] As director of research for the Conference of Major Superiors of Women, Sister Marie Augusta had conducted a survey of some 181,000 sisters in the United States in 1967. In this capacity she sent a detailed response in the form of a report to Cardinal Antoniutti, the author of the "Four Points" letter.

Sister Marie Augusta's survey and analysis of Catholic nuns are still unsurpassed by those of any other sociologist. With 135,000 respondents, her report provided insight both into the dilemma faced by

[37] Ibid.

[38] Sister Marie Augusta Neal, S.N.D. de N., director of the Conference of Major Superiors of Women Research. Letter to Anita Caspary, I.H.M., March 30, 1968. A/IHMCOM.

sisters everywhere and into the innovative spirit of renewal of the IHMs. In her position as a consultant to many religious orders of women and as director of the project for the Conference of Major Superiors of Women, Sister Marie Augusta emphasized the need for women religious to change, thus participating more in the creation of their lives. In her report to Cardinal Antoniutti, she stated:

> The increasing education of women, their more active roles in public life, the reduced time demand of the family and the accompanying freedom to participate in community life, have broadened the expectation of today's young women and increased their critical appraisal of the groups they will join and replace in the professional world, especially in the traditional fields of service. . . . Religious orders have felt this evaluative press in a manner similar to their secular counterparts. But religious orders have felt more than this.[39]

Her report stressed that religious women have trained today's youth, who are far more concerned with social reform and direct involvement in campaigns for peace, civil rights, and solutions to problems of poverty and injustice. These are the very same issues, she noted, "that made Pope John the beloved leader of the value-committed of the world," and which called for the assumption of personal responsibility "to initiate and to reform."[40]

As a competent sociologist trained at Harvard, Sister Marie Augusta reported that two actions on the part of the Sacred Congregation deeply disturbed her. The first was the command that all renewal decrees by religious orders be sent to the Vatican agency. This directive affected all Catholic orders in the world. The second was the specific restrictions placed on the Immaculate Heart Sisters of Los Angeles. In her report Neal explained, from a sociological perspective, her understanding of why we responded so rapidly to the call for renewal issued by the Catholic Church.

> In this study, one of the orders that stand out as richly aware of the directives of the Council and loyally eager to respond to them is

---

[39] Sister Marie Augusta Neal, S.N.D. de N. "Report to Cardinal Antoniutti," Boston, March 30, 1968. Photocopy, 1. A/IHMCOM. A copy of this report was sent to the author.

[40] Ibid., 2–3.

the Immaculate Heart Sisters. Not only did they stand out as genuinely aware and responsive to the Church's concerns and psychologically capable of mature response, but a number of other studies, like the college study of Father Andrew Greeley that is published this year, and the study done by a David Reisman and Christopher Jenks last year, also revealed these sisters as creatively sensitive to human needs today and caring more about servicing mankind in a Christ-like way than in preserving advantage for themselves, and this to a degree greater than most other groups of religious women.[41]

Sister Marie Augusta continued to extrapolate the implications[42] of her findings and the reaction of youth to the tactics of the Vatican. She wrote:

> Young people who half expected that the renewal would be withdrawn by some process are convinced that the response of the Sacred Congregation to the Immaculate Heart Sisters presages similar response to the decrees of any chapter. . . . They have seen and are scandalized by the easy use of character attack against this group of women who have been outstanding for their response in truly Christian ways to human need.[43]

Not surprisingly, perhaps, one of the most striking conclusions of Sister Marie Augusta's work was that "creative and initiating people enter religious orders that initiate, and timid people, fearful of the conditions of the world, enter religious orders that resist response to current world conditions."[44]

Sister Marie Augusta Neal, like a number of other prominent scholars and writers, foresaw long-lasting damage to the Church by the Sacred Congregation's failure of trust and its deferral to the most conservative forces in the Church. Father Andrew M. Greeley, a leading religious-sociologist then at the University of Chicago, phrased it in the starkest of terms:

---

[41] Ibid., 8–9.

[42] In his interview with Marshal H. Mercer on December 10, 1992, Bishop John J. Ward reaffirmed these qualities of the IHM sisters. He stated: "The Immaculate Heart Community was, without a doubt, one of the finest communities of women religious in the United States. . . . I tell you those sisters were among the finest women I have ever met. They were a prayerful group. They were devoted to the school. Just outstanding." Audio-cassette transcript, 42, 53.

[43] Sister Marie Augusta Neal. "Report to Cardinal Antoniutti," 7. A/IHMCOM.

[44] Ibid., 9.

> . . . the decision of the Congregation of Religious to support the
> reactionary Los Angeles chancery office in its battle with the Im-
> maculate Heart Sisters is one of the greatest tragedies in the history
> of American Catholicism. It will not destroy the Church in the
> United States if it is not revoked, but it could easily cripple it for
> the next century.[45]

The chancery office referred to was, of course, Cardinal McIntyre's,
one that Father Greeley noted "tried to resist every step of progress in
the Church in the last decade."[46]

The discouragement felt over how best to proceed was further
sharpened by the knowledge that by now Mother Omer Downing's reporting of the Sacred Congregation's reprimand of our renewal efforts
as well as their codification in the "Four Points" mandate was in every
religious community of the United States. If, as was formerly thought,
humility is taught by humiliation (which I do not believe), then we
should have been renamed the Humble Sisters of Doubtful Status at
this point. But more important, this letter was certain to crush the fine
spiritual impetus that had impelled so many religious women's communities to renew their rules and their lives.

Numerous theologians, educators, faculty members of Catholic
universities, and many others sent us letters of encouragement at this
juncture. Keen analysis of the IHM decrees from a theological and
canonical perspective was the subject of those letters; many of the
analyses were in answer to our request for an opinion regarding our
orthodoxy. We thought of such statements as possibly of use in our own
defense. Some others were unsolicited protests against the manner of
our treatment by hierarchical powers, which was frequently at this
point the subject of media accounts. To reproduce the contents of these
letters would consume many pages of this narrative.[47]

Of particular importance during this period of enthusiasm and
change was the public support we received from Bishop Remi De Roo,
bishop of Victoria, British Columbia. While we received many private
pledges of support from members of the hierarchy and religious men

---

[45] Rev. Andrew Greeley, "No Loss of Faith; But Confidence in Leadership Gone,"
Davenport Messenger (March 28, 1968) 10.

[46] Ibid.

[47] There were over two hundred articles, commentaries, and essays on our struggle
during this period. Letters of support numbered in the thousands. A/IHMCOM.

and women across the United States, Bishop De Roo publicly confronted the stance of Cardinal Antoniutti. He stated:

> I protest this interference with a pastoral matter in my diocese on which I have not been consulted. . . . This decision runs counter to the spirit of Vatican II, and the directives of Pope Paul VI. Moreover, it could adversely affect sisters throughout the world who are in the process of renewing their communities.[48]

He noted that the nuns wore a variety of secular dress, adding that there are some kinds of work "where the habit is not only an impediment but illegal." The IHM sisters

> wear a variety of dress and have taken on diverse apostolic work, such as working with children and families on an Indian reservation. There are many social problems, such as alcoholism and drug addiction, afflicting the Indians, and the sisters have to have flexibility to work in the manner they deem best.[49]

Commenting again on their need for flexibility in the horarium, Bishop De Roo said that it was "impossible for the nuns always to have religious services together, however much the Sisters themselves desire this."[50]

But not only priests and nuns showed their concern for the IHMs' modernization efforts. Catholic laity both in the Los Angeles Archdiocese and throughout the country who had followed the spirit of reform with Pope John XXIII's aggiornamento felt that the momentum for renewal would be lost if the Sacred Congregation's decision to quash experimentation in religious communities was allowed to stand. In 1968, shortly after the "Four Points" ruling was handed down in February, a groundswell of support from laity appeared. And "Project Petition," a drive to collect just five thousand signatures, was launched in the Los Angeles Archdiocese. The IHMs had disavowed any role in the petition drive. Its organizers, Sandra and Robert Strickland of Inglewood, Attorney John Thorpe, Sister Beverly White, B.V.M., and Columban priest Father Robert Brady (who was later recalled by his order for his part in

---

[48] "Fighting Nuns," *Newsweek* (April 1, 1968) 100.

[49] "Continue Experiments, Bishop Tells IHM Nuns," *The Catholic Virginian* (April 12, 1968) 10.

[50] Ibid.

the project), saw a sharp increase of signatures in the five weeks of the drive. By May 3, 1968, and with considerable media coverage, 25,556 signatures had been gathered, of which 16,401 were lay Catholics, 2008 were nuns of different religious orders, 1,195 were priests and brothers, 4,146 were members of other religious denominations, and 1,806 gave no religious affiliation. The signatures, along with a petition asking the Pope "to protect and encourage" the nuns in their modernization experiments, were sent to the Holy Father.[51]

Once again, despite the unusual support from so many and from such widely different sources both within and without the Church, there was no change in the Sacred Congregation's decision. Yet through it all the IHM sisters experienced their own renewed spiritual growth; daily they had to wrestle with challenges to their spirit of charity, hope, and courage, and even of faith, as the institution of the Church, their mainstay for the length of their religious lives, seemed indifferent at best and prohibitive at worst. In addition, a grace of deep friendship was forged among members of the community, greater than had ever existed in my experience. One could say that it was at this juncture that we became firmly supportive of one another—the very goal of the IHM decree on community. Many letters from sisters of other communities who had read the gratuitous communication from the Sacred Congregation (as an example of the fate of disobedience to proper authority) expressed honest indignation that Catholic sisters should have so little respect shown to them.[52]

Through my membership in the Conference of Major Superiors of Women, I realized that there were a growing number of major superiors who were sympathetic to our cause and willing to help us. Among the mothers general who were particularly supportive of our kind of renewal efforts were these: Sister Roberta Kuhn, B.V.M., Mount Carmel, Dubuque, Iowa; Sister M. Luke Tobin, S.L., Loretto Motherhouse, Nerinx, Kentucky; Mother Thomas Aquinas (later known as Elizabeth Carroll), R.S.M., Pittsburgh, Pennsylvania; Sister Anthonita Hess, C.Pp.S., Dayton, Ohio; Sister Bernadine Pieper, C.H.M., Ottumwa, Iowa;

---

[51] John Dart, "25,000 Sign Petition Backing Nuns 'Updating,'" *Los Angeles Times* (May 3, 1968) II:1–2. See "U.S. top crust protests IHM decision to pope," *National Catholic Reporter* (April 17, 1968) 4. Over 190 prominent educators, theologians, and Church laity sent a letter to Pope Paul VI supporting us. The petitions were sent to Pope Paul VI on May 22, 1968.

[52] "3,000 sisters support IHM's," *National Catholic Reporter* (March 27, 1968) 3.

Sister Francis Borgia Rothluebber, S.S.S.F., Milwaukee, Wisconsin; Sister Bernadette Vetter, H.M., Sisters of the Holy Humility of Mary, Villa Maria, Pennsylvania; Sister M. William Murphy, P.B.V.M., San Francisco, California; Mother M. Magdalen Martin, O.P., Racine, Wisconsin; and Mother M. Benedicta Brennan, I.H.M., Sisters, Servants of the Immaculate Heart of Mary, Monroe, Michigan.

On these women I called as a last resort, requesting them to accompany me to the Vatican to place the complicated situation in which we found ourselves directly before Pope Paul VI. I hoped that we could ask him to consider the harm that would be done to the vitality and courage of all American sisterhoods if the "Four Points" were to be unreservedly enforced. The fact that by this time many orders of religious women had gone far beyond the "Four Points" in their renewal made us feel that the Vatican must be out of touch with the ability of American women to make decisions about their personal lives for themselves. They could no longer be intimidated by a few harsh words or even by threats that seemed unreal. They were educated for the most part, able to make a living, efficient, and concerned to serve where there was present need rather than cling to a dead past. Many who saw no alternative had already left their communities, and others would continue to do so.

The women whom I had asked to accompany me agreed—all of them—to this rather risky project. Arrangements were made and reservations confirmed for our small but highly representative delegation of women. We were to meet in New York and fly directly to Rome. But all was to be done in strict confidence. I slept uneasily until very early on that day, March 29, 1968, selected for our departure, when my mind was shaken into consciousness by the sharp ring of the telephone on my nightstand. I heard the voice of a friendly prelate who had been advised of our plans. He suggested that we cancel our plans to go to Rome immediately as a new turn of events had taken place. He was not free to divulge the development to which he referred, but he felt that it would be more helpful than our direct appeal to the Vatican.

My decision had to be made instantaneously. The mothers general who were going to Rome would be leaving for New York in a matter of hours. What should I do? What further development could we expect? The cleric had intimated that our delegation would not be welcome in Rome at this time. Personally, I was told I was persona non grata at the Vatican and should not attempt to accompany my supporters when they went to see the Holy Father.

I took my list of the ten mothers general and decided to tell them to cancel the trip for the moment. I phoned for several hours in the early morning, propped against my pillow, not daring to take time to rise and dress until all the mothers general knew the situation.

The Pontifical Commission: Another Visitation

While I was still completing the phone calls, a special delivery letter dated March 29, 1968, arrived from the apostolic delegate announcing that the Immaculate Heart Sisters were to be investigated by a pontifical commission consisting of three American bishops: Most Reverend James V. Casey, D.D., archbishop of Denver, consultant to the Pontifical Commission for the Revision of the Code of Canon Law and president of the commission; Most Reverend Thomas A. Donnellan, D.D., archbishop-designate of Atlanta and chairman of the Bishops' Liaison Committee for the Conference of Major Superiors of Men; and Most Reverend Joseph Breitenbeck, D.D., auxiliary bishop of Detroit and chairman of the Bishops' Liaison Committee for the Conference of Major Superiors of Women. The fourth member of this pontifical commission was our previous visitator, Very Reverend Thomas R. Gallagher, O.P.[53] This, then, was the new turn of events!

The news seemed to indicate that the Vatican preferred to settle the case on this side of the Atlantic, where worldwide repercussions were less likely. Actually, the case had become a focus of intense interest beyond the United States, but the hierarchy had not yet understood the new interest in self-determination. Was this the new turn of events mentioned by the friendly message? Was it good or bad? We would soon know, I thought.

The IHM sisters were unimpressed by the grandiose titles announcing the pontifical commission. One more visitation could hardly affect them anymore. The first visitations by local priests, and then by Father Gallagher held some measure of fear, as few sisters cared to harm the community by careless words. But we had come a long way since those days—just two years ago. We were not being accused of simple imprudent actions or words but of the charge that our whole carefully thought-out decrees were not only worthless but harmful to the Church and to religious life.

---

[53] Archbishop Luigi Raimondi, apostolic delegate to the United States. Letter to Sister Anita Caspary, I.H.M., March 29, 1968. A/IHMCOM.

In the spring of 1968 we awaited the next extraordinary visitation. The dates are etched in my mind: May 4 to May 7, 1968. Because of the national attention given to our case, the members of the pontifical commission spent some time preparing for their visit. They seemed to have studied the issues carefully and consulted with various parties, both prelates and sisters from other communities. They had already met with Cardinal McIntyre on the occasion of the National Conference of Catholic Bishops that spring in St. Louis. In addition, they invited the participation of a group of twelve mothers general, six provincial superiors, and four sisters who were well versed in religious life to a two-day conference in Detroit.

At this meeting "the upgrading of the status of women was explicitly linked with the rising tension between the Roman hierarchy and American sisters. One speaker noted that there were segments of both society and church for whom the 'upgrading of women is so threatening that they will fight against the changes being introduced in religious life.'"[54]

As the next step of their investigation the pontifical commission arrived in Los Angeles, checked into their hotel rooms in Santa Monica, had dinner with Cardinal McIntyre, received copies of the IHM decrees, and after arranging a meeting with the elected chapter members for early the next day, arrived at the motherhouse on May 4, 1968. The bishops met with me in my office, chatting in friendly fashion.

Archbishop Casey of Denver, as the ranking prelate on the commission, was its chair, a man of fairly short stature, white-haired, serious and dignified. Archbishop-designate Donnellan of Atlanta was an Irish cleric, square-jawed, with a ruddy complexion, and a tendency to make assured pronouncements; he was officially appointed archbishop shortly after the commission's business ended. Bishop Joseph Breitenbeck of Grand Rapids, Michigan, had a national reputation of being understanding and sympathetic to religious women attempting renewal. Despite a bad back problem that troubled him most of his life, he was patient and kind. Long after the commission's business was concluded, the sisters whose duty it was to serve the prelates lunch and dinner in the motherhouse's special dining room for guests remembered his gentle, thoughtful ways. He was the single member of the

[54] Sister Lora Ann Quiñonez, C.D.P., and Sister Mary Daniel Turner, S N D, de N., *The Transformation of American Catholic Sisters* (Philadelphia: Temple University Press, 1992) 106.

commission who seemed regretful of the position thrust upon him. The fourth member, Father Thomas R. Gallagher, who was already well-known to us, maintained his inscrutable, cool demeanor.

The bishops and Father Gallagher went to the Immaculate Heart High School library to talk at length to the chapter members assembled there. Later that afternoon they came to my office and continued their light conversation and questions. Archbishop Casey then arranged for the next day's meeting with the entire community, except for our Canadian members. All day long the sisters from other parts of the state would arrive and be given a meeting time. At each of these hourly meetings of sisters, all three bishops and Father Gallagher, dressed in their dark suits and seated solemnly in front of small groups of sisters, would ask broad, open-ended questions, attempting to gain overall impressions rather than the answers to factual questions. Some of the sisters taped the exchanges for future consultation and sharing.

After their three days of meetings in small groups, the commission members announced that they had not yet reached a conclusion and would return in June to conclude their work, but they hinted that perhaps we had gone too far too fast; they were careful, however, not to condemn us. So we allowed ourselves to hope that all might still turn out favorably.

Upon concluding their follow-up visit on June 4, the commission members returned to their hotel. There they conferred and issued their judgment in a letter dated June 6, 1968. They stated that for practical purposes, and while a final decision from the Holy See was still pending, the commission would officially recognize the internal separation of the two groups of the Immaculate Heart Sisters. Thus they ordered two separate groups, each empowered to act separately. The first and larger group, under my leadership, was to be given some time "to experiment, to reflect, and to come to definite decisions concerning their rule of life to be submitted to the Holy See."[55]

The second group, temporarily under Sister Eileen MacDonald, was to live under the pre-conciliar IHM constitution. Maintaining a pre-1967 lifestyle, they could proceed with their own program of renewal if they wished and could contract agreements regarding the schools with diocesan authorities. In the same letter Archbishop Casey directed that all personal files, personal moneys, and stocks belonging to the

[55] Archbishop James V. Casey. Letter to Sister Anita Caspary, I.H.M., June 2, 1969. A/IHMCOM.

minority group were to be given to Sister Eileen. Further, the sisters were to be polled as to which group they wanted to join; transfer of members between the groups, however, was to be accomplished *only* when both Sister Eileen and I agreed to it. And assurance was given that identification of membership with either group was not to be considered irrevocable.

When the sisters were individually polled as to which group they wanted to join, 455 members, whose average age was thirty-six, indicated that they wished to follow the decrees of 1967 as members of the larger group in our experimental renewal process. Sister Eileen MacDonald's group, numbering some fifty-one members, with an average age of sixty-two, chose to follow the constitution in effect before the Chapter of Renewal.

After the pontifical commission had issued the decree of June 6, feelings between the two groups living under one roof made for a condition even more difficult than before. And so the chapter members who represented the larger group addressed a request to the pontifical commission that the members of the smaller group, who were unwilling to follow the renewal decrees or the authority of the duly elected officers of the larger community, be given separate living quarters so that peaceable daily living might be realized. In short, this petition, dated July 16, 1968, asked for "a definitive canonical separation" so that "steps toward achieving it and also a financial and legal settlement . . . [might] begin immediately."[56] No answer to this request was received at this time.

Once again we sought to ascertain how the Sacred Congregation for Religious intended to respond to the first apostolic visitation of Father Gallagher in January, 1968, as well as to the visitation of the pontifical commission from May 4 to May 7, 1968. We wrote to Father Gallagher, as the apostolic visitator, requesting a copy of the results of his visitation. He responded by saying that the apostolic visitation had not been concluded and that all reports would have to be communicated to us by the Sacred Congregation for Religious in Rome. Our request had been prompted by our desire to know exactly what the charges against us might be, since we felt uneasy after the inconclusive visit of the pontifical commission. The permission to continue experimentation did not leave us in a peaceful state of mind. Perhaps our level of trust had

---

[56] Sisters of the Immaculate Heart of Mary, Los Angeles. Petition to the pontifical commission, July 16, 1968. A/IHMCOM.

been lowered by each succeeding visitation; perhaps we had seen too often that the promises from the Vatican Council sessions had been diminished by successive pronouncements; perhaps we were just waiting for the next curial shoe to drop.

Adding to our unease were the many Roman Catholics outside the community who criticized our explanation of the changes, which perhaps had not been as clearly enunciated as they might have been. Others were very frightened and ambivalent about our choices. One group that struggled mightily with our case was the Conference of Major Superiors of Women. At a meeting of the Conference of Major Superiors of Women held in St. Louis in 1969, with some five hundred sisters in attendance, a resolution of support for the Immaculate Heart of Mary Sisters was proposed. Much lively discussion ensued, until Father Edward Heston, C.S.C., representing the Sacred Congregation for Religious, took the floor, telling the members not to pass the resolution and to cease the debate.[57]

Sister Angelita Myerscough, Ad.PP.S., and Sister Elizabeth Carroll, R.S.M., vice president of the conference, who were among the debaters in favor of the resolution, argued that Father Heston's intervention was out of line and continued the debate. Sister Elizabeth Carroll was herself well known for her active interest in religious women's renewal programs. She had taken a very strong position in her own part of the country, Region 4, presenting a resolution against the abuses being suffered by communities of women as a result of the policies and actions of the Sacred Congregation. In fact, it was on this platform that she was elected vice president of the Conference of Major Superiors of Women with full right of succession to the office of the president the following year.[58]

Sister Elizabeth Carroll spoke forcefully in defense of the Immaculate Heart Sisters, saying that we were the scapegoat of the renewal movement of women religious, and although the majority of superiors present voted for the resolution, the final vote, requiring a two-thirds majority, failed by a fraction of one point. We were gratified, however, by the large proportion of major superiors of women's orders who had expressed their support for us.[59]

[57] Quiñonez and Turner, *The Transformation of American Catholic Sisters,* 153.
[58] Ibid.
[59] See Sister Elizabeth Carroll, R.S.M., "Reaping the Fruits of Redemption," *Midwives of the Future,* ed. Sister Ann Patrick Ware, S.L. (Kansas City, Mo.: Leaven Press, 1985) 64–65.

On the other hand, there was much misunderstanding about our situation. There was little parish education in the Archdiocese of Los Angeles regarding the changes of the Second Vatican Council. The new understanding of the Church itself was not common knowledge among Los Angeles Catholics, even though the Second Vatican Council had been convened by John XXIII some five years earlier. Thus we seemed to many good parishioners, especially in our local area, to be disobedient, disloyal, and rebellious instead of self-determining women who hoped to serve more effectively as adult members within the fold.

To see a sister follow her conscience in stating that obedience to God might supersede obedience to immediate hierarchical authority was scandalizing to some sincere Catholics. The concept of obedience they followed was literal, uncritical, and placed the burden of decision-making on authority, not on the individual. What many Catholics failed to realize was that the primacy of the individual conscience meant that single-minded, blind submission to the will of one's superior and mere execution of his or her orders did not in themselves constitute perfection of the vow of obedience.

We ourselves had not fully understood, I think, that to disagree respectfully with higher authority was a service, not a matter of shame for the person, the community, the church. One of the many editorials written about us sometime later called us the "Sisters of the Loyal Opposition" and examined this idea, noting the toll that such a stance takes on groups of sincere women in the Church:

> . . . the order's life has been strained by the conflict with the Vatican. Originally, more than 480 sisters voted to remain in the progressive experiment, but meanwhile 100 have left and 32 others have decided to leave the religious life altogether. About 50 plan to continue a traditional community discipline under official recognition. But more than 300 I.H.M. nuns have retained their solidarity under the stress of ecclesiastical disobedience for the sake of their common vision of a renewed community of apostolic service encompassing a diversity of life styles.[60]

And in spite of the loss of some of its members to disappointment, even to disillusionment, the editorial continues, the community still displayed a strong commitment to its new vision, even while the controversy over the IHM case swirled around them.

[60] "Sisters of the Loyal Opposition," *The Christian Century* (February 18, 1970) 2.

Neither Protestant opportunists nor Catholic cop-outs will find all they are looking for in this story. What is most impressive about these sisters is not their rebelliousness but their determination to retain their Christian identity. "We are not leaving the church," says Sister Caspary, "but new forms, new styles, are called for in every age. In this way we may actually be of greater service to the church in the long run." It is not the sisters' disobedience that overwhelms: it is their patience in the face of an unrenewed cardinal and an uptight Vatican which won't give consistent support to the forces of renewal.[61]

Despite the lack of support from the original center of renewal, the hierarchy of the Church, the sisters had an awareness of the many other communities of women who faced a similar struggle. Here the editorial quoted my concern: "It is important that other communities do not feel we let them down by opting out. This is not a point of despair, but of new hope." And the editor's final comment restored for many hope in the future: "This is, all told, a stirring epic of what the gospel is all about."[62]

---

[61] Ibid.
[62] Ibid.

Chapter 13

A Test Case for the Vatican

By this time our difficulties as a community with the renewal process were very well known throughout the country. There was strong interest on the part of the media as well as the Catholic public as the controversy heated up. One author, Margaret Rowe, captured the essence of our problem in an article entitled "A Test Case for Renewal,"[1] in which our attempts to experiment with new forms of religious life were placed in the context of other orders that had revised their constitutions or had already begun experimenting.[2]

Most renewal-minded religious men and women, Rowe noted, seemed to be "solidly behind the IHM sisters' enlightened attitude to renewal," and evidence of wide support was provided by group letters, meetings, editorials, and thousands of signatures. Jesuit theology professors in California praised the IHM decrees as "a splendid response to the call for renewal and adaptation of religious life" and were particularly supportive of their "acceptance of shared responsibility, adoption of the principle of subsidiarity, and even more the explicit norms for making these ideals a reality."[3] While another group of Jesuits dissociated themselves from these theology professors' commendations, other orders of both men and women spoke highly of the IHMs' efforts. Women superiors of fifteen different major religious orders in the Archdiocese of Milwaukee, for example, praised our commitment to quality

[1] Margaret Rowe, "A Test Case for Renewal," *Herder Correspondence* 5, no. 5 (May 1968) 155–156.

[2] Ibid., 155. Among those religious orders that had revised their constitutions was the School Sisters of St. Francis, whose superior general was Sister Francis Borgia Rothluebber. Their revised constitution was praised as "inspiring."

[3] Ibid.

education in the education decree,[4] the decree that had so irritated Cardinal McIntyre when he used the term "your high-grade community" derisively.[5]

Indeed, men and women throughout the country, particularly those engaged in the Church's mission, Rowe noted, were aroused by this conflict because it was recognized that this small congregation, so desirous of spiritual renewal as "to have grasped the nettle so far avoided by the major orders," was not a group of "misfits and malcontents, but of dedicated women who sincerely want to involve themselves totally in the service of Christ and their fellow-[men]."[6] In addition to the nationwide petition being circulated about this time, we had received some two thousand individual letters of support while we awaited the Vatican's final decision.

But while the controversy, on the part of both supporters and critics, swept back and forth across the country, the Immaculate Heart Sisters prepared to convene the second session of their 1967 General Chapter, at which the now-famous renewal decrees had been unanimously approved. But now a year later, in the summer of 1968, no one was quite sure what would come of those decrees. Still, the sister delegates had committed themselves to this new session and now had to face even more complex questions. The first such problem, namely the issue of the "Four Points" that Cardinal Antoniutti has sent through Father Gallagher as constituting religious life, was in a sense unanswerable. It was tacitly agreed by the delegates to delay an answer about our decision to remain technically "religious," with the hope that time would bring a happier resolution.

And there were other questions. Our decrees, with the notable exception of the section on education, were considered by ourselves as laying the groundwork, or structural outlines, for our renewal. Should more specifics be stated immediately? Should the time of experiment be stated more exactly so that sisters unused to the degree of freedom now advocated would feel more security?

And what of our ministry? Should the sisters be employed only in projects blessed by the Church? Was it true, as we had thought, that

---

[4] Ibid.

[5] IHM General Council meeting with Cardinal McIntyre and advisors. Notes of meeting October 16, 1967. Archives of the Immaculate Heart Community (hereafter referred to as A/IHMCOM).

[6] Rowe, "A Test Case for Renewal," 156.

"every humanizing work is, consciously or unconsciously, a Christian work"?[7] What of our living situations? If there is choice for sisters to live alone, in small groups, with relatives, or in large complexes, how is communal life sustained? After our years of security and certainty, might we become a group of women scattered in living situations and occupations, no longer following a common schedule, held together only by memories of the past and a weak hope of a new kind of unity—a unity of spirit and goals not yet fully enunciated? Could we, would we, persist in our diversity and still grow into a community? Was our continued existence as a community defined as a "quality of relationships," actually livable or a mere abstraction? Was individual fulfillment, in the sense of strengthening each one's search for God, really attainable by our renewal process? Was a leading objective of the religious renewal—"to give greater value to a person as an individual"[8]—really going to be recognized by the post-conciliar Vatican, as Father Elio Gambari of the Sacred Congregation of Religious believed?[9]

All these concerns and others spoke of a need for a second session of the Ninth General Chapter, whose agenda would be the "institutional" aspects of the community. For this session we asked the help of Dr. Elizabeth Jean Bluth, a sociologist who had followed our community's changes with great interest. She was a professor at Immaculate Heart College and a close friend of many of the sisters. She understood the paradoxical nature of building an authority system reflecting accurately the ideals and values of the decrees.

Dr. Bluth visualized a Center for the Study of Religion for the training of new members as well as for the updating of others. Similar "centers"

---

[7] See Appendix D, p. 248.

[8] Sister Lora Ann Quiñonez, C.D.P., and Sister Mary Daniel Turner, S.N.D. de N., *The Transformation of American Catholic Sisters* (Philadelphia: Temple University Press, 1992) 13.

[9] As early as 1958, Father Elio Gambari, S.M.M., advisor to Pope Pius XII, had given an address to the Fourth Annual Institute for Sisters on the adaptation of religious to the modern world, in which he expressed this concept which was to inform a new perspective on obedience: "No one today will any longer accept the idea of acting without awareness of what he is doing, merely because he has been told to act thus by authority. Each person wants to know his own obligations and to understand wherefrom his duty derives. Consequently, the movement to renew religious life must start by giving to religious a personal and well-founded knowledge and awareness of the theological aspects of the religious state." "Religious Women and the Apostolate in the Modern World," *Sister Formation Bulletin* 5 (Summer, 1959) 3.

open to a wide public would be set up within the living groups of the community, thus allowing participation in the Immaculate Heart spirit beyond the boundaries of the older parish concept.

For many reasons, including lack of trained personnel, the "Center" concept was doomed to fail at this point in time. However, the community saw the appointment in 1967 of area coordinators, who helped greatly to fill the difficult role of communication among all the members, many of whom were still adrift in totally new and sometimes unexpected circumstances. By unceasing travel and devotion to their work, the coordinators in pairs tried to keep communal goals alive in groups of convents. "At their group meetings, the coordinators explained their functions and asked for questions. Most encouraging was the interest in communal prayer in the form of group meditation, Scripture reading or something similar." As Sister Mary Charles Schaffer noted at the time in her letter to the convents, "We could have some good things happen if these work out." And so, as she observed, the sisters were being "very trusting in the hand of God in the whole matter."[10]

For the great majority of IHM sisters, the great change in their lives took place on June 30, 1968, when those who had kept their belief in the value of the renewal decrees were made to withdraw, as Cardinal McIntyre had requested, as teaching sisters from parochial schools in the Los Angeles Archdiocese. In some other dioceses in California and in Canada, however, many of the sisters continued to teach in Catholic schools, but under the rubrics of the new chapter decrees, including a more flexible horarium and secular dress. Those sisters who had been teaching at schools owned and staffed by the IHM sisters, such as Immaculate Heart High School and College, also continued their apostolate under the new chapter decrees. But for the many members of the community who had to vacate their schools at the end of the 1967–68 school year, the transitional period was hectic.

There was, first of all, the painful closing of schools, entailing a final meeting, in the case of secondary institutions, with their student bodies, faculty, and parish representatives, often including the priests who served in the parish or who taught in the school. The superior and principal of one of the largest elementary schools in Los Angeles County, Sister Maria Socorro Meza, told of the day her sisters had to

---

[10] Sister Mary Charles Schaffer, I.H.M. Letter to all the IHM sisters who were studying for degrees outside the Los Angeles area, October 26, 1967. A/IHMCOM.

bid farewell to their pupils at St. Luke's in Temple City. Nine-hundred students and their parents, along with the school's sixteen faculty members, assembled in St. Luke's Church on the occasion of their last graduation. The sisters and their pupils loved their school very much, and the audience was unnaturally quiet during the ceremony. But at the end everyone, it seemed, was crying—parents, teachers, students. The beloved pastor, Father John Birch, whom many of those present had known as students and participants in the Catholic Youth Organization activities that he directed, could not find it in himself to be present. Socorro Meza (formerly Sister Maria Socorro) remembers it as one of the saddest days of her life.

One long-time community member, Noreen Naughton (formerly Sister Mary Noreen), was principal of Cathedral Chapel elementary school in the 1967–68 school year. As part of the ongoing community-wide oral history project undertaken by Doris Murphy (formerly Sister Mary Peter), Noreen recounts her experience.

> We were informed by our Mother General, as well as by our local pastor, that the Sisters must be out of Cathedral Chapel school and convent by June 30, 1968. Once school was out and the children (and parents) had all gone, we had two weeks to put everything in move-in condition. All school records and files were to be put in order, which meant reviewing and updating them; everything in both school and convent, such as equipment, supplies, dishes, etc. must be inventoried and labeled. During this time, parents and pupils stopped by with farewells and reassurances, and the phone seemed never to stop ringing. What seemed most pressing at this time was the thought of finding employment in the next school year just two months away. Resumes had to be sent out, phone calls made, and we all had to start house or apartment hunting.
>
> So, at the age of 50, like so many others, I found myself with no money and no credit. What was worse, we seemed not to be able to get any credit, because we had had to close the Immaculate Heart Sisters' account that our Cathedral Chapel salaries had gone into. The most reasonable rental we could find in the area of the Mother-house, which would accommodate five of us, went for the unimaginable sum of $400.00 a month. How in the world could we come up with that kind of money, we wondered. Then help came. My brother, who worked at a bank in the area, signed for each of the five of us to get the bank's credit cards.
>
> With the help of a loan and credit cards, we moved on July 1 into the three bedroom house on Seventh Street, and called it

Shalom House. Next we applied for our drivers' licenses. Two of us soon found teaching jobs in East Los Angeles schools right away. As a matter of fact, all personnel in the Los Angeles Public School system had respect for the IHMs. The head of Adult Education said the Sisters had such rich backgrounds, he didn't know where best to use us. In September, I had 30 hours a week of teaching, including two night classes a week; I taught there at Garfield High for seven years. Two others in our "house of peace" went back to school to complete their degrees so that they would be employable. Those of us who had jobs each contributed to the general pot. We had to budget very carefully for food, rent, utilities, transportation, and other costs. Another important thing was for each member to take personal responsibility for belonging to a relatively small "prayer group," so that we reinforced the sense of community. Through it all, I had great devotion to the Holy Spirit: He was leading, directing us. If we didn't change, I thought, we won't have vocations in ten years. So we must change. And at the end of that long year, we could look back and know that we could do it.[11]

Many of the IHMs, I think, felt a certain ambivalence toward the necessity for such dramatic change. There were, of course, all the frightening uncertainties of the new life that was about to begin. There was Sister Paula Kraus, for example, who had entered the community in 1932 and had spent the greater part of her religious life teaching in schools in Canada and northern California, far from the motherhouse. When she was asked years later how she felt then about starting over, she said: "I had a question about whether we could remain together. But I chose to go with the community because I felt that even if we went down, we would be making an important statement . . . [about] religious life, the church and the world."[12]

For Gloria Kolarik, who was a delegate at the 1967 Chapter of Renewal, the talks at times were "scary" but at the same time exciting, for "the door was opening." As she looked back, she felt that the restrictions of earlier days were often needless. She commented specifically on the habit as a "period piece," adding that she always felt it restricted understanding by non-Catholics. She quickly obtained a position as personnel director for the community, set up a telephone tree and a

[11] Noreen Naughton, I.H.M. Interview by Sister Doris Murphy, I.H.M. Tape recording, October [n.d.], 1988. A/IHMCOM.

[12] Ursula Vils, "An Experimental Religious Community," *Los Angeles Times* 4 (July 9, 1974) 1.

newsletter, and alerted sisters to job openings in Los Angeles public schools.[13]

But it was also true that to start life over held a certain fascination—adopting a new name (often returning to their original baptismal name[14]), going about dressed in a new[15] way (almost incognito, some said), free to do things differently, to be someone new. The awkward situation in which many sisters found themselves, more or less starting their outward lives over, brought forth innumerable kindnesses from friends and secular colleagues. The wife of the chairman of the Immaculate Heart College board, Polly Plesset, for example, personally outfitted several nuns from her own wardrobe. Mary Mark Zeyen, vice president of the college at that time, still remembers the pleasure she felt when Polly's pink suit actually fit her. For others, like Sister Martin Augustine (now Theresa DiRocco), who was studying for her master's degree in Indiana University's Opera Program, the change of clothing produced unexpected results for the university audience: as a requirement for the degree, she was to perform in four recitals in that transitional year—the first two she gave in her sister's blue and black habit, the second two in street clothes.

Many of the elderly and infirm sisters identified with the new community, not an easy decision for them. Some, like Sister Mary Austin, born in England, was in her nineties when she decided to keep her habit but otherwise adopted the new proposals. There could be no doubt that she wished to have her last reward sooner rather than later. Community members recall that when any elderly member died, Sister Austin would go up to the coffin, walk around it, and finally up to the sanctuary, where she would raise her small fist toward the tabernacle and say loudly, "You forgot me again!" And so each of the sisters dealt with the change in different ways, but always with the hope and belief that it would all come out right.

By far the biggest challenge for those who had served in Catholic schools for twenty, thirty, forty, or even fifty years was job-hunting. Fortunately for many in Los Angeles and nearby areas, the reputation

[13] Gloria Kolarik. Interview by Doris Murphy, I.H.M. Tape recording, February 10, 1997. A/IHMCOM.

[14] Many IHM sisters held similar feelings to those expressed by Sister Mary Charles in a letter she wrote to the sisters living outside the motherhouse. [It was] "sort of imperative to have a feminine name now. " She took the name of Sister Mary Schaffer. Letter, October 26, 1967:1. A/IHMCOM.

[15] By 1967, however, the great majority of sisters wore secular clothes.

of Immaculate Heart College as a teacher-training institution and the shortage of instructors in the area made the search for teachers in the public school systems easier for community members. And the community members were encouraged by the moral support they found among secular colleagues, principals, and parents of public school students. Using the leadership experience acquired in the educational apostolate, some became directors of programs within the public school system. Others worked in adult education, teaching evening classes.

Those who felt that they did not have a vocation to be teachers in the Immaculate Heart Community ventured into new work in which they felt they could be just as effective as in a classroom. Some members were employed in adult religious programs; some did ethnic studies followed by social work; some joined the Peace Corps; some worked with mentally or physically handicapped; some became hospital administrators. One sister, a professional musician, left her classroom to return to playing second cello in the Los Angeles Philharmonic Orchestra. Slowly, out of all the uncertainty and threats, a new idea of religious life began to develop, and with it a new Immaculate Heart Community began to form itself by the faith, courage, and initiative of its members. Those sisters who felt that their vocation to the religious life and teaching in a Catholic school were synonymous left the archdiocese. Some of these suffered a vocational crisis that led to eventual departure from the IHM Community. A number of the very young sisters, alarmed at the uncertainties of the future, left the community when their schools closed.

Before the second session of the Ninth General Chapter closed in 1968, a representative assembly (or chapter) composed of delegates to be elected by January 1969 was planned for that summer. In February 1969 I was elected for a second term by a new method, a printed and secret ballot with full community participation, rather than the customary election by delegates. This term was limited to four years instead of the traditional six-year period, a condition for which I was personally very grateful.

The nomination for this second term brought me much soul-searching and anguish. I was physically tired and discouraged and had to pray daily not to become bitter or cynical. Cynics, it is said, are really disappointed lovers. That sentence kept echoing in my heart. I loved Christ, the Church, the community, the mission; the best of my young energies had been poured into their service. Also, as a sister I had received the special benefits of higher education; I loved to teach, and I wanted to help others.

So, through the years of my teaching, studying, counseling, and administration, I had continued to love my community and had tried to find ways to reconcile my inner conflict between the life of work and the life of prayer. The rejection of our decrees by Cardinal McIntyre, I felt, was only to be expected. But we were deeply hurt by the fact that these decrees, expressive of the new, widened, and deepened spirituality, were openly and harshly challenged by the hierarchy as not proper for "religious."

To allow my name to be placed on the ballot for a second term meant to face the charges of being "not truly religious" once again. To be unable to complete my second term would lead to the charge that the decrees, once in practice, were unlivable or that, in the minds of some, God might be displeased with the Immaculate Heart Sisters and their renewal program. My closest friends and my family were urging me not to be a candidate for the office, for they knew that my internal struggle was beginning to show, and they feared for me and for my health. I felt myself growing irritable and was at times depressed.

Yet our board of directors (formerly known as the IHMs' General Council), in December 1968, had already discussed with Archbishop Casey the legal separation of the two groups and all its implications. I had studied the terminology and the rights of the Church and state with regard to our non-profit institutions, such as the college and the high school, all separately incorporated. I had the advice of excellent lawyers who were personal friends and whose cool logic tempered my own tendency to hurry a financial settlement between the two groups so that our work could go on.

Meanwhile I went to a secluded retreat in northern California provided by kind friends, a haven unreachable by telephone except in dire emergency, to ponder my decision. My conclusion after some weeks of reflection and prayer was that it was my duty to finish the legal and ecclesiastical separation with as much calm and poise as I could muster. The General Council members elected in 1963 were all showing the unhappy effects of the prolonged stress they had endured—nervous strains, serious depression, loss of voice, heart problems, etc. But delegation of the work to sisters not familiar with the intricacies involved was not an option. We needed to finish our task with the help of others and with the understanding that experience had given us.

Perhaps that was the wrong choice both for the new community and for me. Perhaps new personnel with fresh energy and new vision were needed. After further prayer and reflection I allowed my name to remain on the ballot. Others on the council decided to pursue other ministries. The IHMs serving in leadership positions with me during this initial term were exceptional women. Sister Elizabeth Ann Flynn, a courageous educator, was untiring in her efforts to promote the education of the sisters. Sister Regina McPartlin was dearly beloved and an innovator par excellence. Sister Dorothy Lester inspired all with her gentle, consistent, and loyal qualities. Sister Mary Charles showed a remarkable inclusivity with her kindness and concern for all. Sister Eugenia Ward's financial acumen and ease of friendship lessened the burden for all of us.

Upon assuming my second term, the leadership structure was changed from a General Council to an administration with a board of directors. The new chairperson of the board of directors, Sister Mary Mark Zeyen, served as vice-president of the community and of Immaculate Heart College. As a professional musician with a doctorate and professorship in music, she managed, with the gift of her fine analytic mind, to assist me through the final settlement.

Elections were over by early February, and on February 24, 1969, the inevitable request came from Archbishop James V. Casey for information on the implementation of the decrees. As we progressed toward legal separation of the two groups, a listing of the various corporations "owned" by Immaculate Heart, their boards of directors, and the names of those in the new IHM representative assembly was sent to him.

Much of the business of separation of the two groups in financial matters was now being carried on by excellent lawyers each group had chosen. This prevented any personal confrontation over properties between any members of either group. It was clear that Sister Eileen MacDonald's group of sisters wished to acquire the buildings that formerly constituted the IHM novitiate, now called La Casa de Maria Retreat House, located on a twenty-one-acre, old oak grove. The former mother general and novice mistress, Reverend Mother Regina McPartlin, had raised funds to build additional motel-like buildings on that property and personally designed the beautiful chapel. La Casa was to provide retreats for married couples, a new kind of apostolate felt to be sorely needed in the fifties and sixties. But since some members of Sister Eileen's group had been on the staff of the retreat house, the whole setting appeared to be under consideration as a central location for her group.

This rumor, once it had reached the group of sisters I served, caused a real disturbance, since Montecito (as the sisters always referred to it) had been the novitiate for the IHM Community since 1943—that is, for most of the sisters, who were considerably younger than Sister Eileen's members. Even though its current program was not financially successful at this time, Montecito was dear to the hearts of all the sisters. Several of us felt that ceding La Casa de Maria to Sister Eileen's group might provide an easy solution to the division of property. But to even entertain such an idea seemed like heresy to those who had known the Montecito novitiate as their first convent home and who had associated its natural beauty with the spirit of Immaculate Heart. It seemed inevitable that there would be a severe staffing shortage to run and maintain the retreat operation if the smaller group should receive this land.

The final legal agreement, with Cardinal McIntyre in concurrence, was a real tribute to the skill and negotiating power of the two lawyers concerned. The non-profit corporations belonging to the large majority of the sisters—Immaculate Heart College, Immaculate Heart High School, Queen of the Valley Hospital, and La Casa de Maria Retreat House—were to be retained by the new Immaculate Heart Community, which alone could provide staffing for them. Each retained separate boards of trustees, made up of both lay and community (IHM) members. A just financial settlement was made by the lawyers on both sides and by the Immaculate Heart Community, taking into account the disproportionate number of retired and infirm in the group of fifty-one headed by Sister Eileen. It was widely known that as the separation date neared, Sister Eileen, anxious to increase her numbers, visited many nuns individually, inviting them to join her group.[16] When the separation became a reality, many of the infirm who did not want to make a dramatic change and signed with Sister Eileen's group remained at the Hollywood motherhouse for the first year and a half, until adequate housing could be provided them. In the meantime the larger group of Immaculate Heart Community members were happy to care for them.

A year or so later Cardinal McIntyre helped provide Sister Eileen's group with Waverly Villa, located in the Los Feliz hills.[17] The beautifully

---

[16] Rose Eileen Jordan. Interview by author. Los Angeles, January 28, 1997.

[17] For a description of Sister Eileen's group in their new motherhouse, see Ursula Vils, "Sisters Live Now Life in Then Setting," *Los Angeles Times* 4 (November 9, 1971) 1, 8.

appointed and spacious mansion, with grounds carefully landscaped, including a pool and recreational facilities, served as their mother-house. It was located about a mile from our own motherhouse. Officially speaking, we remained ignorant of the origin of this gift but were satisfied that the sisters whom we had all known and worked side by side with for so long were enjoying pleasant surroundings. Sister Eileen served a full term as mother general, and when a new mother general was elected, she and four other IHM sisters left for Kansas to form still another small, diocesan religious community.[18]

At the Villa in the Los Feliz hills, the members who remained behind continued their teaching apostolate under Sister Gabriel Marie Keenan in the Los Angeles parochial schools, offering occasional retreats for women. They continued to recruit new members each year, and a number of the original group still live in the Villa today. On special occasions such as jubilees, anniversaries, and funeral services, members of the two groups come together in peace and friendship.

By this time, the spring of 1969, the larger group of sisters had still refrained from making a final decision regarding acceptance of the "Four Points" and so were still, formally speaking, a canonical community. But pressures were being brought to bear on the group from the outside. Cardinal McIntyre wrote to me on April 2, 1969, suggesting that the chapter decrees be revised and sent to the Vatican for approval. In my reply I stated simply that the IHM board of directors was aware of its responsibility and was taking the matter under consideration. We were, indeed, being unduly tardy, waiting as long as possible, hoping against hope that something might happen to stave off the crisis. That the Vatican might somehow come to understand not only our problem but that of the many communities that had made similar changes in good faith was our hope.

But there was more to come. The Vatican officials were not indifferent to our dilatory tactic and did not choose to ignore the issue, especially since our types of experimentation were now becoming common among other religious communities whose bishops were less rigid and conservative. Such communities included the Sisters of Mercy of Pitts-

---

[18] Ironically, in order to become a new religious community in Kansas, she and her four sisters had to give up their pontifical-right status and become a diocesan order. Years later Bishop Ward told how Cardinal McIntyre facilitated the canonical change. Bishop John J. Ward. Interview by Marshal H. Mercer. Audio-cassette transcript, December 10, 1992, 50.

burgh, the School Sisters of St. Francis, the School Sisters of Notre Dame, the Sisters of Notre Dame de Namur, the Institute of the Blessed Virgin Mary (BVM), the Sisters of Social Service, Sisters of Loretto, and many others.[19]

Soon we were informed that the pontifical commission wished to meet again with the entire community, at least all those living in California, on May 31, 1969. An immediate vote was urged by the bishops to indicate our decision to remain officially "religious" or to form a lay organization without recognition in the Church.

With a sad heart and growing indignation at the injustice that we should become in fact a "test case" or an "object lesson" for Catholic sisters of the United States, I phoned the convents, urging attendance at the meeting and stressing its vital importance. The sisters reacted predictably in different ways. Some understandably did not wish to take time coming to Los Angeles to hear the "same old story" again. Others were eager to face the bishops with the logical questions that had been troubling them. Still others wished to challenge the fact that we seemed to have been singled out among religious communities for censure and to question the apparent imminence of our being forced to leave the canonical structure.

But they came—from the central valley, from San Francisco and the Bay area, from San Diego and El Cajon, from San Luis Obispo, and, of course, the largest number from Los Angeles itself. They trouped in, weary at the end of a long school year and anxious for some decision so that their lives and work could go on.

The pontifical commission, which consisted of Archbishop James V. Casey, Bishop Joseph Brietenbeck, and Archbishop Thomas A. Donnellan, arrived, unaccompanied this time by Father Gallagher. During that unforgettable day in May 1969 we heard over and over from them of a status that seemed more and more out of our reach—that of a recognized religious community.

There was a formal meeting first between the board of directors of the IHM Community and the bishops, at which the long anticipated verdict was handed down as final. The bishops seemed to want to soften the blow by suggesting that we change our status and become a

---

[19] For an analysis of the changes in the case of the Sisters of Social Service, where the Vatican's formal approval did not come until 1989, see Helen Rose Fuchs Ebaugh, *Women in the Vanishing Cloister* (New Brunswick, N.J.: Rutgers University Press, 1993) 72–77.

secular institute, a pious association, or a sodality. Each term held un-favorable connotations for us. The secular institutes were fashioned to allow for religious life lived "in the world." Unfortunately for us per-haps, with the changes adopted at the Second Vatican Council the Church agency in charge of secular institutes was subsumed under the Sacred Congregation for Religious, already so unfavorable to our cause. We were not sure what the definition of a "pious association" might be, but we felt that the title would be received unfavorably by the majority of our sisters as self-proclaimed holiness. A "sodality," for most of us of middle age, meant a high school youth group to which we had pledged adolescent allegiance (the suggestion brought smiles to those of us for whom the word had associations no longer appropriate).

The reaction of the IHM board of directors, at this last meeting with the bishops, was silence, with only a few mild questions, hardly indica-tive of our innermost feelings. The bishops seemed puzzled by our ap-parent withdrawal, evidently expecting a renewed discussion. But we had expected the verdict, and this was hardly the time or place for one more debate.

The atmosphere changed, however, when the bishops stood before group after group of sisters, scheduled at intervals according to their arrival time from the various parts of California. Endlessly the ultima-tum was repeated until it was burned into our memories: Follow the four points or accept a dispensation from your vows. Then become any kind of religious association you choose. Just don't call yourselves "religious."[20]

Actually there was nothing in this message that was not implied after the much earlier visitation report of Father Gallagher. But it had always seemed remote, unbelievable, especially to those sisters living outside the Los Angeles area. For them, the whole episcopal drama was somewhat bizarre. As the truth came home to these sisters especially, there were tears, there was openly expressed anger, there were the burning questions: How had the General Chapter of 1967 lost its right to determine the internal affairs of the community? And what had hap-pened to Pope Paul VI's open invitation to religious communities to experiment? In considering the dire choice between the old lifestyle of the "Four Points" and the forfeiture of their canonical vows, some

---

[20] Any IHM sister who was at this meeting can repeat this demand to the present day.

asked Archbishop Casey difficult questions. Sister Corita Kent must have startled him when she stood and asked simply, "What do you think Jesus would have done if he were given this choice?"

These questions were left unanswered. However, the commission of bishops suggested that our General Chapter to be held in summer of 1969, just two months away, would be an opportune time to reach a decision. This suggestion was motivated most probably by another mandate. The Sacred Congregation for Religious had requested that the bishops "propose a procedure whereby the case would be settled."[21]

The pontifical commission's visit lasted from early morning, with various groups in session, until late at night. Many sisters returned to several meetings to hear the bishops' message repeated. They could not believe what they had heard the first time or even the second. The decision, of course, had come from the Vatican, as the earlier report of Father Gallagher had indicated. So the bishops' message could only be a series of formulas repeated. The sisters were restless, dissatisfied, anxious to convince the bishops that our chapter decrees were not final but only in process. We did not claim the role of prophets attributed to us by the press. We had been faithful only to what seemed right for us at our specific time of renewal, not what should be followed by any other community. Many IHMs who had kept abreast of the Second Vatican Council's more revolutionary changes remembered the wonder they first felt at the teaching on the primacy of the individual conscience. Where, they wondered, was its place, its value now?[22]

The three bishops made a final visit to my office, where I had heard out many of our sisters, trying to calm the atmosphere, trying above all not to reveal to the bishops my vehement reaction to their message. The friendliness they manifested at our earlier meeting, changed by the unhappy day's experience into weariness on both sides, was now carefully disguised as formality. I preferred the distance that had grown between us, feeling that they had really not understood us enough to make a case for us at the Vatican, even if they had the authority to do

[21] Archbishop James V. Casey. Letter to Sister Anita Caspary, I.H.M., June 2, 1969. A/IHMCOM.

[22] *Lumen Gentium*, in *Vatican Council II. The Conciliar and Post Conciliar Documents*, ed. Austin Flannery, O.P. (Northport, N.Y.: Costello Publishing Co., 1981) 1:367, no. 16. Also *Dignitatis Humanae*, ibid., 800–801, nos. 2-3. See Cardinal Leon-Joseph Suenens, "The Nun in the World Debate." From a photocopy of an address given at St. Mary's Symposium, South Bend, Indiana, June 1969. A/IHMCOM.

so. My sense was that they were surprised at the challenges and questions directed to them during the group meetings with our sisters. How could they have been surprised? That I will never know.

Furthermore, the bishops must have felt that some of the sisters' remarks displayed disrespect. The fact that the bishops were dealing rather highhandedly with people's lives did not seem to alter their conviction that the "Four Points" were, irrespective of their merit as rationales for a truly spiritual life, easy to follow. Our struggle to retain our self-determination and our integrity should be made subservient, they said, to unquestioning obedience to higher authority. Then this case would be over and done with. They seemed anxious to conclude their troublesome and time-consuming mission. They appeared to be somewhat moved by the predicament facing us, but they could not reverse decisions made, no doubt, by the Sacred Congregation for Religious. The bishops went to their hotel, preparing to leave Los Angeles the next morning. After asking Archbishop Casey to put in writing the "Four Points," which I thought might have been modified somewhat, I found myself exhausted but peaceful. The officials had met and heard almost every sister in the community.

Archbishop Casey acceded to my request, and a courteous letter recounting the entire situation was soon received. Since there were some slight differences with the original "Four Points" issued by the Sacred Congregation some nine months earlier, I am including that section of his letter below.

June 2, 1969

Dear Sister Anita:

    . . . You asked me in addition to put in writing the four points, as they have been communicated to me. They are as follows:

1. The religious habit may be modified, but cannot be completely abolished; there must remain an exterior sign marking out the wearers as true religious;

2. Life in common, with all that that implies, cannot be entirely dissolved; the religious cannot be permitted to live, each on her own, without any discipline and without the proper spirit of the Community. It does not seem possible to dispense the Sisters from daily participation in Holy Mass and at least some practices of community piety;

3. The active life of the apostolate must be subordinated to the spiritual life, since it is in that that religious life primarily consists;

4. The religious must cooperate with the local Ordinary, who has the responsibility and the pastoral direction of the faithful. . . .

Devotedly yours in Christ,

(Signed) James V. Casey
Archbishop of Denver [23]

Two points, it seemed to me, showed a slight change of emphasis. In Archbishop Casey's version, the first issue was now specified modification rather than outright prohibition of lay clothes, the significant aspect being some "exterior sign" that presumably might be placed on lay clothes. The third point, that "active life . . . must be subordinated to the spiritual life," seemed significant. The sentence was short but the significance was great, and lay behind many of the seemingly superficial disagreements, I believe, between ourselves and the Sacred Congregation for Religious as well as the pontifical commission made up of the bishops. The renewal decrees of our chapter had attempted to follow the lead of the Second Vatican Council in eliminating the dichotomy between apostolic work and spiritual life, indeed to integrate the two so that we could state with assurance that "every humanizing work is, consciously or unconsciously, a Christian work."[24] By this statement we were trying to eliminate the dualism that had marred the spirituality of Catholic Christians for decades. One Roman Catholic theologian had praised this aspect of our renewal decrees in a private letter, stating that "Christ and the life of grace must be shown as natural to the world, so that in attaining them, we do not abandon the natural and the human."[25]

This new concept did not need my explanations; the spirituality, rooted in the gospel message, had been explained in the many books, treatises, and periodicals our sisters had read in defense of our position. There was much about sanctification and the modern secularized world still to be explicated even years later. But the "new look" at a technological society infused by a christological spirit had already brought comfort to innumerable sensitive souls in religious communities torn between the obligation of prayer and the urge to relieve the pressing needs of people both inside and outside convent walls.

[23] Archbishop James V. Casey to Sister Anita Caspary, I.H.M., 1.
[24] See Appendix D, p. 248.
[25] Eulalio Baltazar. Letter to Anita Caspary, I.H.M., January 21, 1968. A/IHMCOM.

But the time for theological discussion was over. Archbishop Casey's letter of June 2, 1969, had stated that we had had sufficient time to experiment. Now each sister would have to make her decision. On June 14, 1969, the community met as a whole to discuss the implications of the message delivered by the bishops. Differing opinions were voiced, as sisters repeated the counsel they had received from various spiritual directors and canon lawyers. Some sisters thought that by our remaining silent, the Vatican might change its opinion. Some felt that each day's delay brought further disillusionment with the Church—to decide soon was the only way to prevent any greater losses among our members and to preserve a community for the future.

The summer chapter of 1969—our tenth—came and went. It resulted in the same division of opinion, but the final vote was that we would delay a decision, thereby indicating that we could not be accused of initiating a process we did not, by any means, desire, that is, to be forced to forfeit our vows and to leave canonical status. This delay was displeasing to Cardinal McIntyre, who, when he discovered our non-committal attitude, wrote to me on August 28, 1969, deploring our "persistence of opinion" and offering his assistance in creating a more "constructive attitude."[26]

The choice could not be delayed much longer, and we knew it. On September 2, 1969, Archbishop Casey wrote, stating that the process of separation of the two groups should be completed. He perhaps was not aware that the process was already in progress legally. Most of Sister Eileen's group had left the motherhouse and were living in parochial convents, preliminary to assuming teaching assignments in the fall.

There were moments of irony during this interlude. One afternoon that same fall, I received an unannounced visit from four sisters of Sister Eileen's group. They told me they wanted me to be the first to know that they had left her group to form a separate community under the leadership of Sister Leonella Lynch, a novitiate companion of mine. I was surprised at this early change of plan, but I was pleased that these sisters had felt they could trust me and that they cared enough to share this information.

Fall also brought a new decision. Urged by a long-time friend, a priest from another California diocese, I was quietly preparing to go to Rome. There, I was told, I might be given a fair and open hearing by the

---

[26] Cardinal McIntyre. Letter to Anita Caspary, I.H.M., August 28, 1969. A/IHMCOM.

Vatican substitute secretary of state, Archbishop Giovanni Benelli, who was considered more liberal than his predecessors and who had spoken informally with me in 1967, before he assumed his position in the Vatican secretariat. Was I grasping at a straw? Perhaps, but we had nothing to lose. I informed the community that a "new creative alternative" had appeared and that we would delay the vote of each sister as to her future for a short time.

The prospect of visiting Rome again brought me no joy. I chose to go unaccompanied by any community member—somehow that seemed the right approach. In this I risked challenging the bureaucracy, the proper way of approaching the Vatican. The innumerable churches and the grandiose façade of St. Peter's Basilica became for me now an unfortunate symbol of triumphalism, hardly symbolic of the Christ who walked among the poor. As a young sister I had felt a thrill of pride in seeing the aristocratic Pope Pius XII carried on the magnificent *sedia gestatoria* down the long aisle of St. Peter's Basilica, his slender fingers outstretched in blessing the surging crowds. But now I spent little time in the vast body of the basilica, instead searching out again the unpretentious tomb of Pope John XXIII, begging his intercession. The white catafalque seemed as short and wide and unprepossessing in appearance as was that great man. I even found a paradoxical awe and comfort among the Italian peasants honoring "their Pope."

On the second day of my stay I approached the arm of the basilica where the offices of the various commissions and congregations are housed. My welcome was rather chilly, I felt. I was in a modest, uniform-looking black dress, but the ubiquitous sister-companion was missing. My halting Italian made my purpose a doubtful one. As a woman, I felt distinctly out of place in this house of male clerics and ecclesiastical attendants.

Although at the time I was unaware of any sympathetic support from any of the many religious groups that lived near the Vatican, a former priest who had been a Jesuit student in Rome at the time of my earlier visit said to me many years later: "We were all cheering for you, Sister—a David challenging Goliath, a David, however, who was bound to lose."

Making my way up a narrow staircase, I came to an official sitting at a desk, handing out forms and tickets. I was given one of the forms, told to explain my purpose in coming, the person I wished to see, my passport number, even the date of my birth and innumerable other items of information. In return for all this I received a small ticket. I was directed up still more stairs, then down wider porticoes, at various junctures being startled by the halberds of Swiss guards halting my progress. Each time my small ticket gave me permission to pass on. The corridors seemed to grow wider and taller as I went, and I felt that I was shrinking, losing height at each step.

Finally I reached the door of the office of the Vatican secretary of state. I explained my mission to the young priest at the appointment desk, and with my heart beating faster as the seconds went by, I found a seat in the fairly crowded waiting room. Soon after, I was admitted to a small, beautifully appointed inner waiting room where a kind-looking Archbishop Benelli stood. After taking our seats, he listened attentively as I explained our situation carefully. In no way did he indicate that he already knew of our case.

At the same time I presented him with the letter drawn up by our community's board of directors, asking him to present our plea directly to Pope Paul VI. The document began with a brief statement of our long altercation with the cardinal archbishop of Los Angeles. We stated that our special Chapter of Renewal had been held and its results promulgated on October 15, 1967, to the dismay of Cardinal McIntyre. In our presentation we had explained the immediate, though not major, rationale for the changes we had made, namely, the prospect of the steady loss of vocations. The letter read:

> . . . the members of the Community are convinced that the basic direction taken by the Chapter in its enactments is vitally necessary to the well-being of the Church and to them, both personally and apostolically. . . . So widespread is this conviction that it will not be possible to follow the directives sent by the Sacred Congregation for Religious without losing from the religious state in the immediate future a large majority of this community. . . .[27]

We identified the impetus for our changes, like those of the special Chapters of Renewal in many communities, as the "spirit and directives of the Second Vatican Council" itself and as the fact that these sisters represent "the youth, strength, and vitality of their respective communities." Further in the letter we then related our case to the whole issue of religious renewal in the United States. It read:

---

[27] Members of the Immaculate Heart Community. Letter to Pope Paul VI, 1969, presented by Sister Anita Caspary, I.H.M., to Archbishop Giovanni Benelli. A/IHMCOM. See Appendix E, p. 263.

Consequently, the course of action taken by the Sacred Congregation for Religious and the resulting directives issued to the Sisters of the Immaculate Heart represent to hundreds in the United States some kind of test of whether or not the Sacred Congregation for Religious will find it possible really to allow communities in this country to renew themselves so that they may present "to believers and to unbelievers alike an increasingly clearer revelation of Christ," (*Lumen Gentium* #46) especially in a society which is predominantly pluralistic and secular. The decision is a blow to the hope of renewal as many communities envision it from the *"Motu Proprio."*

For the above reasons, we petition Your Holiness to grant us permission to experiment with what may be considered a new form of religious life, a life which we believe is highly relevant to our age and society, as well as in keeping with the spirit of the Second Vatican Council. . . .

We ask this privilege of experimenting for a limited time (at least a year) because our Sisters believe so strongly that this type of religious life is needed today. We are also petitioning for this favor because we believe, with good reason, that at least eighty percent of our Community will withdraw from religious life if the institute is required to follow the present directives of the Sacred Congregation for Religious, in order to live a new form of consecrated life outside the canonical structure of religious life or of other ecclesiastically recognized groups.[28]

We concluded by stating once again what we believed to be the significance of our case for all sisters, especially to the communities in the United States.

Archbishop Benelli promised to give the matter his most earnest attention and quietly left the room. I was escorted out to the waiting room by an attendant priest. The whole interview had lasted at most about fifteen minutes. I felt a letdown after the strain of trying with all my being to make the churchman understand. I left the Vatican office, trying to restore my own peace with the thought that I had done my best. I could do no more.

I returned as soon as possible to the motherhouse in Los Angeles. I thought that at least the infinite pains we had taken to have interviews and consultations with Church authorities and canon lawyers, our searching written studies of our renewal process and our educational

[28] Ibid.

situation, our constant effort to make our motives understood, all these demonstrated our desire to serve, even though our efforts had failed to bring understanding. In the BBC film made of our plight a year or so later, the Jesuit Father Robert R. Arrowsmith explains clearly the distribution of power and influence in the bureaucratic structure of the Vatican. In a win or lose situation, we had to lose our petition—the pope could not rule against his own appointees. The structure could not be turned upside down for a small and relatively unimportant religious community—of women! The moral win would be ours, but only if we left the institutional Church.[29]

No communication from the Vatican was ever received after my visit. My own resources and energies were exhausted, even while I realized that I had a natural measure of physical endurance beyond that of most of the sisters. But even I could no longer witness the mental stress, the physical breakdowns, and the heart-rending departures of the disillusioned from the IHM Community. I had made up my mind as to what my next step would be, and I announced my intention to the IHM board of directors.

The board approved my idea of a community assembly, the presentation of all our alternatives, and allowing each sister to vote for her own choice. And so we announced a meeting of all IHM Community members for December 6, 1969. At this meeting I announced my personal decision and asked each sister to make her own decision, understanding that belonging to the group in accord with the Renewal Chapter meant that she had to obtain a dispensation from her vows and would lose her canonical status. I spoke from my heart to each sister.

> I am asking each Sister to write to me by December 15, a letter of intent stating whether she chooses to become a member of a dedicated lay group living according to the Decrees. . . . Such a group may have to ask for dispensation from public vows. . . . Other options open to members of the present group are: to find a more traditionally-oriented community and join it; to obtain a dispensation from vows and disassociate oneself from any group; to form another religious community with the guidelines drawn by the Sacred Congregation for Religious including the Four Points.[30]

[29] "Nuns in Conflict," in the *Man Alive* series, British Broadcasting Corporation, 1970. Sixty minutes. A/IHMCOM.

[30] Sister Anita Caspary, I.H.M. Address to the IHM Community, December 6, 1969. A/IHMCOM. See Appendix F, p. 267.

These and many other thoughts were expressed before this group of sisters whom I had worked with so long and loved so much. Now, at last, each one would have to come to her own personal decision, and I knew this would be unbelievably painful, no matter what the decision would be.

Toward the end of 1969, but before the sisters' final choices had been presented to our community, the major superiors of communities of both men and women in the United States began to protest to the Vatican the threatened interference in the lives of American religious and in particular, the treatment of the Immaculate Heart Sisters' renewal program. The two largest organizations—the Conference of Major Superiors of Men and the Conference of Major Superiors of Women—each presented to their members formal letters and resolutions for approval, and in both organizations an overwhelming majority endorsed these efforts.

In the case of the Conference of Major Superiors of Men (CMSM), Father Paul M. Boyle, C.P., president of the conference, had circulated a formal letter addressed to Cardinal Antoniutti of the Sacred Congregation for Religious and approved in its first draft by a two-thirds vote of the major superiors. After suggested changes were made, a second draft was approved by 73 percent of the members and was then sent to Cardinal Antoniutti. In his letter of November 6, 1969, Father Boyle indicated the deep disappointment of the superiors at the position taken by the Sacred Congregation in its letter of February 21, 1968, in the "unfortunate controversy surrounding the IHM Sisters of Los Angeles, California." The letter of the Sacred Congregation, he wrote,

> [is] indicative of an attitude contrary to the spirit, if not the letter, of the Conciliar and post-Conciliar documents, especially in those sections of the *Motu Proprio Ecclesiae Sanctae* which state that the most important role in the adaptation and renewal of Religious life belongs to the institutes themselves, and, that general chapters have the right to alter certain norms of their constitutions as long as the purpose, nature and character of the institute are preserved.
>
> It is hard for our religious to accept that the Congregation for Religious can appreciate the situation better than responsible religious in this country. Chapters, Major Superiors and thousands of religious in many communities across this country are doing one, or several of the things reprobated by the Congregation for Religious in the letter mentioned above.[31]

[31] Paul M. Boyle, C.P. Letter to Cardinal Antoniutti, November 6, 1969. Father Boyle sent a copy of this correspondence to me. A/IHMCOM.

Father Boyle then expanded his position to include the alarming possibility that some canonical religious orders might disappear if their attempts to renew honestly and in good faith were thwarted, a fate that by this time had already befallen the majority of the Immaculate Heart Sisters:

> Another facet of the situation in the American Church that we feel obliged to bring to your attention is that there is frequent and open discussion on whether entire Religious Congregations will be forced to withdraw from the Canonical Religious State in order to continue their lives as consecrated celibates in the manner which seems to them most fruitful and most faithful to their call. . . .[32]

Meanwhile the Conference of Major Superiors of Women responded similarly, circulating in December 1969 a resolution among all its members requesting that the Sacred Congregation allow our experimentation to continue and referring to the postconciliar commission on religious set up by Pope Paul VI. It urged the major superiors to take "courageous leadership in implementing Chapter decrees and support in sisterly charity sisters of other congregations in their renewal." To amend an earlier resolution that narrowly failed at its spring meeting, this resolution, which required a two-thirds vote of members, fell short of passage by one vote.[33]

Sister Rosalie Murphy, provincial of the Sisters of Notre Dame de Namur, sent a new resolution, dated December 15, 1969, to Father Edward Heston, C.S.C., the official representative of the Sacred Congregation for Religious and Secular Institutes. It read as follows:

RESOLUTION:
WHEREAS Pope Paul VI initiated guidelines developed by the Post Conciliar Commission on Religious for deep spiritual renewal

---

[32] Ibid.

[33] In writing this history, I was told by one of the former major superiors present at this session that she considered the vote on this initial resolution as invalid. She described the meeting as chaotic, in which members were not allowed sufficient time for reasoned discussion. Also, many visitors were participating as voting members, which further invalidated the negative outcome of this initial resolution. I believe that had the Conference of Major Superiors of Women publicly supported our renewal during this spring meeting of 1969, the Vatican and the American bishops would have lessened the pressure on us.

by the prescriptions of *Ecclesiae Sanctae* granting an extensive period of experimentation; and

WHEREAS the Special General Chapter is the highest legislative body for renewal within a congregation; and

WHEREAS each religious congregation should maturely and prudently accept due responsibility through their Special General Chapters for renewal within their Congregations;

THEREFORE BE IT RESOLVED that we the undersigned urge that major superiors take courageous leadership in implementing Chapter decrees and support in sisterly charity sisters of other congregations in their renewal.

BE IT FURTHER RESOLVED that we the undersigned publicly offer support to the Immaculate Heart of Mary Sisters and request that the Sacred Congregation for Religious and Secular Institutes allow them to follow their Chapter decisions during an extended period of experimentation.[34]

This resolution was sent to each member of the Major Superiors of Women in the United States. It carried 190 signatures, each superior acting as an individual. To my knowledge, no reply to this resolution was ever received.

[34] Sister Rosalie Murphy, S.N.D. de N. Letter and resolution of support, December 15, 1969. A/IHMCOM.

Chapter 14

A New Life for Religious Women

After the meeting of December 6, 1969, at which I had requested a decision from each sister as to her choice of Sister Eileen MacDonald's group, living under the pre-renewal Rule, or the community living under the 1967 decrees, my appointment book became extraordinarily full. Sisters waited outside the president's office (formerly the mother general's office) to tell me, each in her own way, that the choice was not a free one, since we had been forced by both the cardinal's intransigence and the uncompromising view of Vatican authority. Some of these sisters had chosen simply to be dispensed from their vows and not to join the "new community." Some doubted that a community could survive without the Vatican's approval. Others felt that they needed time and space to recover emotionally and physically.

For some, however, the decision was still alarming; for others, it was a heartbreaking experience. Sisters who feared the outcome especially of experimentation made appointments to see me, assuring me of their personal regard but of their inability to follow a new way of life. For these I felt great sympathy; they struggled with their consciences over the issue of vows made "forever." They had been taught, even as I had, that infidelity to those vows would bring them God's disfavor as well as a feeling of guilt they might never be able to erase. They had been imbued with the idea that stability meant a static state, and so the changes seemed difficult enough. That the Vatican authority asking for change had now appeared to deny the reality of that change was simply one more barrier they could not overcome. No longer to be a "real sister," a decision they had made years ago, was to them an unthinkable choice.

Many hours were spent in prayer and reflection as all the sisters prepared to choose either the new or the older form of life. At this point, again, some sisters felt that they were showing a lack of courage to try a new way, with all the personal responsibility each sister now had to exercise in matters of conscience. These sisters were wise enough to realize that for them life needed a pattern, a structure, and they were not prepared to cope with the new freedoms. For some, the training of years of convent life had made this their pattern; for others, the realization that the "world" they were about to re-enter would demand adjustment they could not yet predict. Yet they knew that they could not return to the rigid life they had left. They chose, it seems to me wisely, to leave the community. A few sisters sought out other canonical communities that seemed peaceful and without our painful polarization. They transferred to other communities without repeating the novitiate or making vows again.

There were others who had been leaders of thought in making the new decrees. To have those sisters leave the community seemed to be an irreparable loss to its future growth and development. But their minds and hearts had been shaken by the treatment received from the Church. They were exhausted by hours of explanation to hierarchical officials and even to their own sisters as to what the decrees were all about. They were appalled at the lack of understanding on the part of laity and clergy of the significance of the Second Vatican Council. Trained to think and to write, they were hurt by hearing the decrees called "abstract," "impractical," "hopelessly idealistic." But each sister's leaving, for whatever reason, was to me a matter of sorrow, not simply of numerical loss.

The most publicized separation was certainly that between those who had objected to the new decrees, and indeed to the renewal plans in general. This group, now directly responsible to Sister Eileen, had fifty followers, while the group who professed loyalty to the decrees of renewal had about three-hundred fifty members, a number having left the community altogether or relocated to another religious community by the end of 1969.

On December 30, 1969, a letter was sent to Cardinal Hildebrand Antoniutti, reminding him that we had received no reply to our latest plea regarding community status. However, we added, the local diocesan paper had made a public announcement of a new pontifical institute called Sisters of the Immaculate Heart. The use of the title "Sisters of the Immaculate Heart," applied to the group led by Sister Eileen, led us to believe that we were already regarded in the Vatican's eyes as being no longer real religious. Thus we were no longer under the jurisdiction of the Sacred Congregation for Religious, no longer a "canonical community." But yet we were still bound by our vows.

Because of the unusual nature of our situation, we inquired in this same letter to Cardinal Antoniutti how the formal severance of our community from canonical status might take place. More important, how was the usual dispensation to be carried out in the case of the majority of the community, none of whom had petitioned for release from her vows? To be dispensed from final vows normally required the express desire of the sister herself or the proof of the community that she was considered "incorrigible." We added that if we received no further correspondence from the Sacred Congregation for Religious, we would simply regard ourselves by our own definition as a "lay community of religious persons." We would also send the signatures of those constituting this community to Cardinal Antoniutti before February 1, 1970.

No letter of reply was received, but instead auxiliary Archbishop Timothy Manning asked for an appointment with me. He was quiet and cordial, as was his customary way. He appeared utterly calm as he explained that those desiring to become members of the "new community" based on the decrees of renewal could turn in the forms for dispensation to him rather than to the Vatican. Each sister following this course of action was thus obliged to seek dispensation from her vows and to sign that application without delay. But in the application form was the statement that the petition for dispensation was made freely. Virtually every sister, without consultation with the others, took one final, important step: she crossed out the word "freely."

The date of this interview, January 18, 1970, was meaningfully close to the press release announcing the resignation of His Eminence James Francis Cardinal McIntyre from the Los Angeles Archdiocese. Some sisters felt that the appointment of a successor might mean a change of our situation, perhaps a more understanding view. But a more sympathetic change either locally or at the Vatican was not to be. Indeed, the more sophisticated view was that the cardinal's departure from office was a bargain struck by the Vatican because His Eminence had not found a diplomatic solution to the problem of the IHM community. The controversy, now international in scope, had displeased the Vatican as far back as April 1968, as could be seen from the Sacred Congregation's complaint about the IHMs, inveighing as it did against "a wave of disedifying publicity . . . stirred up around points which are not open to question. . . ."[1] It goes without saying that a more sympathetic hearing of our renewal plans initially would have merited little or no press notice. So the Ordinary, it seems, would have to bear at least some of the responsibility for the debacle.

Of course, the process of giving each sister a piece of paper for dispensation and seeing her reaction was hardly a simple one. This whole episode partook of the surreal for most of us. The controversy seemed dead. The anguish of division was over. There were no newspaper stories on the bulletin boards. Each person called at the appointment desk of the general secretary of the Immaculate Heart Sisters to receive a plain, mimeographed sheet. And that sheet left no space for the reasons or arguments for renewal. The case was closed, and each person's signature marked the end of her chosen way of life. To many, the signature written on the paper seemed to be the final touch in a deeply personal and communal tragedy.

Besides these personal problems, there seemed to be a harsh insensitivity toward us on the part of some Catholics, who considered that our former commitment was valued so lightly by us. Some wondered how seriously we had adhered to our tradition of service to the Church. They could not fathom that hours of meditation and prayer had been involved in the decision. Suddenly persons who had been our friends seemed to be saying, "Because you are accepting the legal dispensation, you are no longer religious in any sense," as though the legal status were all-important, and the personal ideals, commitment, and way of life counted for nothing. This hurt all of us deeply.

On the other hand, I was amazed at the courage and dedication of some of the older sisters, some in their seventies and eighties. They had lived through the anxiety of the separation of the California province from its Spanish origin and realized that the stress of waiting for ecclesiastical decisions was to be expected and need not inspire guilt or fear in the petitioners. Such, for example, was Sister Emmanuel, who had been part of the Spanish province and made a difficult choice in the 1920s. In the California province were many stalwarts who chose to join the "new community" of these days. Numbered among them were Sisters Ancilla O'Neill and Isabelle Larkin, Albertine Campbell, Anita

---

[1] Archbishop Luigi Raimondi, apostolic delegate to the United States. Letter to members of the Conference of Major Superiors of Women, April 9, 1968. Document No. 1068/68, 2: no. 4. Archives of the Immaculate Heart Community (hereafter referred to as A/IHMCOM).

and Patricia McRae, as well as the former mothers general Eucharia Harney and Regina McPartlin.

I remember the first sister who came into my office with her signed acceptance of her dispensation. She was over seventy and was still wearing her entire habit, without modification of any kind, and she wore it to the day of her death years later. Documents showed that she had made her vows before I was born, and I marveled at her serenity as she handed me the official forms. Then I read her note appended to the application for dispensation: "I have signed this, but just after I did, I went into the Chapel and renewed my promise to God." I marveled at Sister Anna Musante's faith and smiled to myself at the simplicity that triumphed in that single line of hers.

Although this sister, and no doubt others as well, were not in complete agreement with some of the decisions the Chapter of Renewal had made, no legal status could interfere with their lifetime commitment to God through the community they had joined. That this community had made lawful decisions seemed clear to them. For her and for many sisters the commitment was different in form now but unchanged in the depth of conviction that their community—call it what you will—was the means by which they would continue to serve God.

Eventually our group, which identified with the changes approved by the Chapter of Renewal, took as its legal title "Immaculate Heart Community," a title recorded by the state of California on October 1, 1970, and wrote a contract that would constitute our commitment to the Immaculate Heart Community. The contract began:

> Motivated by a desire to explore the mystery of God and man [sic]; a desire to carry out Christ's redemptive work and manifest His presence in the world by whole-hearted service of others; a desire to contribute of my time, talent, and material goods to the Immaculate Heart Community and its works . . .[2]

Then followed a brief section on the structure of the new community, the conditions of its membership, authority, and government, the expected participation in community events, and financial contribution according to one's means, and so on.

To bring home to both community members and to the various groups among the general public the fact that we were seriously binding

---

[2] IHM 1970 contract sample. A/IHMCOM.

ourselves to a new form of religious life, we solemnized the contractual agreement with a liturgical celebration and a prayer incorporating our communal promises. This prayer we recited for the first time together at the evening Easter Vigil services in 1970. The time was considered appropriate because it brought together the renewal of our baptismal promises at the vigil ceremony and our commitment to the Immaculate Heart Community.

This first "commitment ceremony," held on Holy Saturday, March 28, 1970, seemed as impressive to our friends who had gathered to witness it as it was deeply stirring and inspirational to us. The traditional Easter Vigil liturgy is highly symbolic as the opening chants are begun in darkness, with all lights extinguished. Then as the Easter fire is enkindled at the door of the church, each person holds a candle set aflame as the light passes from person to person. A feeling of joy, peace after a long struggle, and communal unity were ours. The long period of indeterminacy had found resolution in this meaningful ceremony. For me and for others as well, there was an upsurge of hope, with a tremulous yet real assurance that we were walking together in the presence of the Spirit.

At the chapter in that summer of 1970, a bold new step was taken when we decided to allow married persons to be admitted to the community. At no time did the community propose a commune, but rather a religious commitment, without celibacy as a necessary condition for membership.[3]

Some members felt that in taking this step we were denying the single-mindedness of service, often a strong argument for the celibate state. The outcome of this step cannot be finally evaluated at this time. But in the relatively small number of married couples who are community members, or in the case of one partner of a marriage entering the community, or of one who was already a member and chose to marry, we have instances of continued full and active membership, loyalty, and generous service to the community.

Since no mention of the term "Roman Catholic" was made in the contract, the delegates of the IHM chapter also moved to open its doors for the first time to Christians of all denominations, not solely Roman Catholics. The new community began to call itself "ecumenical" while still a bit unsure of the dimensions of the term. The Christian members

---

[3] See Jo Ann Kay McNamara, *Sisters in Arms* (Cambridge, Mass.: Harvard University Press, 1996) 1–6, for historical precedents.

who are not Roman Catholic are few in number, but they have brought a disproportionate broadening of perspective to our community. Our use of the term "ecumenical" has brought some deserved criticism for many reasons. Some criticize our choice of the Catholic Mass as our basic worship service. The outcome of our choice to become ecumenical cannot at this time be fully evaluated, and a new understanding of Christian community as a broad term is being explored in this fourth decade of our existence.

With both legal and financial arrangements concluded, and with the choices of individual members having been made, there was now a peaceful atmosphere in the new Immaculate Heart Community. There were of course an infinite number of problems to be settled, but at least they were our own problems. The rather bland announcement of the establishment of the new community to the Catholic public was made known by Archbishop Manning's proclamation in the official Catholic newspaper. "A number of sisters, previously members of this community, have received dispensations from their canonical vows of poverty, chastity and obedience. This aggregate has grouped together to conduct certain educational and welfare enterprises." And he added, "In view of these negotiations, we are happy to write a terminus to these anxious events and to pray God's benediction on all those who so charitably sustained the members of both groups until this end."[4]

This serene period was shattered, however, by a letter to us from Archbishop Manning announcing that a non-canonical community could no longer have a chapel or reserve the Blessed Sacrament in the motherhouse chapel. The infirmary chapel and the college chapel were notably missing from this order. It will be recalled that one of the points that Cardinal McIntyre had insisted upon was the *communal* use of the motherhouse chapel for morning Mass. We had tried to explain why the problem was insurmountable for us, since the Los Angeles Fire Department had limited the number of persons at one time in the chapel, a number much smaller than our community. Had the chancery office's disfavor found a vulnerable spot—our spiritual practice of praying before the presence of the Blessed Sacrament in the chapel?

We quickly formulated a petition addressed to the archbishop calling his attention to the chapels the Vatican allowed for families, dedicated

---

[4] Archbishop Timothy Manning, "Announcement," *The Tidings* (December 25, 1969) 1. See also "Archbishop Thanks Immaculate Heart Nuns" and "Sisters To Form Lay Community," *The Tidings* (February 6, 1970) 1.

groups, etc., only to be met with the reply that an indult for public ora-
tories must be obtained from the Holy See. We were sure that such permission would not be given to us. Yet it was essential for us to have our
chapel, our sacred space, to which we could have access in the midst of
our busy lives. We were trained to appreciate morning Mass, and we
relished a place of silence where the Presence could be renewed within
us.

Now Mass had to be said in the community room. The tiny infirmary
chapel, still exempt from the archbishop's ruling, was the place we
might visit for a few moments on a busy day. Thus the indomitable
spirit of the sisters in the midst of deprivation was once more demonstrated.

And so the Immaculate Heart Community, a new entity without official ecclesiastical recognition or approbation, has continued to grow,
slowly but steadily. Does the community, as we see it now, embody that
first vision that energized the initial Chapter of Renewal? We were attempting to establish a new set of conditions that would preserve individual spiritual growth while providing the bond of community. The
tension of person and community did not originate in the thinking of
Vatican II. Modern thinkers have found in it a rich paradox: a passion
for freedom and a certain desire for unity, if not conformity.

The community has as its central bond an open, loving concern for
the other, a willing investment of time, service, caring, and personal
sacrifice. Such a community's existence, because of its constant need to
reinforce its ideals, remains a rarity. Society itself operates to turn communities into institutions. The Church's structures operate to regain
control of the single direction of a task force. Loss of prestige, it is
thought by advocates of a strong institutional authority, results when a
uniformed band of people are no longer seen marching in tune to an
unquestioned command. The renewed community thus lived with the
subtle fear, especially in the beginning, of an inability to sustain the
loyalties that the initial "revolution" engendered.[5]

So the ability to continue the life of the Immaculate Heart Community or of the individual member to remain within that community re-

---

[5] "Out of the Convent, into secular sisterhood," *Time* (February 16, 1970) 84. See
also "The Immaculate Heart Rebels," *Time* (February 23, 1970) 49–50; "You've Come
a Long Way Baby," *Time* (February 23, 1970) 55. James P. Shannon and I share the
front cover of this issue under the banner "The Catholic Exodus: Why Priests and
Nuns Are Quitting." These articles give a U.S. cultural context to our decision.

quires a sturdy faith, an undaunted courage, a reliable sense of humor, a belief in the intelligence of the common effort and of its fulfillment in dedication. All these require the members' constant reaffirmation and reinforcement of each other and in communal acts of worship and celebration.

This is the vision we dreamed of. If our vision is meant to survive, God will see that it does. If it should not, it may provide a glimpse of what humankind might gain in exchanging the comfort of well-trodden roads for the often imaginary terrors of the path not taken. Perhaps only by the latter path, with its risks and insecurities, will the splendor be found for us and for our times.

Chapter 15

The Immaculate Heart Community

The Immaculate Heart Community was born out of a religious idealism, a faith perspective, deep relationships, a collective resistance to unjust authority, and an unwavering Christian commitment to the individual conscience of each sister. Yes, we paid a high price. The lost relationships of some family, friends, colleagues, and institutions still pain many of us. Our renewal, which was ultimately a revolution, was accomplished only by an insistence on trusting our collective participation, which led us to a communal and practical vision. We believed that the Spirit of God was with us.

To some we are seen as having paved the way for renewal of Roman Catholic religious orders of women in the United States. What we lost in canonical recognition we gained in public witness to resist an authoritarian and abusive Church system of control. We gained joy and peace and freedom to worship, serve, and love.

As a Christian ecumenical community, our rituals are open and not confined by male-privileged rules and prohibitions. We are free to serve in the public and private realms of life. As attorneys, educators, ministers, professors, nurses, mothers and fathers, social workers, foster-mothers, scholars, musicians, secretaries, retreat and shelter directors, we continue to expand our understanding of being a Christian in the world. We are free to love and form committed relationships that enhance our service to the world.

Change holds both pain and possibility, fear and freedom. Thirty-three years ago we chose possibility and freedom. Today we exist and celebrate our future which is the present. Our freedom gifts us with laughter at the hurts of the past.[1]

Characteristic of our beginnings was the experience of our oppression as women. Pitted against a powerful patriarchy through years of petty criticism and overwhelming condemnation, we emerged conscious that the ecclesiology in which we lived could not tolerate our vision of liberation or of a relationship of equals.

But it was not only ourselves who were in this position. Slowly we came to realize that what we claimed for ourselves—the right to make decisions affecting our personal lives—we could not surrender. If we did, we yielded as well the right to self-determination as a community. We also realized the implications of our decisions for religious women everywhere. They, too, were present to us as we made our decision.

It was not a single cardinal who forced us to abandon canonical status in the Catholic Church. It was a vast ecclesiastical system that for centuries has used every ploy to keep women beholden to its curiously antiquated rules and regulations. Bishops, cardinals, priests have inherited the legacy of domination over women, especially over women religious, who by built-in dependencies of their lifestyles were made subservient to male clerics. This is not to say that some priests and bishops are not fully appreciative of the inequality and, whenever possible, try to relieve the immediate pressures on women, especially religious women. But the system itself remains intact.

Since the present history is concerned with a climactic effort to defeat and disempower one group of women devoted to the Church, more space will not be allotted here to other forms of systemic oppression. It is enough to point out that systems of oppression are often

---

[1] The current archbishop of Los Angeles, Cardinal Roger Mahony, in his Lenten address, issued a public apology for the sins of the California Catholic Church. Among those he acknowledged was the "unfortunate dispute" between his predecessors and the Immaculate Heart Community. He apologized to those "who felt hurt and rejection by the church during these years." Larry B. Stammer, "Mahony Offers Apology for His, Church's Failings," *Los Angeles Times* (March 8, 2000) sec. B:1.

Although these words may seem timid, the fact that the reigning Los Angeles Catholic archbishop felt he should make a public apology to the IHM Community discloses the deep feelings surrounding this historic event. This apology was given thirty years after we were fired collectively from service to the Catholic Church. The IHM leadership team acknowledged this apology in a letter to Cardinal Mahony.

linked; thus our conscientious inability to submit to one ecclesiastic led to our dismissal from our teaching ministry and thus, for a time, to economic hardship and deprivation of the sacramental presence of the Eucharist.

What is also worth noting in the IHM history is the bonding of male power figures so that once the patriarchal system is in operation, every activated link cooperates with every other. What bands of inquisitors ferreted out at visitations in our community was rubber-stamped "True" by the Los Angeles chancery office; what a single male clerical figure protesting support of the IHMs did in St. Louis at the Leadership Conference of Women Religious meeting was communicated to all religious in the country; what a single conservative priest condemned gave rise to the infamous "Four Points" issued by the apostolic delegate in Washington; what three bishops failed to understand called forth the silence of non-approval in the chambers of the secretary of state at the Vatican. And so it went.

The only way to escape the oppression was to exchange the term "religious" by opting for "religious person," and thus become a "non-canonical" community.[2]

Out of this experience of disempowerment was to come empowerment. Out of a predicted demise there was to come unexpected life and growth. Out of an unjust condemnation of our renewal was to come a renewed commitment to the works of justice.

Our mission statement sums up our understanding of our values and ideals:

[2] Sandra Schneiders, I.H.M., wrote: "The most disturbing case was probably the destruction of the Los Angeles I.H.M. congregation by Cardinal McIntyre when the congregation refused to revert to a preconciliar lifestyle. Although no full-scale history of the event is yet available, it is described in Quiñonez and Turner, *Transformation*, 152–153."—*Finding the Treasure: Locating Catholic Religious Life in a New Ecclesial and Cultural Context*, Religious Life in a New Millennium 1 (New York: Paulist Press, 2000) 392, note 22. Unfortunately, in pronouncing our "destruction" Schneiders misinterprets our experience. Moving from canonical to non-canonical status was not a destruction of our community. On the contrary, it gave us a new life and freedom. However, this type of interpretation also does a disservice to the history of Roman Catholic orders of women. There can be significant life and gospel living in communities with non-canonical status. Frequently I get inquiries from communities investigating this as a possible option.

We the members of the Immaculate Heart Community
rooted in Jesus Christ
and united with the people of God,
commit ourselves
to build relations in society
which foster access of all persons
to truth, dignity, and full human development,
and strategically to change
practices and situations
which impede such access.
In our choice of work and living style,
and in our use of
time, talent, and money,
we hold ourselves accountable to God
and one another
for effecting this goal
and supporting one another in this effort.

Epilogue

Dear Immaculate Heart Community Members,

To Destiny with You

Today I
Thought and I
Thought again as the
Lecturer announced
In learned tone
"We are destined—all"
As in D E S T I N Y
For a future no one
Can clearly see.
I cannot know
Or under-
Stand this, really
Nor can you—
But there it is.
So without a doubt
We know ourselves
Destined, you and me
For other things
Than our petty loves
And careless follies
Now this we share
Immediately

Our destiny is
An unknown thing.
A wondrous thing.
And this I hug
To my aging breast
With solemnity
To me, my dears,
You are destiny.

—Anita Marie Caspary, I.H.M.

To My Other Readers,

It is not fair to the Immaculate Heart Community to stop at the story of our struggles and the subsequent readjustments in our lives. At first our numbers decreased, our resources were limited, our institutions gradually were no longer staffed by community members, and our goals required rethinking by debate and discussion. And yet, somehow in all this the new community continued to grow, to listen to the great flood of counsel given by would-be advisors, to assimilate what fit our needs and to dismiss the rest. If there was always one consistent thing, it was our belief that the Spirit continued to enlighten and enliven us. Among our numbers, loving concern for one another's welfare was at the forefront, making us true successors of our bold and caring foremothers.

Perhaps the most hopeful sign of our continued existence and growth is the number of candidates who have joined us in the last several years. They come, women and men, the majority Roman Catholic, but with a growing number of Christians of other denominations linked in prayer groups, in committees, in celebrations. They are women and men of multiple talents and achievements searching for community, searching to transform their daily work into ministry, searching for God. They are persons learning to live humbly, to risk, to dare, and to be stirred by a passion for justice and peace. I believe that our next task is to renew the Christian life by living in the present moment, knowing that God's loving Spirit is always with us, no matter what happens.

SISTERS OF THE IMMACULATE HEART
LOS ANGELES, CALIFORNIA

Background of the Ninth General Chapter's Decree on Education

The Decree on Education, directed to the Immaculate Heart of Mary community and more specifically to its general government, was adopted in an attempt to solve two very serious problems of the community. The first is the inability to provide a sufficient number of teachers for the schools because of previous commitments to staff schools, a smaller number of candidates for religious life, and a larger number of sisters leaving the community than was the case a decade ago. The second problem lies in the fact that, in order to answer the requests of pastors, school superintendents, and bishops for new schools or for the maintaining of the usual number of sisters in existing schools, the Immaculate Heart community has not been able to educate its sisters to even a minimum level of professional competence in terms of degrees and licenses before sending them into professional apostolic work.[1]

For more than a century, the Sisters of the Immaculate Heart have had a deep commitment to Christian education. Although the sisters

---

[1] Full certification of elementary and high school teachers in California requires five years of college or university work, one of these being after the baccalaureate degree. Teachers may hold the certification on "postponement of requirement basis" if they have completed the baccalaureate degree and a certain amount of professional training. Certification held on a postponement of requirements basis may be renewed for seven years if a suitable amount of post-graduate work is pursued yearly. California's Compulsory Education law exempts from full-time attendance at public schools those children who attend a private school in which "teachers are capable of teaching." "Capable of teaching" has been defined by the State Attorney General, whose opinion has force of law, as holding the California license or having equivalent levels of preparation.

began their apostolic work in Spain as catechists to the indigent, they secured government approval as soon as they undertook to teach and maintain schools. For some time after coming to the United States from Spain in the nineteenth century, the sisters employed American lay teachers for the major school subjects, confining themselves to teaching sewing and the arts.[2] This they did because, having been competent teachers in Spain, they realized the injustice which would be done to students should they attempt to teach before becoming fluent with the language and recognized as American educators in their own right.

As the secondary and higher institutions which they owned and/or staffed were established, the sisters strove immediately to see that they were duly approved by the State Department of Education or by appropriate accrediting agencies. Thus, Immaculate Heart High School, accredited by the University of California in 1908, was the first high school in Southern California to be so recognized. Cathedral High School, under the direction of the Sisters of the Immaculate Heart, was the second. Cathedral High School retained its "A" entrance rating with the University until its accreditation was transferred to Los Angeles Catholic Girls High School—now Conaty Memorial—opened in 1923. Likewise, all the parochial high schools administered by the Sisters of the Immaculate Heart have been granted full recognition by accrediting agencies.

Immaculate Heart College was chartered by the State of California in 1916, the first baccalaureate degree being granted in 1922. The Graduate School, opened in 1950, offers over fifty Master's degrees annually in the fields of library science, English, professional education, biology, music, and religious education. At each stage in its development, Immaculate Heart College has received accreditation of its various programs and of the college as a whole. In addition to accreditation of the entire degree granting program by Western Association of Colleges and Secondary Schools, the college has been awarded full recognition by the American Chemical Association, American Association of Schools of Music and similar professional accrediting bodies. It is empowered by the California State Department of Education to recommend its graduates for immediate certification in elementary and secondary teaching, administration, supervision, and school librarianship. The teaching, administration, and supervision programs were

[2] Marian Sharples, I.H.M., *All Things Remain in God* (Los Angeles: Unpublished manuscript) 264.

also accredited in 1960 by the National Council for the Accreditation of Teacher Education, a distinction frequently reserved to much larger institutions.

The recognitions which institutions under the direction of the Immaculate Heart sisters receive attest to the continued living out of a tradition of striving to maintain high quality education, whether in matters of teacher education or of programs. In order to make such education readily available to priests and religious of other congregations, Immaculate Heart College offers its services to such students at considerably reduced tuition rates. Within recent years, this assistance has also been made available to lay teachers employed in parochial and diocesan schools. Reduced tuition rates for those employed in Catholic schools, other than Sisters of the Immaculate Heart, constitute an annual contribution to Catholic elementary and secondary education of one hundred thousand dollars annually.

The Sisters of the Immaculate Heart have a second quality imbedded in their history and, by implication, in their spirit. This is the traditional readiness to adapt to meet: the exigencies of time, situation and the needs of others. Thus, during a time when the sisters taught children of Catholic families who were not highly educated, many of whom were first-generation Americans, they found it necessary to send into classrooms teachers who were not prepared according to the standards of the day. Because of the backgrounds of the people in those early days, this kind of service was possibly sufficient. Indeed it was often superior by comparison with other schools then in existence. As time went on, however, and as a more highly educated public evolved, as sisters were asked to take on a larger and larger number of schools, both the degree of competence of the sister teachers and the lack of ability on the part of the community to supply numbers of teachers demanded by the increasing population became apparent.

The community made several attempts to meet the situation that evolved. It took steps also to follow the directives of Pope Pius XII, his successors and the Sacred Congregation of Religious that communities provide for their members an education at least equal to that of their secular counterparts.[3] In 1957, the Seventh General Chapter established a scholasticate (juniorate) for the newly professed sisters, the purpose

[3] Pius XII, "Nous Vous Adressons," September 15, 1952, delivered during the International Congress of Superiors General of Orders and Congregations of Women: On Religious Vocations.

of which was "to stabilize the formation begun during the novitiate, to provide for the spiritual, intellectual, and professional education of the sisters and to help them acquire the desired balance between prayer and study in the preparation for their apostolic work in the Institute" (Article 44, Constitutions). . . .

In principle the community committed itself to use all possible means, in keeping with its own traditions and the directives of the Church, to meet the problems of educating its sisters. Nevertheless, as late as 1963 because of outside pressures the community still found itself (1) agreeing to staff some new schools because of their proximity to other institutions of the community or for other special reasons; (2) providing additional staff for existing schools which, because of the influx of population to California had greatly increased their enrollments; (3) assigning some sisters to study for advanced degrees so that the young sisters, as soon as they could be released for full-time education would study under competent teachers at Immaculate Heart College. In spite of the attempts to educate, statistics showed that in May of 1967 seventy Immaculate Heart sisters were still without baccalaureate degrees, thirty-five of whom had been professed for ten years or more. . . .

By the time of the Ninth General Chapter, the tension between the desire to adapt to the need for teachers in the various dioceses and the necessity of preparing teachers for their work before assigning them to the classroom reached a point beyond which decision could not be delayed. The fact that this point had been reached is attested to by the study and reports of the Committee on Elementary Schools and the Committee on Secondary Schools of the preparatory Commission on Apostolic Works whose recommendations were presented to the chapter for action. In preparing their recommendations, these committees sent questionnaires to and interviewed every sister teaching in elementary and secondary schools. They likewise conferred with principals and supervisors and analyzed records of various kinds. Each month from October, 1966, until June, 1967, they reported to the total Commission on Apostolic Works and received its evaluation of their progress and the results of their study. Not unrelated to their concern were the consistent reports from doctors and from the sisters themselves that sending sisters into apostolic works for which they were not prepared was associated with deep discouragement, frequently accompanied by bitterness (especially when sisters had been teaching ten or more years without the minimum preparation required for professional beginners), illness, and leaving the community altogether. Coupled with these adverse effects on the sisters themselves, adverse effects in some children in some classrooms can only be imagined.

Using this and similar data, the Commission on Apostolic Works adopted the recommendations on education to be made to the Ninth General Chapter. The decree on education promulgated by the chapter was essentially the same as the recommendations made by the Commission on Apostolic Works (See Decrees of the Ninth General Chapter).

December, 1967
Sisters of the Immaculate Heart of Mary
5515 Franklin Avenue
Los Angeles, California 90028

Actions on the part of the Ordinary which have created difficulties for the Sisters of the Immaculate Heart

1. Denial of that academic freedom necessary to effective operation of an institution of higher learning and to the life of the community in general.

   References: Letter from His Eminence to Mother M. Humiliata, 9/11/65, regarding description of Immaculate Heart High School innovations in teaching of religion, *Ave Maria* article by Edward Fisher (4/17/65).

   Correspondence between His Eminence, Bishop Ward, and Mother M. Humiliata regarding Mary's Day publicity, 5/6/66; 5/10/66; 6/20/66.

   Correspondence between His Eminence, Mother M. Humiliata, and Sister William, 11/66, with regard to attendance of Sisters at lecture by Hans Küng and informal meeting with him at the college.

   Correspondence between His Eminence, Mother M. Humiliata, and Sister William in regard to article in college publication *On the Move.* Request that publications of the college and expressions of opinion by members of the community or its representatives be submitted to the Chancery Office for approval before publications, 7/15/67; 7/24/67; 8/2/67.

   Correspondence between Bishop Ward, and Mother M. Humiliata, and Sister William regarding status and function of Dean of Faculty—date [sic].

   Letter from Rt. Rev. Joseph F. Sharpe to Sister William, 5/8/64 ". . . to make it a matter of general policy to clear the names of guest speakers with the Chancery Office before inviting them to appear under the auspices."

Correspondence between His Eminence, Rev. Eugene Gilb, and Sister William, 4/9/67 and 4/24/65, regarding commencement speakers.

Sampling evidence of requests for clearance of the names of prospective theology instructors; correspondence between Sister Richard Reif and Vicars for Religious, 12/17/62; 12/27/62; 3/3/65; 3/10/65; same between Sister William and Sister Inviolata and Bishop Ward, 5/67 and 6/67, with reference to Rev. Eugene Burke, Rev. Mangin [sic].

2. Excessive curtailment of ecumenical and civil rights activities of any sort.

References: Letter from His Eminence to Mother M. Humiliata, 4/17/64, relative to Sisters' attending lecture sponsored by Catholic Human Relations Council; response to same 4/21/64.

Letter from His Eminence 7/6/67, regarding participation of Sister Camilla Edwards in ecumenical program; acceptance of misinformation from newspaper with consequent canceling of her activities before inquiring into the truth of the news account.

Correspondence between Bishop Ward and Sr. St. Anne Dunne [sic], 9/29/66, regarding talk to inter-church group.

Correspondence between Bishop Ward and Mother M. Humiliata, 3/23/66, regarding Sr. M. Jean Pew's participation in conference at Pomona (Pacem in Terris Conference).

Correspondence between Bishop Ward, Sister Richard Reif, Sr. M. Jean Pew, 3/66, with reference to cooperation with the Los Feliz Jewish Community Center; letters of 2/28/66; 3/1/66; 3/3/66; 3/7/66.

Correspondence between His Eminence, Rt. Rev. Msgr. Edward Wade, and Neil C. Sandberg on Sister Richard Reif's participation on a panel discussion on Catholic-Jewish Relationships, under sponsorship of American Jewish Committee, Los Angeles Chapter; letters of 3/30/65; 12/7/65; 12/9/65; 12/10/65.

3. Interference with affairs related to the internal life of the community especially:

   a. claiming the right to make General Chapter decrees dependent upon the approbation of the Ordinary; demanding, through his vicar, the list of chapter delegates and the agenda of the Ninth General Chapter;

   References: Appeal of the Sisters of the Immaculate Heart to the Sacred Congregation for Religious, 1/66.

   Report to Ninth General Chapter, 10/22/67, of meeting of members of general government with His Eminence, 10/16/67.

   Correspondence of Bishop Ward and reply of the Ninth General Chapter as cited under #4a below.

   b. ordering three visitations since April, 1965, one to the general government of the community, one to all of the IHM convents in the diocese, one to all members of the motherhouse, college, and high school staffs, as well as to the postulancy and novitiate staffs.

   References: Book of Minutes of the General Council, 5/65.

   Appeal to Sacred Congregation: see above.

   Correspondence among His Eminence, the Vicars for Religious, and Mother M. Humiliata, 11/65; 2/7/66; 3/23/67.

   c. issuing specific "recommendations" with regard to community prayer schedule and its content, silence, time of retirement, garb worn within the house, etc. (These "recommendations" have been given particularly as a result of visitation, but also at other times as well.)

   References: Appeal of IHM Sisters to the Sacred Congregation, see above.

   Letter from His Eminence of 12/28/65 and Mother M. Humiliata's response of 2/7/66.

   Correspondence from Bishop Ward, 5/15/67, and response of Mother M. Humiliata, 5/26/67.

   d. conducting follow-up visitation to see that "recommendations" were carried out; ignoring new legislation of Eighth General

Chapter in making inquiries during the visitation, even though decrees of same had been submitted to His Eminence in response to his request, 2/66.

References: Correspondence between His Eminence and Mother M. Humiliata, 12/28/65 to 2/7/67; interview with His Eminence, 2/67, at which Mother M. Humiliata presented Decrees of Eighth General Chapter.

Letter from Bishop Ward, 3/15/67, and response of Mother M. Humiliata 3/23/67. Denial by His Eminence and Bishop Ward that either had received decrees: see report of Mother M. Humiliata to Ninth General Chapter, 10/16/67.

e. *de facto* denial of right of Mother General to dispense within accepted limits in matters of religious discipline.

References: Questions sent by Rt. Rev. Msgr. Augustine O'Dea to Sister M. Carol Carrig, 11/15/65.

Letter from His Eminence, Cardinal Antoniutti, to Mother M. Humiliata, 7/67, as result of report of visitation.

Report to Ninth General Chapter of interview with His Eminence of 10/16/67.

f. making almost unshakeable judgments against the community on the basis of anonymous letters and other reports from Sisters and laymen.

References: Reference under #1 above to correspondence of 5/67.

Letter from Bishop Ward to Mother M. Humiliata, 7/11/67, and response of Ninth General Chapter, 7/18/67 (anonymous letter).

Correspondence between Bishop Ward and Mother M. Humiliata, 6/19/67 and 6/29/67.

Informal testimony of pastors regarding His Eminence's expressed view that decrees of Ninth General Chapter are result of minority coercing majority into a new way of life, that expression of dissent will be followed by recriminations on the part of the general government or/and of the community itself.

Questions asked by visitors to Motherhouse and college community as assembled during the April 1967 visitation.

Letter from Sisters of Motherhouse Community to His Eminence, 4/67.

4. Somewhat continued harassment in matters highly specific and/or at times technical, e.g.,

a. complaint of Bishop Ward that he was not notified of the Ninth General Chapter;

References: Letter from Mother M. Humiliata to His Eminence, 6/9/67, giving courtesy notification of chapter: to Bishop Ward, 6/29/67.

Letters from Bishop Ward, 6/7/67 and 6/14/67: response of Ninth General Chapter.

b. questions regarding approval of Mass books used at final vow ceremony when ceremony had been approved by predecessor of present Vicar for Religious;

References: Letter of Bishop Ward to Mother M. Humiliata, 8/16/67, and return correspondence from Sr. Gregory Lester, 8/24/67.

c. reprimand for having Mass outdoors at Montecito when so required because of lack of space indoors, even though such permission had already been given for the motherhouse and college; same with regard to concelebration;

References: Letter from His Eminence to Mother M. Humiliata, 7/17/67, with threat "that any recurrence of this kind will oblige us to an action which I am certain would be very restrictive to your community."

d. constant questioning of the Mother General's right to dispense in matters related to necessary experimentation (but restricted as to time and/or group) in the year before the General Chapter.

References: Letter from Bishop Ward concerning habit, 5/5/67; letter from His Eminence to Mother Regina, 6/5/67, regarding modified habit worn by hospital Sisters at Queen of Valley.

5. Disruption of the peace of the community and demoralization of its members as a result of #3 and #4 above.

6. Interpretation of decrees of Ninth General Chapter, especially those related to education, on the one hand, and those concerned with prayer, government, clothing on the other, as an "ultimatum" to the Ordinary with consequent:

   a. ordering of community to withdraw from the parochial and diocesan schools by June of 1968 (with some phasing out allowed until the end of the following year):

   b. forbidding the Sisters' meeting with the parents of students to discuss the decrees of the Ninth General Chapter.

      References: Session of the (meeting) Ninth General Chapter, 10/16/67.

      Correspondence between His Eminence and Mother M. Humiliata, with subsequent response of the Ninth General Chapter and its president, 10/67.

7. Implying, in spite of the order given in #6 above, that the community is choosing to withdraw from the parochial schools.

   References: as for #6 with emphasis on correspondence between His Eminence and Mother M. Humiliata, President of the Chapter, October 23, 24, 26, 30/67.

In all this, the community recognizes that the viewpoint of the Ordinary is influenced by two groups of Sisters:

   a. a relatively small group (possibly 25 to 50) who are very much opposed to the principles of renewal which have been held by a very large majority of the community and incorporated into the decrees of the Ninth General Chapter. (This group has registered its views repeatedly at the Diocesan Office.)

   b. an even smaller group who, wittingly or unwittingly, have taken advantage of the principles of renewal espoused by the community in order to perform imprudent acts.

It is likewise recognized by the community that the views expressed by group "a" above coincide with those of the Ordinary, and that the acts occasionally performed by group "b" above furnish some evidence that the principles espoused by the Ninth General Chapter, e.g., subsidiarity, responsibility, freedom, acceptance of diversity, respect for the human person, can and almost inevitably do allow for the possibility of abuse and evidence of human weakness.

Appendix C

Psychological Influences on the Sisters of the Immaculate Heart

Anita M. Caspary, I.H.M.

In Chapter 6, "The Sixties and the Sisters of the Immaculate Heart," there is reference to the influence of psychological principles on post-Vatican II spirituality, especially for religious women and men. This new way of thinking about our relationship to God and others began for the IHMs with the retreat-workshop given by the distinguished Father Noel Mailloux, O.P., in 1961. This introduction to psychological information filled a gap in the education of many IHM sisters. Many yearned for retreats and educational events that addressed the integration of psychology and religious belief, especially related to community life. This led to a series of prominent retreat masters visiting the IHM community. Following the retreat of Father Mailloux, we hosted Adrian Van Kaam, Gregory Baum, Eugene Kennedy, and many others.

Of all the influences on the IHM community and the changes we chose to make, the work of the eminent humanistic psychologist Carl Rogers received wide attention. By 1959 Rogers had developed a human relations theory that he called his dream. The applicability of this theory to educational systems was widely recognized, but its possibilities in other group contexts were yet to be tested. For this purpose, Rogers needed a system that included a women's college heavily invested in the training of teachers and a system that also staffed several high schools and a large number of elementary schools.

Briefly it proposed the intensive group experience (encounter group: T-group: human relations workshop) as a tool for educational change. "Individuals come to know themselves and each other more fully than is possible in the usual social or working relationships; the climate of openness, risk-taking and honesty guarantees trust. . . ."[1]

Immaculate Heart Community provided the ideal location to test Rogers' dream. Workshops were planned for the faculties of college, high schools, and elementary schools staffed by the IHMs. But preceding these meetings, a special workshop was organized for the delegates to the ninth general chapter of 1967 (the chapter of renewal).

Rogers' workshops centered on change and communication skills. Therefore it is accurate to state that the 1967 chapter of renewal proceedings were affected by Rogers and his staff. In the workshops before and after the chapter, Rogers was assisted by members of his staff, followers of his psychological theories. They spent valuable time with the IHM community and the faculties of our many institutions. Through the years many have speculated as to the direct influence Rogers' theory of change and communication his staff and the workshops had on our ultimate decision to change our status with the Catholic Church. If there was any influence, it was indirect. The decision of the chapter delegates in 1967 to write the decrees and embrace the process of experimentation was rooted in a deep commitment to the gospel, the directives of the Second Vatican Council, and the urgent need to educate the sisters in order to continue the IHM tradition of excellence in education at all levels.

Dr. William Coulson, Ph.D., an ardent follower of Rogers', was at one time the project coordinator for the implementation and facilitation of Rogers' theory in the workshops with the IHMs. However, at no time did Coulson supersede the leadership of Rogers during this period. For several decades Coulson has written about his role with the IHMs as one of a central figure during this time of transition. Since 1971, in a remarkable "conversion" from his former self-understanding and adherence to psychotherapy, Coulson has written and spoken ceaselessly of his role in the "destruction" of the Immaculate Heart Community. He speaks of the initial workshops of Rogers as time for a community ready for "an intensive look at themselves with the help of humanistic psychology. We overcame their traditions, we overcame

---

[1]Carl Rogers, *Freedom to Learn* (Columbus, Ohio: Charles E. Merrill Publishing Co., 1969) 718.

their faith."[2] His more recent writings convey a boastful knowledge about the IHM community that is false and inaccurate.

Coulson, with the fervor of a repentant sinner, describes the current population of the Immaculate Heart Community: "There may be a couple of dozen left all together, apart from whom, *kaput,* they're gone."[3] And in another passage he states: "We thought we could make the IHMs better than they were: and we destroyed them."[4]

In consideration of the above blatantly false statements, it is of interest to know how Carl Rogers evaluated the program with the IHMs. In an evaluative article entitled "The Project at Immaculate Heart," Rogers criticizes the lack of competence of some facilitators working in his program for the IHM institutions.[5]

Rogers' biographer and co-editor, Howard Kirschenbaum, counters Coulson's opinion that Rogers repudiated his project with the IHMs. A passage indicating Rogers' unchanging faith in his system is quoted by Kirschenbaum: "In 1986, the year before he died, Rogers wrote: 'What do I mean by a client centered or person centered approach? For me it expresses the primary theme of my whole professional life, as that theme has become clarified through experience, interaction with others, and research. . . .'"[6]

In these and even later personal reflections Rogers shows no signs of retracting his theory. Why Coulson persists in denigrating Carl Rogers and insisting on the demise of a healthy and growing religious community are matters for speculation and also for protest in the name of justice.[7]

[2] William Coulson, "We Overcame Their Traditions, We Overcame Their Faith," *The Latin Mass* (January–February 1994) vol. 3, no. 1:14.

[3] Ibid., 15.

[4] Ibid.

[5] Carl Rogers, "The Project at Immaculate Heart: An Experiment in Self-Directed Change," *Education* 95, no. 2 (1974) 181.

[6] Howard Kirschenbaum, "Denigrating Carl Rogers: William Coulson's Last Crusade," *Journal of Counseling & Development* 69 (May–June 1991) 412.

[7] Joyce Milton, in *The Road to Malpsychia* (San Francisco: Encounter Books, 2002), continues to repeat the myth of the destruction of the Immaculate Heart Community. See a promotion of the book at the website www.conservativebookclub.com.

Appendix D

Decrees of the Ninth General Chapter of the Sisters of the Immaculate Heart of Mary

PREFATORY STATEMENT

Los Angeles, California
October, 1967

Following the second Vatican Council Pope Paul VI issued a *Motu Proprio* dated September 2, 1966, entitled *Norms for the Implementation of the Council Decree on the Appropriate Renewal of Religious Life.* In the document the Pope exhorted all religious to examine and renew their way of life and to engage in wide-ranging experimentation in achieving this renewal. He directed each religious community to convoke a special Chapter of Affairs as soon as possible, in no event later than three years from the date of the *Motu Proprio.*

The document which follows, written by the delegates to the Ninth General Chapter of the Sisters of the Immaculate Heart, is based upon schemata prepared by commissions composed of a wide spectrum of community membership. Commission deliberations were in direct response to Pope Paul's request which was promulgated to the entire community on October 15, 1966. Meeting regularly from that date until the convening of the general chapter on July 2, 1967, these commissions labored to interpret the life of the Sisters of the Immaculate Heart and to relate that life to both Church and world in a manner which will be deeply religious and fully human.

Thus the following document suggests a way of life by which the Sisters of the Immaculate Heart wish to live during the period of experimentation requested by the Holy Father. Though it represents our best efforts to date, it is in no way final or conclusive. Rather it is a provisional document to be reflected on throughout the coming year and evaluated at the summer, 1968, session of the Chapter. The general decrees (I, II, III, etc.) are descriptive statements which incorporate the spirit underlying the more specific decrees (I.1, I.2, I.3, etc.) following them. The latter are always to be viewed in the context of the former, more general decrees.

Prologue

I. Decree on Apostolic Works

II. Decree on Person in Community

III. Decree on Apostolic Spirituality

IV. Decree on Authority and Government

V. Decree on Preparation for Life in Community

VI. Epilogue

PROLOGUE (1967)

We live in an era marked by decreasing formalism and increasing candor; more and more things are being called by their names. We see the world, with its mixture of beauty and sadness, as the only one we know and the only place in which we may live and work. We see the church as the extension of Christ's body, instituted by Himself, meant to be of service and a yoke to no man. Christ came that we might have life, and He showed us by His own choices, by unhesitatingly transcending traditional categories and separations, that life is to be abundantly fulfilled only in the freedom to make difficult and consequential decisions which confound some of the people at least some of the time.

Women, perhaps especially dedicated women, insist on the latitude to serve, to work, to decide according to their own lights. Our community's history from its beginning, including its early missionary activities in California and its eventual separation from a Spanish foundation which was inevitably removed from and indifferent to peculiarly American conditions, speaks of our readiness to abandon dying forms in order to pursue living reality. It expresses, also, our willingness to seek human validity rather than some spurious supernaturalism.

Women around the world, young and old, are playing decisive roles in public life, changing their world, developing new life styles. What is significant about this new power for women is not that it will always be for the good, nor that it will always edify, but that there can be no reversing of it now. Women who want to serve and who are capable of service have already given evidence that they can no longer uncritically accept the judgment of others as to where and how that service ought to be extended. American religious women want to be in the mainstream of this new, potentially fruitful, and inevitable bid for self-determination by women.

What all of this affirms is the pulpit message often preached but seldom perceived, that we have not here a lasting city, that we are pilgrims on the move. We must be ready to weigh the value of any change, and ready to choose it without regard to the cost, if such change appears to be in order. This is not to canonize change for its own sake, but to insist that change be rational and directed rather than happenstance and reactive, for there is no life without change. The question is whether we will ourselves determine the course of change, or submit to it passively.

We would miss much of the world's wonder if we were to suppose that change is limited to the measurable: production rates, population growth, the phenomenal increase in the power of lethal weapons. But these measurable elements of growth are seen in a less overwhelming perspective when we compare them with the potential significance of changing modes of communicating and learning, of new dimensions in awareness of self, awareness of others, and, ultimately, awareness of God. It would seem that the ability to change, to evaluate and direct change, must soon become prized human goals if we are not to become a generation of automata, controlled by an array of forces of change—political, technological, ideological.

Most active religious communities, including our own, had their origins in the spontaneous response of sensitive men and women to particular needs in their society which were not being adequately met: teaching and healing the poor; providing for the indigent, the destitute and dying, the incurable; catechizing; witnessing to the Church's concern for the life of the mind in higher education and scholarship. It was the work, and the way in which the work was done, which attracted new members to these communities, and in time the work became more or less fixed.

At the same time these communities tended to become less responsive to new and more acute needs in their societies. Their zeal had bounds set on it by their commitments to tasks no longer clearly needed, and to tasks which were being performed on a more comprehensive and far-reaching basis by agencies funded by public monies. Even buildings themselves, some of them highly specific in terms of the kind of work which could be performed in them, set limits on the apostolic imagination of those who had come to religious life in order to serve their neighbors as simply and directly as possible.

It can be confidently asserted that there is a providence in the events and trends of Church and world in the last ten years as these affect members of religious communities. The documents of Vatican II summarize the spirit of these events and trends in their emphasis on the centrality of Christ, on the unity of the human community, on a renewed conception of the dignity of man and of the respect which must be paid to the voice of the Spirit speaking through human history.

Again and again, these documents recall the Church and its members to Christ's intention in establishing the Church: "to give witness to the truth, to rescue and not to sit in judgment, to serve and not to be served."[1]

The pilgrim quality of the Church is undeniably affirmed. The injunction to travel light is implicit in this, as is the willingness to listen to the outcry of man who, generation after generation, finds himself in the position of destroying his young, denying access to the truth, neglecting the neglected, despising the ignorant, fearing the man who is different in color and belief.

In all of this religious today hear a desperate cry for their relevant response. By relevant the world means a response which really touches its need for peace, which leads to an end to the senseless amassing and destructive use of lethal weapons, for an end to the artificial separations of the colored peoples of God's one human race, for an end to the legalistic, judgmental, self-serving exclusions of beliefs, customs and conditions not corresponding to our own.

What the world desperately needs is bridges, individuals and groups who, like Christ Himself, put an end to all the distances which divide men and which hinder their access to truth, dignity and full human development. This is another way of saying that the world needs community; it needs models of community to convince it that the diverse and warring elements in the human family can be reconciled.

Implicit in the will-to-community is a readiness to respond and a desire to move on. These become a demanding discipline and asceticism, and endow with renewed meaning the life of the evangelical counsels. They reconstitute the religious life as an effective and affec-

---

[1] Pastoral Constitution on the Church in the Modern World in *The Documents of Vatican II*, ed. Walter M. Abbott, S.J. (New York: America Press, 1966) no. 3:201.

tive expression of service and praise. They are the voice of our founders speaking clearly again in our own time through the Church to the world.

The virtue and talents and inner strength of our community give hope that we will endure and continue to contribute significantly to Church and world. The will and ability to serve implicit in this hope depend upon the widening or removal of some of the institutional bounds currently set on apostolic zeal.

We wish to remain faithful to our long-standing and beneficial commitments to teaching and healing. There are some, however, who can no longer see the compatibility between the spirit of Vatican Council II and parochial education when it is conducted in such a way that the generally accepted aims of education are obstructed, or with healing as it is exercised in hospitals which are often caught in bureaucratic entanglements. There are aspects of both which seem to them to have little to do with charity or religion, with the city of man or the city of God.

The documents and decrees which follow say some introductory things about some of the changes which we believe must be made if our life and work are to be satisfying and significant and worthy to be called religious. They have to do with the spirit in which we are to render service (apostolic works, education, health services, other works); with the spirit in which we live together (person in community) and pray to our Father (apostolic spirituality); with the spirit and regulations by which we live in common according to the counsels (local and general government); with the spirit and manner in which we incorporate new members (preparation for life in community); with the whole manner in which we give "splendid witness" by our communal life and service to our faith in the possibility of fulfilling the two great commandments.

I. Decree on Apostolic Works

We Sisters of the Immaculate Heart of Mary are united by our faith in Christ and our dedication to carry out His redemptive work. The two great commandments of the gospel provide the total meaning and direction of our dedicated life; the beatitudes and the counsels implied in them give it form. What this means is that our dedication exists in and exercises itself through loving service of neighbor, thereby manifesting the presence of Christ in our world.

As the Second Vatican Council made clear, this service of neighbor is extended not only to members of the Church but to the whole family of man.[2] Through the Council, the mission of the Church was viewed as essentially that of reconciliation,[3] of creating human community,[4] of helping to solve the world's urgent economic, social, and political problems.[5] If every humanizing work is, consciously or unconsciously, a Christian work, then every humanizing work would seem to be a proper apostolate. The dignity of the human person, rooted in his call to communion with God,[6] makes the service of the human community an obligatory one for the People of God who, in this service, show forth and exercise the mystery of God's love for men.[7]

Moreover, we believe that our direct and immediate participation in the mission assigned by the Council Fathers to the laity calls for a new style of communal existence— one which will not rigidly separate us by customs, cloister, or clothing from those we serve. We wish to identify ourselves intimately with the life and concerns of our fellow man, to share with them the richness and strength of our community life. In effect, what we desire is community—but community without walls.[8]

We seek, therefore, a recognition of this new conception of our apostolate and of the life-style which it demands. This vision of religious life and work, foreshadowed by the ecumenical zeal of Pope John XXIII, will enable us to join with other men of good will in healing the divisions which rend the human family.[9] It will also meet the urgent need of young people today, who yearn to serve by assuming their share of responsibility for shaping the world and its corporate life. We offer this new vision of religious life as a partial answer to the vocation crisis within our own community, and perhaps to the general crisis of religious life in America today.

Faithful to the spirit of their founders as well as to the promptings of Vatican II, the Sisters of the Immaculate Heart will strive: 1) to determine the most urgent social, economic, intellectual, and spiritual needs of the family of man; 2) to satisfy these needs insofar as they are within the aims and the spiritual and material resources of the Immaculate

[2] Ibid. no. 1:199–200.
[3] Rom. 5:8; 2 Cor. 5:18.
[4] Pastoral Constitution on the Church, no. 42:242.
[5] Ibid., no. 31:229; no. 55:261.
[6] Ibid., no. 19:215; no. 26:225.
[7] John 4:16; Col. 3:14; and Rom. 13:10.
[8] Pastoral Constitution on the Church, no. 32:230.
[9] Decree on the Church's Missionary Activity in *The Documents of Vatican II*, ed. Walter M. Abbott, S.J. (New York: America Press, 1966) no. 7:594.

Heart Community; and 3) to provide the opportunity for each sister to experience her own fulfillment as a person by adequate preparation and continued education to meet these needs.[10]

For greater apostolic effectiveness the sisters are offered freedom and opportunity to respond to the needs of Christ in the world today in apostolic endeavors in addition to those already undertaken by the community. Such authentic response to contemporary needs may include involvement in diverse political and social actions. In such actions sisters act as individuals according to conscience, but the corporate ramifications of their acts should be a consideration in the making of their decisions. They have the rights and responsibilities of every citizen and are no more and no less exempt from the consequences of their free actions than any other citizen.

Finally, the sisters should continuously evaluate their works in an effort to make them more relevant to and effective in contemporary society. The community and its individual members are mutually responsible for determining priority of needs and for assuming only those works and obligations which are consistent with their capabilities and limitations.

Education

The work of education has been a main concern of the Sisters of the Immaculate Heart since their foundation in 1848. Our conviction of the centrality of the educational apostolate is based on the belief that every human person has an inalienable right to an education enabling him to develop his full potential as a human person and to contribute positively and creatively to the building of a better society. But the conception of the goal and process of education has necessarily undergone modification by reason of the rapid and constantly accelerating changes in all areas of modern life.

In a world of increasing diversification and specialization, problems arise daily to which there are no ready-made solutions. The goal of education, therefore, is not only to impart information. It is also, and more importantly, to develop flexible, adaptive individuals, open to change and willing to learn continuously. Accordingly, the process of learning must become an increasingly dynamic one in which teacher

---

[10] Decree on the Appropriate Renewal of Religious Life in *The Documents of Vatican II*, ed. Walter M. Abbott, S.J. (New York: America Press, 1966) no. 20:479.

and student cooperate in inquiry, experimentation and discovery. Only by such active participation in the learning process can the student develop an adequate awareness of his complex world and the ability to respond critically and lovingly to its challenges. Furthermore, such participation provides the most effective means through which beliefs and values are made one's own.

Although we believe that effective Christian education must, in the future as in the past, hold an important place in the teaching mission of Christ' s Church, and of our own congregation within the Church, we have become increasingly aware that our own efforts have been falling short, by a widening margin, of our objectives and aspirations in this field. We observe political, economic, educational and religious trends in our American and Catholic society which must inevitably raise our aspirations further and make them even more difficult to obtain. We are persuaded in particular that financial realities will impose restrictions on the relative size of the Catholic school system and will suggest a reorientation toward a smaller system of more distinguished quality. And we are persuaded that in an ambience of strongly supported and generally sound public education, only distinguished quality in both religious and secular fields can retain for Catholic education the persevering support of Catholic parents and other elements of the Catholic community. We are convinced also that the forces cited have brought us to the threshold of creative initiatives for more nearly integral Christian education in our schools.

These changed perceptions of education in general are especially true of formal religious education. There, too, the goal is conceived less in terms of imparting a body of doctrine than in the formation of a certain type of person: one open and responsive to the love of God revealed in and through Christ. And the process, mysterious though it be, is a cooperative one. It involves a reciprocal personal witness, possible only where thoughts and experiences are shared.

Given the paramount importance of education in the life of man, we pledge to take every means possible to insure its excellence. For to the degree that any kind of education is deficient, to that extent it is less Christian.

Health Services

In 1953 the Sisters of the Immaculate Heart voted by secret ballot to extend their apostolate to include hospital work, in order to manifest

Christian love to the sick, injured and dying, to increase vocational opportunities for the sisters, and to provide an additional source of revenue for the community. As a result of rapid changes in the concept of medical care as manifested in the larger society, the present trend is for hospitals to expand their services, so that in addition to being facilities to which persons come for treatment, they also serve as bases from which satellite programs can be offered, e.g., home nursing services, family counseling, preventative medicine, rehabilitation, and other social services.

The sister in the health services should be adequately trained prior to pursuing her task, just as she should realize her need for continued education in her field in order to remain competent in her work.

Sisters should be free to follow the lead of the Spirit in their care for the sick and injured as the needs of the People of God are manifested to them. This commitment may be on an individual or community basis and in community-owned or other institutions. However, requests to be released for individual commitments should be made with a responsible awareness of the need for adequate staffing of existing community commitments.

II. Decree on Person in Community

The theme of person in community inspires many of our contemporary prophets, both within and outside the Church. Their stress on the sacredness of the human person and his fulfillment within community seeks to avoid both the extreme of isolating individualism and that of repressive collectivism.[11] Realizing that an over-emphasis on either person or community can so easily occur in an age marked both by a passion for freedom and a need for conformity, we as persons freely joined in community desire to reiterate this contemporary theme as it relates to our Christian communal existence.[12]

An emphasis on persons developing in community is deeply rooted in the message of Sacred Scripture.[13] Christ's unique reality as Son,

---

[11] Declaration on Religious Freedom in *The Documents of Vatican II*, ed. Walter M. Abbott, S.J. (New York: America Press, 1966) no. 1:675; The Pastoral Constitution on the Church, no. 12:211.

[12] Pastoral Constitution on the Church, no. 17:214.

[13] Declaration on Religious Freedom, no. 1:676.

realized in the triune community of the Godhead, is the primary instance of that fundamental paradox: one's radical selfhood, his very constitution as a person, is realized only in and through his relation to other persons.[14] This reciprocity of person and community became manifest when Christ dealt with human persons in community.[15] Whether he stressed the disciples' relation to their heavenly Father or to Himself or to one another, Christ ranked the inviolability of the person over the demands of conformity, while exalting fraternal union over isolating self-fulfillment.[16] Thus, His earthly actions speak profoundly of the dignity of the human individual and the primacy of community, but never of the person in isolation, nor of the community through coercion.[17]

Recognizing this creation of community as the universal vocation of Christians, and appreciating the diverse ways of achieving such a goal, we as Sisters of the Immaculate Heart dwell together with the explicit intention of fostering the conditions which make community possible.

Starting with our own religious family, we strive to create those human situations wherein individuals can develop not in spite of, nor at the expense of, but because of the common good of community.[18]

Community, as a value in itself, consists in a quality of relationships based in part on the mutual recognition of shared personal needs for affection, inclusion, privacy, inner discipline, and external limits. Indeed, the relation of person to community is a reciprocal and developing one. Just as the community has a responsibility to foster unique personal talents, so the individual person comes to realize that her talents are to be used for the larger good.[19]

These convictions regarding persons in community—the sacredness of human persons, the importance of diversity, the priority of the common good, and community as a quality of relationships—point to some of the fundamental values of our life in common.[20] But any communal life presupposes some organizational form or structure through which these values may be realized. Thus within the community there is need for some business-like relations, quite compatible with proper

---

[14] Pastoral Constitution on the Church, no. 19:215.

[15] Ibid., no. 12:211.

[16] Ibid., no. 23:222; no. 31:229.

[17] John 14:10-17.

[18] Pastoral Constitution on the Church, no. 40:238–239.

[19] Rom. 15:1- 6.

[20] Acts 6:1-4.

respect for person. For our community of persons is also a working organization wherein the personal and functional levels of existence are interrelated.

The particular form or structure of a community is not simply an historical legacy. It is the ongoing creation enjoined upon all its members. Hence, this structure is a matter to be carefully considered and continually evaluated in the light of the shared values. Every particular goal, custom, norm, rule, practice, or role expectation is good only insofar as it is a positive means for affirming those values. In response to situational exigencies, the structure may have to be altered in some or many of its particulars. This alteration may create new problems which, in turn, call for further structural change. Only with this kind of flexibility is a religious community able to satisfy its members' desire to serve with justice and love the changing needs of the larger community of mankind.[21]

III. DECREE ON APOSTOLIC SPIRITUALITY

The kind of religious community which we envision is rooted in the gospel and in Christ's own life.[22] This evangelical meaning is affirmed by Vatican II as the dedication of the whole human person to Christ.[23] Since Christ is our risen Lord, the entire universe is alive with His presence.[24] Through the gift of His Spirit, God dwells in the midst of mankind, revealing Himself to us not only in Sacred Scripture and in the life of the Church, but also in every aspect of our human circumstance.[25] Thus any dedication to the person of Christ implies a dedication to all men.[26] As Sisters of the Immaculate Heart we "gather in His name" and through this explicitly communal manner help others and ourselves to become the full human persons who celebrate and serve in this Christian way.[27]

[21] Pastoral Constitution on the Church, no. 55:260.

[22] Dogmatic Constitution on the Church in *The Documents of Vatican II*, ed. Walter M. Abbott, S.J. (New York: America Press, 1966) no. 43:73; See also Decree on Religious Life, no. 1:466.

[23] Decree on Religious Life, no. 6:470-471.

[24] Col. 1:18-20; Phil. 2:9-11.

[25] Dogmatic Constitution on Divine Revelation in *The Documents of Vatican II*, ed. Walter M. Abbott, S.J. (New York: America Press, 1966) no. 8:116.

[26] Pastoral Constitution on the Church, no. 1:199.

[27] Mt. 18:19-20; I Thess. 5:17.

All Christian prayer is orientated principally toward a deepened awareness of our filial relationship to God. In prayer the full, concrete reality that we are, in whatever situation we find ourselves—joy, sorrow, hope, despair, struggle, peace, emptiness, boredom, or confusion—is brought into the presence of God and exposed to Him. Prayer is thus a fully human activity. It does not deny or destroy anything that we are. It is not something imposed on our lives as a superstructure, nor arbitrarily inserted into them at certain times or places. Rather it enters into the total rhythm of our lives so that in what we are and do there is a joy and completeness and hope which proclaim our belief in the risen Christ. To the degree that through our prayer we allow ourselves to be open to the Holy Spirit leading us into an unknown future, to that extent we will have reached an authentic wholeness between life and prayer. Apostolic work, therefore, is not only the fruit of Christian prayer, but also its stimulus and nourishment. It is through prayer that our work has that depth and richness of meaning which makes it radiate the spirit of Christ.

Prayer takes many forms, and in all of them, both liturgical and personal, God is revealed and a response of faith is inspired. Yet the supreme prayer of the Christian community is the Eucharistic celebration.[28] It is both the source and the sign of that profound familial unity between men and God and between man and man which is the presence of the Holy Spirit.[29] As religious women we manifest in a communal way this presence of the Risen Lord in our world, a presence intensified by the Eucharistic celebration.[30] Sacred Scripture, too, nourishes our life of prayer.[31] For it is the living word of God, speaking to us with force and power, able to effect in us what it proclaims.

Finally, in our community life we turn to Mary, the most holy Mother of God. As one of the faithful in community who heard the word of God and pondered it in her heart, she made His interests her own; in her service, concern, and compassion for others Mary extended Christ's redemptive work. Thus she exemplifies the believer in whom the Spirit dwells, celebrating Christ's risen presence in our world.[32]

---

[28] Constitution on the Sacred Liturgy in *The Documents of Vatican II*, ed. Walter M. Abbott, S.J. (New York: America Press, 1966) no. 10:142.

[29] John 6:51.

[30] Decree on Religious Life, no. 15:477.

[31] Constitution on the Sacred Liturgy, no. 33:149.

[32] Dogmatic Constitution on the Church, no. 53:86; no. 56:88.

We must remember, however, that God dwells with us as with those who are on the way. We are women on pilgrimage who recognize our need, personally and communally, for conversion of mind and heart.[33] The greater openness to reality in any conversion often entails pain.[34] Therefore, we accept a constant dying for the sake of more abundant life in the human community.[35]

In sum, we aspire to a kind of prayer which unites us with God and gradually opens us to the full meaning of our Christian existence. All our prayer is a gift from God, though God's action in us is dependent upon our response to Him. We recognize that development in prayer gradually unfolds in the life of each person; we spend our entire lives becoming women of prayer.[36] Though we find ourselves at times separated from those of other religions in the forms our prayer may take, we aim to unite ourselves with all mankind as we pray to the Father, through the Son, and in the Spirit.[37]

IV. Decree on Authority and Government

The concepts of authority, obedience, and community are correlative and interdependent. The notion of authority which emerges from a study of the New Testament is that of service. By virtue of baptism all Christians share this responsibility of service according to their various gifts and callings. Thus, in a true sense, every Christian "authors" the salvation of the whole body; every Christian has authority. The emphasis is not so much on laws and control as on love and leadership in promoting the mission of the Church: the proclamation of the gospel by word and work.[38] It is only by virtue of this mission that any authority in the ecclesial context is empowered to act, and it properly acts by freeing the individual Christian to respond with generosity and joy to the call of Christ manifested in the needs of mankind. The scriptural concept of obedience is complementary to and inseparable from that of authority. It, too, is a form of service. It consists not so much in the

[33] Ibid., no. 41:70.
[34] Pastoral Constitution on the Church, no. 22:221.
[35] Ibid.
[36] Decree on Religious Life, no. 8:472.
[37] Decree on Ecumenism in *The Documents of Vatican II*, ed. Walter M. Abbott, S.J. (New York: America Press, 1966) no. 7–8:351.
[38] Mt. 28:18-20.

fulfillment of precepts as in the active acceptance of Christ's invitation to cooperate in His mission. While authority is our share in the mission and power of Christ, obedience is our active response to the demands placed upon us by that participation. And, since it is the Spirit who clarifies for us what Christ's mission is,[39] it is by listening to the Spirit speaking to us through Scripture, through each other, and through human events that we both author and obey.

In a religious community whose members are united in a communal effort to carry out Christ's humanizing mission, authority serves both by embodying and promoting the loving communion of persons and by coordinating the actions of the group through appropriate rules. To expedite the attainment of these communal goals the members of the community exercise the authority which is theirs by delegating it to various offices or by group decisions. In both cases there is need for open interchange and mutual consultation so that the insights of all are brought to bear on the decisions of authority.[40] Our religious obedience consists not in passive submission but in cooperative interaction with other members of the community. The obedient sister enters wholeheartedly into common deliberations and accepts the decisions arrived at thereby; for, assuming that mutual consultation has taken place and that authority desires to promote the common good, she has a legitimate basis for trust in its dictates. However, since each person is responsible for her actions and for their effect upon community, in substantive decisions the obedient sister may not abstain from judging whether these are really in the service of the common good, nor from acting in accord with this judgment. Even when she judges by thoughtful questioning of or considered opposition to such decisions, her stance does not necessarily deny or weaken authority. Rather, she may strengthen authority by helping it to overcome the limitations in its actual exercise.[41]

Such a notion of obedience is much more demanding than uncritical compliance with precepts, since it involves unremitting concern for the common good and the effort to act always in love. Such love entails a constant process of self-purification: from egoism, precipitous judg-

---

[39] John 14:26.

[40] Decree on Religious Life, no. 14:476-477; Dogmatic Constitution on the Church, no. 37:64.

[41] Robert O. Johann, "Authority and Responsibility," *Freedom and Man,* ed. John Courtney Murray (New York: P. J. Kenedy & Sons, 1965) 148–151.

ment, narrowness of view, and prejudice. Constructive, loving criticism of authority presupposes an even more profound self-criticism.

In order to realize the above conceptions of authority and obedience in our community, we think it necessary to make some changes in our present government. We seek to develop a governmental structure which will reflect our beliefs in broad participation in decision-making, subsidiarity, personal freedom and responsibility, and open and free communication.

The Fathers of the Second Vatican Council with their emphasis on collegiality, as well as the findings of psychologists, sociologists, and political scientists all emphasize the importance of subordinates involving themselves in decision-making processes. Whether one looks to the group decision-making which characterized the older monastic tradition, or to the newer political impetus to participatory democracy, one finds that purposeful involvement in the life of the community is best achieved when there is structural provision for this involvement and when significant decisions are made by those affected by them.

The principle of subsidiarity holds that decisions should be made whenever possible at the level at which they are to be implemented. We believe that this principle should operate in our community. Only when demands on the local unit (whether individual sister or separate living group) are beyond the resources of the unit should there be referral to higher authority. Outside counsel may with profit be called in to facilitate the making of decisions by the local group. Ordinarily, however, there should be no need for someone from another level of authority to intervene in the carrying out of these decisions, since reliance on outside intervention often tends to undermine the necessary autonomy and responsibility of the smaller unit.

Personal freedom is exercised in the choice to join and subsequently to remain with the community. No coercion is possible in this choice. But from this choice there follows a personal responsibility for continuing active participation in the community's work. Each sister is expected to help determine, achieve, and evaluate community goals.

The open, free, and continuous communication which we desire in the total life of our community is especially needed if the above characteristics are to become operative in our governmental structure. This communication is important on all levels: among the sisters themselves, between the sisters and those in positions of authority, between the sisters and those with whom they work, whether clergy or lay. We want to keep open all the channels through which the Spirit speaks to us so that our common deliberations and joint decisions will produce a Christian community attentive and responsive to the needs of (men).

Administration of Funds

The area of finance can with profit be related to our beliefs about person and community. In order that the services of the sisters may be generously extended to apostolates which cannot be self-supporting, community resources are apportioned by those to whom stewardship has been given as a trust by the community. This does not preclude the advisory function of those representative boards whose statements should reflect the thinking of the total community.

The community has special and privileged obligations to its own members who are ill or retired or in full-time preparation for the apostolate. These obligations rest on the community as a whole and may entail, at times, the sacrifices of certain material advantages for the individual sisters. Therefore, the sister in the active apostolate ought to consider carefully her personal expenditures for clothing, vacations, retreats, advantages in education, special plans, etc., in the light of community projects and community obligations. If the individual sister finds her independent judgment in these areas modified, she accepts this situation knowing that her freedom from preoccupation with material goods in the spirit of Christian simplicity is one measure of her availability for the apostolate. By such sacrifices she freely and lovingly acknowledges her indebtedness to the past and her hope and vision for the future of the community.

V. Decree on Preparation for Life in Community

Various traditions exist by which men express personal commitment to Christ and fidelity to the Church in the service of mankind. Among these is our pattern of life in community. We are convinced that community is an entity beyond the sum of individual qualities within the group, and that Christian community bears a special witness to the presence of Christ in the world. For, under the guidance of the Holy Spirit, when the powers released by communal interaction are directed toward the needs of mankind, that service acquires a Christian dimension impossible to an individual worker. "Where two or three are gathered in My name, there am I in the midst of them."

Women who choose this kind of communal witness will find it demanding. For there will be no fixed pattern or structure nor even a permanent involvement in one type or manner of work. Within community, they continually examine and evaluate their concerns and commitment, developing sensitive awareness and compassionate response to the needs of the world.[42] They find their commitment to Christ deepened and strengthened by communal and private prayer. They find Christ at work in the world wherever there are those who bear the burdens of others, wherever there are those who love and suffer for one another, wherever there is need for community.[43]

To incorporate into our Immaculate Heart community women intent on a life of service to the larger community of mankind is no small challenge. For, as stated elsewhere, community is created out of the dynamic relationships among its members. Such dynamism causes continual change in the complexion of the community, change which stems from and affects each member.

The new member comes to our community from the wider community of mankind, often bringing with her a distinctive spirituality, a background of communal service and worship, specialized training, and a particular knowledge of the needs of mankind.[44] The personal attitudes and goals developed through these experiences moved her to dedicate herself to a life of service in the first place. Therefore, with this contemporary understanding, to consider her a "novice" in these areas and to attempt to "train" her accordingly is to set her introduction to community on a false basis. Formerly, a style of initiation for new members developed which was based upon the presupposition that withdrawal from contemporary society was a better way to live a Christian life of service. This belief in turn indicated a more or less uniform pattern of induction which came to require a closed and isolated environment, constant supervision and control, and discipline aimed at behavioral conformity. Since many of the values implied in this style are no longer in accord with our vision of community, such a novitiate now seems not only inadequate but detrimental.[45]

[42] Decree on Religious Life, no. 2:468–469.

[43] Message to Humanity in *The Documents of Vatican II*, ed. Walter M. Abbott, S.J. (New York: America Press, 1966) 5.

[44] Declaration on Christian Education in *The Documents of Vatican II*, ed. Walter M. Abbott, S.J. (New York: America Press, 1966) 638.

[45] Pastoral Constitution on the Church, no. 7:205; Decree on Religious Life, no. 3:469.

The once clear distinctions underlying these values are, in fact, now blurred. The great themes of Vatican II have called into question, if not denied, a disjunction between the secular and the sacred, between law and spirit, between church as institution and church as body of pilgrims, between lay and religious.[46] Hence, those patterns of living and attitudes of mind which separated religious in a divisive way from the general body of the faithful must be carefully scrutinized when formulating any change in training for community life.

Our scrutiny thus far convinces us that there are certain values inherited from the past, yet no longer viable in the forms of the past, certain values implied in contemporary society, yet suffering for lack of development in that society. Hence the modern community woman must add a new dimension to that generosity, endurance, and fidelity which characterized her predecessors in religious life. She needs as well a sense of personal autonomy, independence of judgment and tolerance for adversity if her service in the contemporary world is to have any significance or effect. Further, she needs so to make community her own that from the outset she is capable of building up community in the tradition of Immaculate Heart.

This continuously flexible tradition in our ever changing world demands, then, certain qualities of a mature, independent and resourceful woman: a sensitive self-knowledge and acceptance of others; an ability to grow in giving and receiving love; an adaptability to changing situations; a self-discipline required by her work and common life; an initiative and courage in contributing to the growth of the community. Her early experiences in the community, then, far from stifling her independence or narrowing her vision, must increase her sense of worth and provide her with the tools to help build community.

Thus, preparation for life in community is the process by which each individual, with her personal background and experience, talents and differences, inserts herself into the complex of dynamic relationships which make up community. The individual differences of all members create the richness of community, and the community experience enriches each individual. With the help and support of more experienced members, especially those of the Committee on Community Membership, the new member makes her own the community

---

[46] Decree on the Apostolate of the Laity in *The Documents of Vatican II*, ed. Walter M. Abbott, S.J. (New York: America Press, 1966) no. 5:495; Dogmatic Constitution on the Church, no. 9:25.

goals and spirit, while contributing substantially to their development. She may require professional training so that she may participate in the community's service of men; she will need to integrate her past and present experiences; she will need to receive the gospel message and, by reflection and prayer, contribute to her own and others' growth in Christ. For her increased commitment to Christ and the Church through community is her personal responsibility. In a sense she must prepare herself, a process which is life-long.

VI. Epilogue

Our vocation as persons in community implies first of all a realization of our humanity, not an escape from it. For only in community does the human person adopt a life pattern of creative response to circumstances. Even more does the religious community involve the person in a permanent engagement with the world, rather than flight from the world or protection from its concerns. For witness to the risen Christ is given in self-sacrificing service to the world. And the best service we can bring to our industrial, urban, mechanized society is the creation of community.

Though our pilgrimage may be through space or time or continuum of ideas, the essence of our pilgrim state is the inability to rest in the status quo, with the consequent insecurities and limitation this journey may bring. This theme of search inherent in the pilgrim Church does not contradict the intentional creation of community, but expands it. Community no longer carries the image of fixed abode but rather signifies the working out of ever new relationships in varied contexts.

Those who search for ways to build community cannot be strangers to change. They must not only be open to change but also imaginative and resourceful in creating this new type of community in the midst of profound change. For this task, each member needs the shared experience of Christian community. This strengthens the individual with the personal courage necessary for a life painfully open to awareness of need. Support from fellow-religious is given and received in communal genuineness, friendship and loyalty. Since such experience is rare to modern life, our religious community chooses to create community today by opening itself to others, by becoming a community without walls, by relating to the larger community in varied, complex and rich ways. Interaction at first will be chiefly within the newly expanded religious community where the situation will provide the place for interaction on many levels. But those who share such human, religious, intellectual and liturgical resources will then move out into other areas of life and work with incentive and directions for forming community life wherever they are.

Our religious community becomes thus a witness to Christ by being a witness to community. It assists society at the very point where the tensions are greatest. It shows the beauty of cohesiveness, the intelligence of the common effort. It can offer useful patterns for interpersonal relationships, for building common life.

Where the religious community becomes complacent, indifferent to mankind's need for communal life, for the reassurance of brotherhood, there is infidelity and abdication of the group vocation. The faithful religious community bases its hope for renewal of society on man's search for a new social reality, a search for peace, reconciliation, and communal love.

Appendix E

Most Holy Father

The Mother General of the California Institute of the Sisters of the Most Holy and Immaculate Heart of Mary humbly asks, in the name of the Ninth General Chapter, to bring the following matter to the personal attention of Your Holiness.

On October 15, 1967, the Sisters of the Immaculate Heart of Mary, an institute of pontifical right, promulgated the major decrees of its Ninth General Chapter, a Special Chapter of Renewal called for by the *Motu proprio Ecclesiae sanctae* II. His Eminence, James Francis Cardinal McIntyre, Ordinary of the Archdiocese of Los Angeles, in which the motherhouse is located, expressed his displeasure with these decrees and ordered the community to either change drastically its legislation with respect to internal life, government and apostolate or to leave the schools and convents of the Archdiocese. Within two weeks after the date of promulgation and at the instigation of His Eminence Cardinal McIntyre, an Apostolic Visitation of the community was ordered by the Sacred Congregation for Religious. Four months later, the accompanying directives were given to the community.

The General Chapter acted in direct accord with the informed wish of a very large majority of the community. That the decrees are necessarily experimental and open to revision during the next seven years, in accordance with the *Motu proprio*, is well recognized. Nevertheless, the members of the community are convinced that the basic direction taken by the Chapter in its enactments is vitally necessary to the well-being of the Church and to them, both personally and apostolically. The directives effectively reverse this direction. So widespread is this conviction that it will not be possible to follow the directives sent by the Sacred Congregation for Religious without losing from the religious state in the immediate future a large majority of this community which has five hundred forty members.

The renewal program of the Sisters of the Immaculate Heart has received notable attention among communities for several years. Over two thousand requests have been made, chiefly by religious communities of men and women, for the documents of renewal which were a result of the first session of the General Chapter. The Special Chapters of Renewal in many communities, including some with several thousand members, have adopted or are about to take measures similar to or even more basic than those set up by the Sisters of the Immaculate Heart. They are acting in accord with what they believe to be the spirit and directives of the Second Vatican Council. They are also responding to the fact that large numbers of their members are asking for basic and immediate steps toward renewal of religious life. These Sisters represent in most cases the youth, strength, and vitality of their respective communities. Consequently, the course of action taken by the Sacred Congregation for Religious and the resulting directives issued to the Sisters of the Immaculate Heart represent to hundreds of religious in the United States some kind of test of whether or not the Sacred Congregation for Religious will find it possible really to allow communities in this country to renew themselves so that they may present "to believers and unbelievers alike an increasingly clearer revelation of Christ," (*Lumen gentium* #46) especially in a society which is predominantly pluralistic and secular. The decision is a blow to the hope of renewal as many communities envision it from the *Motu Proprio.*

For the above reasons, we petition Your Holiness to grant us permission to experiment with what may need to be considered a new form of religious life, a life which we believe is highly relevant to our age and society, as well as in keeping with the spirit of the Second Vatican Council. The accompanying decrees of the first session of our Chapter of Renewal contain, in preliminary form, the outline and orientation of the form of dedicated life which we ask to be permitted to live as religious. We realize that such a permission appears not in accord with the present thinking of the Sacred Congregation for Religious. Nevertheless, we ask this privilege of experimenting for a limited time (at least a year) because our Sisters believe so strongly that this type of religious life is needed today. We are also petitioning for this favor because we believe, with good reason, that at least eighty per cent of our community will withdraw from religious life if the institute is required to follow the present directives of the Sacred Congregation for Religious, in order to live a new form of consecrated life outside the canonical structure of religious life or of other ecclesiastically recognized groups. We do not think that we are mistaken in calling to the attention of Your Holiness the fact that this is likewise the feeling of religious across the United

States, and we fear that a mandatory return to the monastic tradition for religious institutes will sound the death knell for religious life as we know it in this country.

At this point in history, Your Holiness is the only one who can grant the permission we so urgently need. We therefore, petition sincerely that you look kindly upon our request. We further respectfully ask that Sister Anita Caspary, mother general of this community, be granted an opportunity to present this matter in person to Your Holiness. This request is made for the well-being and peace of soul of thousands of religious women in this country.

With confidence in the pastoral care and concern of Your Holiness, I have the honor to be, Your Holiness,

Respectfully in Mary,

Sister Anita Caspary, IHM
President of the Ninth General Chapter

Appendix F

Talk to Immaculate Heart Community

Sister Anita M. Caspary, IHM—December 6, 1969

Recent developments in our checkered history of the last few months are centered about the notion that our life as a religious community was marginally, if at all, acceptable to Rome. What the role of Church diplomacy and the role of conflicting personalities have had to do with this is not completely clear, nor even relevant at the moment. The fact remains that the notion of self-determination and the ability of a community to listen to the word of God and to find an historically relevant response is not acceptable presently to the institutional Church under the Sacred Congregation for Religious to whom we are presently subject.

For almost all of us this position became obvious with the final visitation of the Bishops on May 29, 1969. Disappointment was universal among the Sisters in that we sincerely believed that we were working at the direction of the *Motu proprio*, "Norms for the Implementation of the Council Decrees on the Appropriate Renewal of Religious Life." There was, however, a difference in response between those who wished to initiate the steps to sever relationships with the Sacred Congregation and those who wished Rome to initiate this process of settlement.

Meanwhile, very recently, a new possibility opened itself—that of petitioning Rome to becoming a dedicated group of lay persons—serving the Church, continuing our present apostolates but enlarging and enriching them, a group free to exercise the prophetic role of social criticism, a group practicing meditation and contemplation out of which all good works flow. Such a possibility became a kind of creative alternative somewhere between our own declaration of purpose and reception of a punitive statement from higher authority. This alternative has been explored to its limits within the past few weeks, with the consent and hope of the Board of Directors.

However, on the best and highest authorities I have searched out, I am now morally certain that our designation as a lay group is inevitable.

267

I am hopeful, but not positive, that a letter of encouragement to form a more flexible community than the Sacred Congregation can admit, may be on its way to us. That we will no longer be known as a religious community seems already to have been decided; that the Church will welcome our society as a form suitable to do her work in these new times is still a "consummation devoutly to be hoped for." The advantages of this "creative alternative" are many. Among them are the ability of those who so desire to work unabashedly with cooperative ecclesiastical hierarchy, and the ability of the general public to understand our posture as one of service to the People of God, not of rebellion.

Perhaps it is important here to reflect on the term "religious" and "religious community." You will remember that at the meeting of Major Superiors at St. Louis, Father Edward Heston, Secretary of the Sacred Congregation for Religious, clearly defined a religious community as conforming to the famous "four points." Yet he was most careful to state that neither he nor anyone else could judge a person as "religious" or "not religious." Such a judgment would be presumptuous and beyond the competence of any judicial group. It refers to a quality of dedication, an intense devotion to the living God and a firm intent, a call, to serve Him and neighbor at the cost of self. Anyone can determine conformity, but the quality of dedication is intangible and partakes of the transcendent.

Thus I think we can with impunity call the community described in our last three sets of Decrees a community of religious persons, as I did in my letter to you. The legalistic description of ourselves as "religious community" may be taken from us—the impact of what we are doing as religious persons and its ultimate meaning as a service to the Church remains. The times call for a group such as this. By a series of circumstances which I think of as providential, we, the IHM's, seem to be chosen to form such a group.

The historical background that has brought us to this point is well known to all of you, but I suspect if you were writing the actual history as I had to summarize it recently, you would see the events in dramatic relief.

No one, looking at the size and geographical spread of our community would have assumed that it was to be the "cause célèbre," the example considered symbolic in the struggle for renewal within religious communities. The severe tests of endurance and purpose are not yet over, but that they must end soon to allow our community to live and grow seem imperative at this point in history.

The witness to integrity is a difficult role—it demands purification of one's motives, a rejection of all the means by which one can manipulate others; it calls for just anger without erratic outbursts of temper, for steadiness of purpose cleansed of stubborn immobility. Surely we have not survived the test without fault. But, surely, too, our weaknesses stemmed from our personal inability to face the fact that the inspiring actuality of the Gospels constantly asks for renewal.

Our Decrees pledge us to an unending search for personhood, relevance and Christian community. They deny the attainment or even the ideal of human perfectibility. They demand an asceticism we have never before been asked for—an unselfconscious devotion to the truth, a vigilant and constant concern with the destructive forces in our society, a sensitive response to the needs of others, a willingness to welcome diversity not merely to tolerate it, and a condemnation with the clarity of Christ of the primary evil— hypocrisy, especially religious hypocrisy.

When I reflect on the Decrees and the degree of dedication they demand, I remember Father Bernard Häring's comment on them before the community saw them. After a careful reading, he said: "These Decrees demand women of extraordinary strength. Do you have such women?" My response was hesitant. It seemed to me, and it still seems, that a complete re-thinking of community life, a real nakedness of the spirit before God can alone yield the answer. Growth in the spirit is indeed a part of such a life—and the growth is found in prayer, in silent contemplation and exchange among ourselves on the things of the spirit that concerns us most.

There are, of course, those who feel that such a lay group is only a negation of what we are—not a promise of becoming something of which we have seen only the beginnings. Actually and somewhat ironically, the lay group I visualize is the kind of community many religious in this country are striving to rebuild for themselves within canonical structure.

A Dominican priest who recently left his community in his disillusionment indicates the vision of Christian community as I think it can be—call it what you may. He writes:

> I realize that a lot of my trouble in the order stems from my conception of the purpose of an order, what it can do, and why I'm in it. I'm in the order to accomplish something I couldn't do by myself, to tackle problems that are too big for one man, to work on problems that will yield only to an organized attack. I'm interested

in changing the patterns and practices of society that keep man from living in dignity—poverty, discrimination, war, crime, corruption, ignorance, and the like. This kind of change can usually be made only by people working together in organizations, teams, movements.

It seems to me that the order is admirably suited to engage in this kind of work: where men work in teams, eat, sleep and drink the problem, supporting one another in fraternity and prayer, and free to engage in work that others cannot or would not do; work that is too dangerous or too hopeless or too thankless, but vitally necessary for the dignity of men. I would think that almost any problem in society would be fair game for such teams: wherever there's a need and we can do something about it, we'd move in, do what we can, and move on. It goes without saying that if someone is already doing it, or hiring people to do it, or where we're in competition with someone who wants to do it, we'd move on.

It is this conception of communal life, supportive, respectful, sometimes corrective of the vision of others which is desperately needed in the world today. If we can make the idea, paradoxical though it is, of "person in community" succeed, then, even though our numbers are small, we have in hand the Archimedes' lever that can move the world. Certainly such a group, Gospel-oriented, combining various types of membership in charity, can affect this impersonal, mechanized, technological world of ours which has become cruel and tragic even while it yearns for redemption. And in so doing we will serve the Church—which is the People of God—humbly and honestly, asking no special distinctions, receiving no special privileges, glorying in our anonymity.

Now let us be more practical. Even though every effort has been made vis-à-vis Rome, no reply has yet been received. I had hoped to be able to have such a communique for you today, but I suspect it must wait until the second group of IHM's becomes a recognized religious community. But those of us responsible for a financial plan, for retirement plans, for requesting members to live up to the expectations of the 1969 Decrees are living in the unknown as to the persons with whom we should deal.

I am asking each Sister, therefore, to write to me by December 15 a letter of intent stating whether she chooses to become a member of a dedicated lay group living according to the Decrees. It is possible that such a group will have to ask for a dispensation from public vows and then take private vows or promises.

Other options open to members of the present group are,

to find a more traditionally oriented community and join it

to obtain a dispensation from vows and disassociate oneself from any group

to form another religious community with the guidelines drawn by the Sacred Congregation including the four points

If the first option is chosen, hopefully with some recognition by the Church, then the Decrees are our way of life. No one should write such a letter of intent unless she is prepared to become a member

deeply engaged in daily searching for God through prayer

intensely involved in the modern scene with its problems of peace, poverty, race, alienation and despair

readily responsive to the needs of community, giving of her services and her goods, her financial assessment, to the larger group

We are, of course, trusting that this decision does not offset the obligations for which we are responsible this year, the people with and for whom we work and those with whom we live. We shall need the rest of this year for careful evaluation, for study commissions on internal government and on our communications system, as well as on social responsibilities and attitudes. The financial plans that we can make when we have facts from you need implementation and the retirement plan needs further study and action.

Older Sisters need to see their place in such a community as vital for the stability and healthy balance of the group. We need to find out if we are recruiting new members and how this can be done.

I have felt for some time that the IHM's, for no reason one could analyze, are being asked in a special way to read the signs of the times, to forge ahead, to begin with enthusiasm to work at a community of hope. Anxiety, losses, personal sufferings have accompanied this unsought request. Invitations to painful action when passivity is comfortable have to be read with care. The Church has been characterized more often, I think, with failure to act than with making mistakes. I hope we can avoid such a condemnation.

With confidence and peace, I choose to go ahead. If you believe that you can make this choice freely and willingly, I ask you to join me.

Bibliography

Albertson, Clinton. Interview by Fidelia Fleming Dickinson. Notes. Los Angeles, 19 December 1997.

Antoniutti, Cardinal Hildebrand. Letter to Thomas R. Gallagher, 21 February 1968. Document no. 493/65. Archives/Immaculate Heart Community, Los Angeles. (A/IHMCOM).

"Archbishop Thanks Immaculate Heart Nuns." *The Tidings* (6 February 1970) 1.

Arrowsmith, Robert. Letter to Cardinal James McIntyre, 30 January 1968. A/IHMCOM.

Baltazar, Eulalio. Letter to Anita Caspary, 21 January 1968. A/IHMCOM.

Bernstein, Marcelle. *The Nuns.* New York: J. B. Lippincott, 1976.

Boyle, Paul M. Letter to Cardinal Hildebrand Antoniutti, 6 November 1969. A/IHMCOM.

"A Cardinal Conservative." *Newsweek* (24 June 1968) 65.

Carroll, Elizabeth. "Reaping the Fruits of Redemption." In *Midwives of the Future.* Ed. Ann Patrick Ware. Kansas City: Leaven Press, 1985.

Casey, Archbishop James V. Letter to Anita Caspary, I.H.M., 2 June 1969. A/IHMCOM.

Caspary, Anita (Mother M. Humiliata). Undelivered letter to Cardinal McIntyre, 1 February 1966. A/IHMCOM.

_____. (Mother M. Humiliata). Letter to Bishop John J. Ward, 10 May 1966. A/IHMCOM.

_____. (Mother M. Humiliata). Unpublished speech to IHM sisters, 31 October 1966. A/IHMCOM.

_____. (Mother M. Humiliata). Letter to Bishop John J. Ward, 18 July 1967. A/IHMCOM.

_____. Letter to the IHM community, 22 October 1967. A/IHMCOM.

_____. (Mother M. Humiliata). Letter to Cardinal McIntyre, 18 December 1967. A/IHMCOM.

_____. Letter to all persons served by the Immaculate Heart sisters, 8 January 1968. A/IHMCOM.

_____. Letter to IHM community, 4 March 1968. A/IHMCOM.

_____. (Mother M. Humiliata). Speech given in the Christian Culture Lectures, sponsored by the Paulist Fathers, Boston, 31 October 1968. A/IHMCOM.

_____. Address to the IHM community, 6 December 1969. A/IHMCOM.

_____. "The Making of 'Servant Community.'" Speech delivered at Tacoma, Wash., 14 June 1973. A/IHMCOM.

"The Catholic Exodus: Why Priests and Nuns Are Quitting." *Time* (23 February 1970) cover.

Chittister, Joan D. "No Time for Tying Cats." In *Midwives of the Future.* Ed. Ann Patrick Ware. Kansas City: Leaven Press, 1985, 4–21.

_____. "Rome and the Religious Life." *The Ecumenist* (July–August 1985) 72–76.

"A Christian Gentleman." *Newsweek* (19 January 1970) 85–86.

Christus Dominus. In *Vatican Council II: The Conciliar and Post Conciliar Documents.* Vol. 1. Ed. Austin Flannery, O.P. Northport, N.Y.: Costello Publishing Co., 1981.

The Constitution on the Sacred Liturgy. In *Vatican II: The Conciliar and Post Conciliar Documents.* Vol. 1. Ed. Austin Flannery, O.P. Northport, N.Y.: Costello Publishing Co., 1981.

Constitution on the Sacred Liturgy. In *The Documents of Vatican II.* Ed. Walter M. Abbott, S.J. New York: America Press, 1966.

"Continue Experiments, Bishop Tells IHM Nuns." *The Catholic Virginian* (12 April 1968) 10.

Cooney, John. *The American Pope: The Life and Times of Francis Cardinal Spellman.* New York: Times Books, 1984.

Coriden, James, Thomas Green, and Donald Heintschel, eds. *The Code of Canon Law: A Text and Commentary.* New York: Paulist Press, 1985.

Coulson, William. "We overcame their Traditions, We overcame their Faith." *The Latin Mass* 3 (January–February 1994) 12–17.

Curran, Charles. "What Can Catholic Ecclesiology Learn from Official Catholic Teaching?" In *A Democratic Catholic Church: The Reconstruction of Roman Catholicism.* Ed. Eugene C. Bianchi and Rosemary Radford Ruether. New York: Crossroad, 1992.

Dart, John. "25,000 Sign Petition Backing Nuns 'Updating.'" *Los Angeles Times* (3 May 1968) II:1–2.

Declaration on Christian Education. In *The Documents of Vatican II.* Ed. Walter M. Abbott, S.J. New York: America Press, 1966.

Declaration on Religious Freedom. In *The Documents of Vatican II.* Vol. 1. Ed. Walter M. Abbott, S.J. New York: America Press, 1966.

Decree on the Appropriate Renewal of Religious Life. In *The Documents of Vatican II.* Ed. Walter M. Abbott, S.J. New York: America Press, 1966.

Decree on the Church's Missionary Activity. In *The Documents of Vatican II.* Ed. Walter M. Abbott, S.J. New York: America Press, 1966.

Decree on Ecumenism. In *The Documents of Vatican II.* Ed. Walter M. Abbott, S.J. New York: America Press, 1966.

De Roo, Bishop Remi. Letter to Mary Mark Zeyen, 25 September 1969. A/IHMCOM.

Dignitatis Humanae. In *The Documents of Vatican II.* Ed. Walter M. Abbott, S.J. New York: America Press, 1966.

Dogmatic Constitution on the Church. In *The Documents of Vatican II.* Ed. Walter M. Abbott, S.J. New York: America Press, 1966.

Dory, Robert C. "Ban on Cremation Is Relaxed by Pope." *New York Times* (6 June 1964) sec. 1.

Dunn-Smith, Dorothy. Letter to Anita M. Caspary, 21 June 1997. A/IHMCOM.

Ebaugh, Helen Rose Fuchs. *Women in the Vanishing Cloister: Organizational Decline in Catholic Religious Orders in the United States.* New Brunswick, N.J.: Rutgers University Press, 1993.

Ecclesiae Sanctae II. In *Vatican Council II: The Conciliar and Post Conciliar Documents.* Ed. Austin Flannery, O.P. Northport, N.Y.: Costello Publishing Co., 1981, 624–633.

Ellis, John Tracy. "The Formation of the American Priest: An Historical Perspective." In *The Catholic Priest in the United States: Historical Investigations.* Collegeville, Minn.: St. John's University Press, 1971, 3–110.

"15 Milwaukee superiors back IHM's." *National Catholic Reporter* (6 March 1968) 6.

"Fighting Nuns." *Newsweek* (1 April 1968) 100.

Fitzgerald, Kathleen W., and Claire Breault. *Whatever Happened to the Good Sisters?* Lake Forest, Ill.: Whales' Tale Press, 1992.

Flynn, Agnes E. Interview by Doris Murphy. Audio-cassette recording. Los Angeles, 15 May 1988.

Flynn, Sister Elizabeth Ann. "Background of the Ninth General Chapter's Decree on Education," 1 December 1967. A/IHMCOM.

Ford, George Barry. *A Degree of Difference.* New York: Farrar, Straus & Giroux, 1969.

Frankel, Jack. *A Lion at the Door.* Play judged at Siena College, Loudonville, N.Y., 1994. Previous title *The Mother General,* 1990.

Gallagher, Thomas R. Letter to Sister Anita Caspary, 12 January 1968. A/IHMCOM.

Gannon, Michael V. "Before and After Modernism: The Intellectual Isolation of the American Priest." In *The Catholic Priest in the United States: Historical Investigations.* Ed. John Tracy Ellis. Collegeville, Minn.: St. John's University Press, 1971, 293–383.

Gitlin, Todd. *The Sixties: Years of Hope, Days of Rage.* New York: Bantam Books, 1987.

Greeley, Andrew. "No Loss of Faith; But Confidence in Leadership Gone." *Davenport Messenger* (28 March 1968) 10.

Gremillion, Joseph, ed. *The Gospel of Peace and Justice.* Maryknoll, N.Y.: Orbis Books, 1979.

Häring, Bernard. Letter to Anita Caspary, 28 November 1967. A/IHMCOM.

Hill, Gladwin. "Cardinal McIntyre of Los Angeles, Retired Archbishop, Is Dead at 93." *New York Times,* Biographical Services (July, 1979) 950.

Immaculate Heart College. *On the Move: a publication devoted to the exchange of ideas and opinions.* A/IHMCOM.

"The Immaculate Heart Rebels." *Time* (23 February 1970) 49–50.

Implementation of the Decrees *Christus Dominus, Presbyterorum Ordinis and Perfectae Caritatis.* In *Vatican Council II: The Conciliar and Post Conciliar Documents.* Ed. Austin Flannery, O.P. Northport, N.Y.: Costello Publishing Co., 1981.

Jordan, Rose Eileen. Interview by author. Los Angeles, 28 January 1997.

Katzenstein, Mary Fainsod. *Faithful and Fearless: Moving Feminist Protest Inside the Church and Military* (Princeton: Princeton University Press, 1998) 224.

King, Margot H., ed. *A Leaf from the Great Tree of God: Essays in Honor of Ritamary Bradley, SFCC.* Toronto: Peregrina Publishing Co., 1994.

Kirschenbaum, Howard. "Denigrating Carl Rogers: William Coulson's Last Crusade." *Journal of Counseling & Development* 69 (May–June 1991) 411–413.

Kolarik, Gloria. Interview by Doris Murphy. Tape recording. Los Angeles, 10 February 1997.

Krebs, A.V., Jr. "A Church of Silence." *Commonweal* 70 (10 July 1964) 473.

Leckey, Hugo. *Immaculate Heart.* Play performed in Los Angeles, October 1985.

Lumen Gentium. In *Vatican Council II: The Conciliar and Post Conciliar Documents.* Ed. Austin Flannery, O.P. Northport, N.Y.: Costello Publishing Co., 1981.

Lynch, Thomas L., and others. Letter to Sister Anita Caspary, 11 March 1968. A/IHMCOM.

MacDonald, Sister Eileen. Letter to Cardinal Hildebrand Antoniutti, 26 February 1968.

MacGuigan, J. Elliott. Letter to Sister Anita Caspary, 21 November 1967. A/IHMCOM.

Mahoney, John F. "Is Convent Life Fundamentally Unchristian?" *National Catholic Reporter* (6 March 1968) 10–11.

Mailloux, Noel. "Ascetical Workshop for IHM Sisters." 24 March–2 April 1961. A/IHMCOM.

Manning, Archbishop Timothy. "Announcement." *The Tidings* (25 December 1969) 1.

Massa, Mark. "To Be Beautiful, Human, and Christian—IHMs and the Routinization of Charisma." In *Catholics and American Culture.* New York: Crossroad Publishing Co., 1999.

McGucken, Archbishop Joseph T. Letter to Mother M. Humiliata, I.H.M. 27 February 1968. A/IHMCOM.

McIntyre, Cardinal James F. Letter to Mother M. Humiliata, 28 December 1965. A/IHMCOM.

————. Undated memorandum. December 1965 or early 1966. A/IHMCOM.

————. Letter to Mother M. Humiliata, 7 February 1966 (a). A/IHMCOM.

————. Letter to Mother M. Humiliata, 7 February 1966 (b). A/IHMCOM.

————. Letter to Mother M. Humiliata, 12 May 1966. A/IHMCOM.

_____. Letter to Mother M. Humiliata, 4 November 1966. A/IHMCOM.

_____. Letter to Mother M. Humiliata, 23 March 1967. A/IHMCOM.

_____. Letter to Mother M. Humiliata, 24 October 1967. A/IHMCOM.

_____. Letter to Mother M. Humiliata, 30 October 1967. A/IHMCOM.

_____. Letter to Archbishop Joseph T. McGucken, 2 November 1967. Archives of the Archdiocese of San Francisco.

_____. Letter to Mother M. Humiliata, 19 December 1967. A/IHMCOM.

_____. Letter to Anita Caspary, 28 August 1969. A/IHMCOM.

McNamara, Jo Ann Kay. *Sisters in Arms.* Cambridge: Harvard University Press, 1996.

Mercer, Marshal H. "'You People Don't Pray Right.' A Study of Organizational Power and Superordinate Goal Conflict." Ph.D. dissertation, Claremont Graduate School, 1994.

Message to Humanity. In *The Documents of Vatican II.* Ed. Walter M. Abbott, S.J. New York: America Press, 1966, 3–7.

Murphy, Sister Rosalie. Letter and resolution of support, December 1969. A/IHMCOM.

Naughton, Jim. "James Shannon: A Former Bishop." *The Washington Post* (17 September 1987) sec. C, 1–3.

Naughton, Noreen. Interview by Doris Murphy. Tape recording. Los Angeles, October 1988.

Neal, Sister Marie Augusta, S.N.D. de N. Letter to Anita Caspary, 30 March 1968. A/IHMCOM.

_____. "Report to Cardinal Antoniutti." Boston, 30 March 1968. A/IHMCOM.

Norms for Implementing the Decree: On The Up-to-Date Renewal of Religious Life. In *Vatican Council II: The Conciliar and Post Conciliar Documents.* Ed. Austin Flannery, O.P. Northport, N.Y.: Costello Publishing Co., 1981.

"Nuns in Conflict." In *Man Alive* series, British Broadcasting Corporation, 1970. A/IHMCOM.

O'Grady, Desmond. "Ildebrando Antoniutti: II IM Case Figure 'Gets What He Wants.'" *National Catholic Reporter* (19 June 1968) 2.

"Out of the Convent, into Secular Sisterhood." *Time* (16 February 1970) 84.

Pastoral Constitution on the Church in the Modern World. In *The Documents of Vatican II.* Ed. Walter M. Abbott, S.J. New York: America Press, 1966.

Pastoral Constitution on the Church in the Modern World. In *Vatican Council II: The Conciliar and Post Conciliar Documents.* Ed. Austin Flannery, O.P. Northport, N.Y.: Costello Publishing Co., 1981, 903–1001.

Paul VI, Pope. "Address to the General Assembly of the United Nations, October 4, 1965." In *The Gospel of Peace and Justice.* Ed. Joseph Gremillion. Maryknoll, N.Y.: Orbis Books, 1979.

Pearce, Lucia. "Sister Corita: Bringing Art into Learning." *National Catholic Reporter* (4 November 1964) 5.

Perfectae Caritatis. In *Vatican Council II: The Conciliar and Post Conciliar Documents.* Ed. Austin Flannery, O.P. Northport, N.Y.: Costello Publishing Co., 1981, 611–633.

Pfisterer, Robert B., and others. Letter to Dan Thrapp, religion editor, *Los Angeles Times* (1 February 1968). A/IHMCOM.

Pius XII, Pope. "Nous Vous Adressons." Speech delivered during the International Congress of Superiors General of Orders and Congregations of Women: On Religious Vocations, September 15, 1952.

Pizzardo, Cardinal Joseph. Letter to Sisters of the Immaculate Heart, 13 July 1967. A/IHMCOM.

"Pope Sees Cardinal McIntyre." *New York Times* (1 October 1964) 25, col. 6.

Quiñonez, Lora Ann, and Mary Daniel Turner. *The Transformation of American Sisters.* Philadelphia: Temple University Press, 1992.

Raimondi, Archbishop Luigi. Letter to Mother Mary Humiliata, 6 November 1967. A/IHMCOM.

_____. Letter to members of the Conference of Major Religious Superiors of Women, 9 April 1968. Document no. 1068/68, 2: no. 4. A/IHMCOM.

_____. Letter to Sister Anita Caspary, 29 March 1968. A/IHMCOM.

Ransing, Bernard E. Letter to Mother M. Humiliata, 25 March 1965. A/IHMCOM.

"Religious Women and the Apostolate in the Modern World." *Sister Formation Bulletin* 5 (Summer 1959) 3.

Renovationis Causam. In *Vatican Council II: The Conciliar and Post Conciliar Documents.* Ed. Austin Flannery, O.P. Northport, N.Y.: Costello Publishing Co., 1981.

Rogers, Carl. *Freedom to Learn.* Columbus, Ohio: Charles E. Merrill Publishing Co., 1969.

_____. "The Project at Immaculate Heart: An Experiment in Self-Directed Change." *Education* 95 (1974) 181.

Rowe, Margaret. "A Test Case for Renewal." *Herder Correspondence* 5 (May 1968) 155–156.

Rynne, Xavier. *Letters from Vatican City.* New York: Farrar, Straus & Co., 1963.

Schaffer, Sister M. Charles. Letter to the sisters in IHM convents, 26 October 1967. A/IHMCOM.

Schneiders, Sandra. *Finding the Treasure.* New York: Paulist Press, 2000.

Seidler, John, and Katherine Meyer. *Conflict and Change in the Catholic Church.* New Brunswick, N.J.: Rutgers University Press, 1989.

Shannon, James Patrick. *Reluctant Dissenter.* New York: Crossroad Publishing Co., 1998.

Sharples, Marian. *All Things Remain in God.* Los Angeles: Unpublished work, 1963.

Shelley, Thomas. *Dunwoodie: The History of St. Joseph's Seminary.* Christian Classics. Westminster, Md., 1993.

Sisters of the Immaculate Heart of Mary, Los Angeles. General Chapter. Minutes of the General Chapter of 1963. A/IHMCOM.

_____. General Chapter. Decrees of the Ninth General Chapter, October 1967. A/IHMCOM.

_____. General Chapter. Minutes of Ninth General Chapter of Affairs: Minutes of Meeting Eight. In *Sisters of the Immaculate Heart of Mary, Los Angeles: Community History Part II. October 13, 1967–March 25, 1968,* 22 October 1967. A/IHMCOM.

_____. General Chapter. Minutes of Ninth General Chapter of Affairs: Minutes of Meeting Ten. In *Sisters of the Immaculate Heart of Mary, Los Angeles: Community History Part II. October 13, 1967–March 25, 1968,* 22 November 1967. A/IHMCOM.

_____. "Background of the Ninth General Chapter's Decree on Education," December 1967. A/IHMCOM.

_____. General Council. "Community Objectives: Five-Year Plan," 2 July 1964. A/IHMCOM.

_____. General Council. Minutes of the meeting of Cardinal McIntyre and Monsignor Edward Wade, 13 May 1965. A/IHMCOM.

_____. General Council. Minutes of meeting, 12 November 1965. A/IHMCOM.

_____. General Council. Minutes of meeting with Cardinal McIntyre and advisors. 16 October 1967. A/IHMCOM.

_____. General Council. Minutes of meeting with officials of the Archdiocese of Los Angeles. 7 December 1967.

_____. "Basis for Changes and Adaptations of Custom Made by the Sisters of the Immaculate Heart," 1963–65. A/IHMCOM.

_____. Minutes of the meeting of Sister Elizabeth Ann and Mother Humiliata with Cardinal McIntyre, 27 December 1965. A/IHMCOM.

_____. Members of the Sisters of the Immaculate Heart. Letter to Cardinal McIntyre, 2 April 1967. A/IHMCOM.

_____. Letter to Cardinal McIntyre, 25 January 1968. A/IHMCOM.

_____. Petition to the Pontifical Commission, 16 July 1968. A/IHMCOM.

_____. Letter to Pope Paul VI, 1969, presented by Sister Anita Caspary to Archbishop Giovanni Benelli. A/IHMCOM.

_____. 1970 Contract sample. A/II IMCOM.

"Sisters of the Loyal Opposition." *The Christian Century* (18 February 1970) 2.

"Sisters to Form Lay Community." *The Tidings* (6 February 1970) 1.

Stammer, Larry B. "Mahony Offers Apology for His Church's Failings." *Los Angeles Times* (8 March 2000) sec. B:1.

Suenens, Cardinal Leon-Joseph. "The Nun in the World Debate." Address given at St. Mary's Symposium, South Bend, Indiana, June 1969. A/IHMCOM.

"30 L.A. sisters support IHMs." *National Catholic Reporter* (6 March 1968) 6. A/IHMCOM, 38–78.

Thompson, Margaret Susan. "The Validation of Sisterhood: Canonical Status and Liberation in the History of American Nuns." In *A Leaf from the Great Tree of God: Essays in Honor of Ritamary Bradley, SFCC*. Ed. Margot H. King. Toronto: Peregrina Publishing Co., 1994.

"3,000 sisters support IHM's." *National Catholic Reporter* (27 March 1968) 3.

Tobin, Mother Mary Luke. Letters to Anita Caspary, n.d. Personal files.

Turner, Sister Mary Daniel. Letter to Sister Anita Marie Caspary, 26 April 1968. A/IHMCOM.

_____. Letter to Most Reverend Luigi Raimondi, apostolic delegate to the United States, 26 April 1968. A/IHMCOM.

"US Top Crust Protests IHM Decision to Pope." *National Catholic Reporter* (17 April 1968) 7.

Van Kaam, Adrian. *Religion and Personality*. Englewood Cliffs, N.J.: Prentice-Hall, 1964.

Vils, Ursula. "An Experimental Religious Community." *Los Angeles Times* (9 July 1974) sec. 4:1.

_____. "Sisters Live Now Life in Then Setting." *Los Angeles Times* (9 November 1971) 1, 8.

Ward, Bishop John J. Letter to Mother M. Humiliata, 6 May 1966. A/IHMCOM.

_____. Letter to Mother M. Humiliata, I.H.M., 5 May 1967. A/IHMCOM.

_____. Letter to Mother M. Humiliata, 15 May 1967. A/IHMCOM.

_____. Interview by Marshal H. Mercer. Audio-cassette transcript. Los Angeles, 10 December 1992.

Ware, Ann Patrick, ed. *Midwives of the Future*. Kansas City: Leaven Press, 1985.

Weber, Msgr. Francis J. *His Eminence of Los Angeles: James Francis Cardinal McIntyre*. 2 vols. Mission Hills, Calif.: St. Francis Historical Society, 1997.

"You've Come a Long Way Baby." *Time* (23 February 1970) 55.

Yzermans, Msgr. Vincent, ed. *American Participation in the Second Vatican Council*. New York: Sheed and Ward, 1967.

_____. *The Unwearied Advocate: Public Addresses of Pope Pius XII*. 2 vols. St. Cloud, Minn.: St. Cloud Bookshop, 1956.

Index